HARPER ESSAYS

# Harper Essays

EDITED BY

HENRY SEIDEL CANBY, PH.D., LITT.D

*Editor of "The Saturday Review of Literature"*
*Member of the English Department*
*of Yale University*

KENNIKAT PRESS, INC./PORT WASHINGTON, N. Y.

HARPER ESSAYS


Reissued 1969 by Kennikat Press by arrangement
with Harper & Row, Publishers, Incorporated

Library of Congress Catalog Card No: 69-16483
SBN 8046-0520-3
Manufactured in the United States of America

ESSAY AND GENERAL LITERATURE INDEX REPRINT SERIES

# ACKNOWLEDGMENTS

*The editor acknowledges with thanks permission to reprint the following essays:* THE FRIENDLY ROCKS, *by* John Burroughs, *by permission of and special arrangement with Houghton, Mifflin Company, authorized publishers;* WHY IS A BOSTONIAN? *by* Harrison Rhodes, *Robert M. McBride Company;* WHEN THE CITY WAKES, *by* Simeon Strunsky, *Henry Holt & Company;* KHAKI CONFIDENCES AT CHATEAU-THIERRY, *from* THE DAY OF GLORY, *by* Dorothy Canfield Fisher, *Henry Holt & Company;* SPECULATIONS, *by* John Galsworthy, *Charles Scribner's Sons;* WITHIN THE RIM, *by* Henry James, *by special permission from his literary executor;* TOLSTOY, *by* William Dean Howells, *by special permission of his literary executors;* AMERICAN APHORISMS, *by* Brander Matthews, *Charles Scribner's Sons;* THE HARVEST OF WILD PLACES, *by* Walter Prichard Eaton, *W. A. Wilde Company.*

# CONTENTS

CONTENTS

# INTRODUCTION

For a book of essays by so many distinguished writers, a preface is scarcely needed except to indicate some reasons for the preferences of the editor in choosing these essays from among the rich variety available in the files of *Harper's Magazine.* He has, indeed, followed his own taste with an especial regard for interest of subject matter and excellence of writing, but a conscious reference also to the swing of opinion, prejudice, and the sources of emotion, over one of the great transitional periods of the Western races. For these essays begin to be written in the last years of that stable era which we call the end of the nineteenth century, although it projected into the nineteen hundreds and down into the sharp alterations in literary taste which came about 1910. They cover the war years. They reach into reconstruction. Only ultra modernism is absent—for that is indeed still in its infancy and does not belong in a book drawn from tested intellects writing in their maturity.

It was not the idea of the editor that this book would be read and studied as an index of a changing civilization. He felt that the essay—which is essentially comment, not dogmatism; literature, not science—should be read for what might be called its permanent values, good for us, good for Horace Walpole could he read this book, good for Bacon. But inevitably, in years wracked by war and dissension, the immediate reference to passing events which one finds in good essays only when the events are great and the writers a part of the major intellectual life of their time, would creep in, would sometimes be the heart and substance of the essay.

Hence this collection is rather surprisingly different from those books of "examples" chosen from the Victorians and the New Englanders which we used to study in college rhetoric classes. In style it will be found not inferior, in subject matter it is as varied, but by its closeness to history it takes on a vividness and actuality of passing life itself which, now that the essays are brought together, seems to the editor somewhat remarkable.

This is due, in part, to the choice of essays from the files of a decade and a half of a magazine that for three quarters of a century has reflected tastes and opinions of the intelligent in America and Great Britain. With a shorter period, or with the intention to illustrate every kind of modern writing, this would have been a limitation, but for the purpose of this book—to present a flow of ideas excellently set down—it provides a kind of living unity which will be felt by the reader. These authors—diverse themselves in race, in opinion, in interest and intention, have addressed a single audience, wide in its range, and yet with that homogeneity which belongs to men and women who live upon a common plane of civilization. It was such a group that Emerson lectured for, to which Booth and Henry Irving played, for which colleges were founded. Whoever the writers, these essays were addressed to a typical and recognizable audience of Americans.

The essays were selected for their intrinsic interest and excellence, from nearly two hundred numbers of a monthly magazine, yet this selection has resulted in a very typical grouping of the American essay. There is the familiar essay of personality, excellently illustrated by Professor Genung's study of his friend, a dog, Captain Mahan's reminiscences of men at sea, and Edward S. Martin's surprising prescience in the matter of the new young girl. There is the nature essay, in which Americans have always excelled, here represented by the veteran John Burroughs, Walter Prichard Eaton, the exotic William Beebe, and that specialist of the road, Hilaire Belloc. There is the acute study of a town, or a country's characteristics, a theme peculiarly congenial to the essay: Arnold Bennett on the United States, Harrison Rhodes on Boston, Simeon Strunsky on New York. Through the conversational pattern of the essay personal grief breaks, without marring the fabric, in Mark Twain's poignant "The

Death of Jean," a worthy successor to those elegies in prose as well as poetry which have been the best monuments to the departed.

With the approach of 1915, the war, which had been philosophical in American magazines, became concrete, personal, as disturbing to the emotions as to thought. Dorothy Canfield on the men who fought, Margaret Deland on minds muddied by the conflict, Galsworthy on its broader issues, Henry James on one fine brain's reaction, all belong to a moment, though a terrible one, of time, and yet are lifted above journalism by the intensity and the art of the writers.

With William Allen White on the country newspaper, the essay returns to its favorite field of literary criticism richly tinged by life. In F. M. Colby's "The Gentleman's Review," irony slips in; W. L. George on the novelist is a typical literary essay. Mr. Alden and Mr. Howells, out of the richness of long experience, comment on literature from the aspect of eternity. Finally, American scholarship, which came to maturity during the decade and a half, touches literature in the sound and brilliant studies of the tongue we speak by Brander Matthews and Thomas R. Lounsbury.

It is, one submits, a rather remarkable collection, and it is to be doubted whether substituting here and there some brilliant article by an author unrepresented or on subject matters not touched upon would compensate for its value as a record of a single forum in which so many minds spoke with assurance that they would be understood. For the magazine in America has been one of the great institutions devised in the history of civilization for the promulgation of literature. It is in the best sense an *organon,* a means for assembling harmoniously literary thought.

This book, of course, is only one man's selection from such a magazine; yet it is the reader's memory that makes for each of us the best anthology, and it is hoped that the taste here exhibited is sufficiently catholic, and sufficiently alive to sincere expression, to justify the choice.

Finally it is the rise and fall from the peak of intensity of 1910 that the editor, without conscious intention, has represented in this book. This, like all true anthologies, is a record of the past—the fruits of the past, of the immediate past—not a guess at the present and future. The years 1910, 1918, 1920, even, are already in perspective. We can know of them certain things which can only be guessed in current reading. An essay collection like this one is therefore a modest contribution to the continuity of literary history. These selections are among the first literary products of essayists we have known and may still know, to emerge into the steadier light which shines upon things done, thoughts accomplished, and records not washed out, as soon as written, from the sand. Herein is expressed how we felt when the century was just a little younger.

HARPER ESSAYS

# MY LOWLY TEACHER[1]

*By* John Franklin Genung

*Professor Genung was a beloved professor of rhetoric in Amherst, author of a widely used textbook on rhetoric, excellent of its kind, and an authority on the Bible as literature. He was a great personality as well as an admirable scholar. Born in 1850, he died in 1919. This essay appeared originally in* "Harper's Magazine" *for May 1911.*

I SUPPOSE WE ALL STUDY theology more or less earnestly as long as we live; I do not see how we can help it. That is to say, our thoughts about the great Reality above us and our relation to It, or Him, fall into a definition and order to which we attach our sense of truth, feeling that, whatever any one else believes, we can feel sure of this and this. Our divinity-school teachers, indeed, cannot go with us through life, but then perhaps we ought not to expect it. If we have open minds, our teachers need not to have had ordaining hands laid upon them; they may be any one or any thing, and they teach as though they taught us not.

I have a teacher who probably has no idea that he is giving me lessons. He does not belong to that class of characters who set themselves up to instruct or persuade or even to do good; what he does he does by just existing in his own natural way. His antecedents, I am well satisfied, have been good. His heredity has not been twisted; his education, though not topped off with ornamental accomplishments, has been such as to have given a naturally sweet disposition free course. His name is Caleb. The fact that he has no surname is not to be reckoned against him, for we do not ordinarily give surnames to dogs. Perhaps the way he came to give me lessons in theology may be explained by some words of Tennyson, in which the poet avers that

> " . . . love in which my hound has part
> Can hang no weight upon my heart
> In its assumptions up to heaven."

This would seem in a manner to shift the teaching to me; and doubtless I am receiving through my reflections much more than he consciously gives; but at any rate, there is a power of education in the little fellow, with his unfailing good-will and loyalty, which seems to deserve grateful acknowledgment.

Some years ago one of our American bishops wrote a sonnet about his dog, who must have been a noble animal. I have forgotten how the sonnet ran; all I can recall is the first line:

> "I well believe he thinks that I am God."

When I read it and some of the good bishop's personal traits came rather vividly to mind, my first mental response was that it was no wonder the dog thought so, if he had seen the bishop, as I had, in the dignity of full canonicals. Then I chided myself for being so impudently profane; and, of course, that was not the reason at all. The church vestments had nothing to do with it. I have seen dogs look up with equal devotion to men in overalls. We read of dogs that licked the sores of beggars; and we know what poor apologies for masters dogs will be faithful to, even though their worship goes wholly wasted. A very significant thing when you think of it; it became one of my first lessons in theology. For it seems to reveal that such an emotion exists in the core of creation, even in the strata below us. There are creatures in actual existence in whom has been put the instinct to look upward from their station to beings higher in the scale, to choose these for friends and masters, to stand by them and reverence them, not for what they can gain by it—for too often, abating no jot of fidelity, they get but kicks and hard words—but purely as a spontaneous, intrinsic outflow of dog nature. I like to contemplate a creation that is rich enough to include such a thing as this; to contain disinterested affection as a wide-spread elemental fact; it gives me a better opinion of the universe. Some things, scholars tell us, are more fully evolved in the animals than in man; the eye in the eagle, the swift foot in the stag. I should be sorry to think that, because the lord of creation gets things so tangled up with reason and selfishness, the dog should have got the start of us in this virtue. I am glad he is not self-conscious; that would spoil it all.

Many times a day Caleb comes to my armchair, as I sit studying, with no apparent purpose except just to say, "How do you do?" and, never without waiting for the word of permission, he jumps up on my knee, remains a minute, and then goes about his affairs. And many a time I have been half startled by a wondering yet wholly loving expression in the great brown eyes so inquiringly searching mine. Only asking me to drop the prosy book and go walking with him? No; that expression is quite different. Those eyes look as if they were searching for something that we two might hold in common and so have a silent understanding of each other. Is it something higher than can enter his dog consciousness? I am often moved to respond "It's you and I, Caleb. We do know each other in some things, don't we?" And there comes a twinge of pathos in it, too; and, oddly enough, it sets me thinking of what an apostle once said about a whole creation groaning in pain and travail together, waiting for some adoption which should redeem the body. I am sometimes silly enough to ask him: "Do you too, Caleb, belong to that vast continuous line of upward-looking, onward-looking things?

Are you, too, dimly conscious of waiting for something which is destined to come somehow by the way of the higher orders? Does the First-born of every creature make his relationship felt in some far-off way even to you?" He never answers me except by that wistful look, which vanishes as soon as I begin to theologize; but the look has on me the strange effect of worship, so that I am almost afraid to recall the bishop's sonnet. Who am I, to be scrutinized so? What is man's office in the sum of things, when such great liquid eyes are gazing up at him from below?

He wants to assure himself, it would seem, that the lines of communication are still open and that the current of love and care is flowing as ever. That is enough. If I admit him to my knee he does not take it out in caresses, for he is no sentimentalist. If I grant him the supreme felicity of his life, to go walking with me, the sense of being with me is all he wants. He turns his head away or gives attention to other things, as if he were indifferent; he is off on his own affairs, attending to his canine world; from which, however, he comes with ready alacrity at my whistle. Let him keep connections clear with my focus of humanity, and the rest is perfect freedom and perfect content to be a dog.

Sometimes he sports in my presence; as an ancient sage was naïve enough to represent Our Lady Wisdom, who was for him symbol of the eager intellect of man, as sporting always in the presence of God. For pure joy of existence he will course round an open field, round and round, returning always to headquarters to report his joy and perhaps jumping up in ecstasy. I cannot break him of that, though I have to brush off much soilure on account of muddy paws. I ought to be sterner with him; I own that. Sometimes, too, he playfully assumes hostility or gives his master a scolding, as if for once he and I had changed places; growling and barking in ironical laughter. But with my hand once in his mouth he is infinitely gentle; nay, he immediately releases it, and would rather die than bite. Yet how savagely he will bite a stick or a rope's end, and how strenuously he will hang to it until his jowl is bloody, as if it were a foe to conquer. It makes me think of the way men sport with the laws of nature and of their own talents, cuffing them about and making audacious demands of them; doughty vanquishers subduing the earth as if they were sole masters of it; yet when this energy faces the calm Reality above, only exploding how much of it in ironic play!

Sometimes a curious fit of the histrionic seizes him; for he loves to astonish, and he is fond of exhibiting his paces before company. He has become aware of his special bent and aptitude: those strong bulldog jaws and that bulldog tenacity must needs render account of themselves. The "stunt" in his case is not hunting or swimming, for he is not trained to the practical services; not carrying baskets or newspapers or slippers, for his ornamental training, too, has been neglected. But in the performance with a stick or rope's end he knows his abilities and takes pride in them; and to have an admiring and exclaiming audience is dear to his heart. Is it childish for us or is it natural and right, even at the risk of some vanity, to exhibit our arts before high Heaven, the things that we can most cleverly do, being thereby made a spectacle to the world and to angels and men? Perhaps we may as well accept the situation, and if we must act a part, act it like men. The wrong is not in this, but in the hypocrisy of it, the counterfeit; trying to seem what we are not. It foots back, after all, to truth of nature; and with all his vanity of histrionism Caleb's nature is true.

Sometimes he sins. He gets into dirty and malodorous places; he rolls and revels there. It is his nature, I suppose; and he comes back to me resembling Achilles, who, according to the schoolboy's composition, "was dipped into the Stynx and became intolerable." Yet he comes up proud of his achievement; as proud as we are when we have been eating Limburger cheese. His punishment, which cannot possibly be dispensed with, is an immediate bath; and he submits to it patiently, yet with keen disappointment, feeling in some dim way that he has wronged the standard of the sphere above him, yet in his heart clinging still to the bad odor and ready the next moment to roll in it again. That is a sin, I suspect, arbitrarily imported into his life from the sphere above him and encountering no moral principle to which it can appeal. I do not know that it is amenable even to education. He is a dog, after all, and his conversance with humanity does not obliterate the dog nature. Is there something here, *mutatis mutandis*, for the next being in the scale to ponder? Is *his* nature as clean as the Reality above would have it be? And may there be sinful tendencies and tastes in him for which the fitting punishment is not stripes and prison, not even blame, but —washing?

Then at other times he sins through impulse; will rush after a bird or a cat, perhaps, when warned not to do so. He does not mean to sin. But he is a bulldog, and when once embarked on an action, however impulsive, his bulldog momentum impels him to carry it to the finish. It is his nature to hang on; and sometimes this gets the better of his sense of right—which is to say, the sense he gets from his master's will. The sin seems to come from a certain lack of equilibrium; a trait in itself good, or at least not bad, imperfectly balanced. He sins through disinclination, too, and this is rather more serious. He is tardy and keeps me waiting sometimes when I call him from a pursuit or investigation in which he is particularly interested. He knows that he ought to leave his unsavory occupation and come, for the master's call is his chosen law; but the dog nature is so strong, the affairs of his life are so sweet, it is hard to give up.

Alas! I find I am excusing all his sins, or what I have chosen to call such. As soon as I look behind them they become venial. Am I thereby misrepresenting that ideal which his dumb worship tacitly imputes to me and making the only deity he knows a weak and indulgent one? Or, as we press the imputation onward to the Reality above, do we come in sight of the truth that He who knows all forgives all? It is a hard question to answer, because I have only my very imperfect self to answer by. Yet I, too, see that sin is sin, an ugly actuality which, however it may be explained, cannot be explained away. And I hold, however pliable my disposition, by an old idea which has somehow come among men, of One who will by no means acquit or concede that a sin was not committed when it was, and yet in full view of all does forgive. It is not a bad ideal, on the whole, to live by, for it maintains the eternal standard and order of the universe; it calls things by their right names and deals with them on that ground.

There is no spirit of rebellion in Caleb. The master's will, coming from the standards of a higher sphere which he has never entered, must needs be to him purely arbitrary. It is only by a native spirit of blind obedience (if we can attribute spirit to a dog) that he obeys at all. But he never questions or resents its arbitrariness. It belongs to the order of nature for him. Once in a great while he has deliberately taken matters into his own hands. One day in camp, for instance, nearly all of our party took an excursion to a place five miles away, where there was to be a large company and a dinner; and I desired him to stay at home with me. But the attraction of the majority, the sweetness of going with the crowd, was too much for him. He remained with me a little while; then, when my back was turned, quietly disappeared. When, however, he returned with them in the evening he brought back no apparent sense of guilt. Was this a nonchalant carrying off of disobedience with a high hand or was he presuming on my easy nature to say nothing more about it? I had not leashed him; had only told him I wished him to stay with me; and for once he had let a keen desire override a mild restraint. The incident made me think of that large sphere of things morally indifferent and of our attitude toward them; things not laid down in a code, but perhaps established by convention, or drifted into by the crowd, or deduced by interpretation of a higher will. We have the advantage of Caleb, because we can in some measure penetrate the sphere above us; far enough, at least, to see that the Will up there is not arbitrary or capricious and to reduce it to sound reasons. We are the better able, therefore, to take things into our own hands and to revise or accommodate our conventions to suit the occasion. Perhaps, indeed, all our morality, which we trace to a source outside the world, may turn out to have come by the way of our own devising, or what seems such. It need not, therefore, deny the higher source if we have all along appreciated the value of the best in us. The hitch comes when we drift so passively with the crowd as to outrage our better judgment; or when in deliberate perversity we transgress the law of being; or even when we abjure the practicability of the best and take up with the second best. It is thus that we can understand that whatsoever is not of faith is sin.

Fortunately, Caleb drifted with a good crowd, so there was no harm done that time. With us it does not always turn out so.

Once in a while Caleb gets lost, and has, on his primitive dog scale, to be sought and saved. It is not that I lose him; rather he loses me. It amounts to the same in the end, losing or lost. Away from home somewhere with his master, suddenly he wakes to the sense that he has missed the presence of the higher will on whom he depends for bearing and direction. And the cause, I suspect, is much the same as when men get lost; namely, that while he is immersed in immediate allurements—in his case generally connected with back yards and scullery doors—his superior being has passed on out of sight. He does not belong to that class of dogs who would use their nose to find the master again; or else his education has suffered neglect. But one thing I can surely reckon on. As soon as he becomes aware of his plight he drops his scavenging interests and stays right where he last saw me. No other person, however friendly or well known, can entice him away from there. Hours may pass and home may be near, but there he stays, watching and hoping. Of course that imposes on his master the duty of remembering and returning to the place—which is to say, of seeking and saving the lost; but this to his canine theology is what masters are for. To find or to be found (the sum is equal, active or passive) is to be where the master is, and it is for the master to determine where that shall be. He is unconsciously—or shall I say cleverly?—reading me a lesson in my function as a deity. And if I in turn pass on the lesson to the Reality above, I can do it in no better spirit, surely, than by emulating the perfect faith by which Caleb knows not only that he is lost, but that he will full surely be found. Such faith looks like worship, the worship that avails, though its only outward expression is waiting.

On the whole, Caleb's nature, as toward me and the species I represent, is all compact of loyalty, patience, trust, and love. This last seems really to be the key to the whole. I confess I do not see that the soul of Shakespeare could *love* me more. He is below me in thought and power, inexorably below me in sphere and range of being; but in this one respect of love he seems to emulate me. A significant thing when we think of it, that there should be this perfectly understood bond of communion between the two species. Love seems to be a thing neither animal nor human by any exclusive claim; a thing stretching away beyond both species, above and below; and both species seem to be strung on it like beads on a string. His love is as self-forgetting as mine is, and all the more single-hearted for not being tangled up with reasons and expediency. It draws into itself his whole being as mine does not. "I cannot understand—I love;" that is what I have often caught his great brown eyes saying. And in that unstudied consciousness he has freedom for his own affairs and grants me freedom for mine.

Having always lived in an atmosphere of good-will and love, he tacitly measures all humanity by it, never dreaming but that his individual deity is a type of all that walks on two feet. He received a sharp cuff once from a two-legged brute who "wa'n't a-go'n' to have no dogs a-suckun *his* fingers." He had licked the man's hand (I couldn't admire his taste), supposing that, being in the form of man, he was a being of good-will, and he got his first experience of a malignant disposition. He could not understand it; he yelped and fled to his master. I do not believe he laid it up against our race. His data were too few as yet to make so sweeping an induction. But some dogs have had to make it; have had to learn that there are men *and* men, or even that men as a race are a poor lot. One cannot but be sorry to see a snarling, suspicious, cowering cur; to think how much reason he has for being so and how he has had to belie his nature, perhaps even before he was born, to have become so. And there are snarling, suspicious, treacherous men; dreadful deities these for the species below them. They are made so, it would seem, partly by the sins of their own kind and partly by what they supposed the sins of their gods. We really cannot dissociate the two, for to lay the wrong on that abstraction called the world is to lay it virtually on the Power that made the world what it is. All this, of course, is only their own ignorance of the gods and their own evil bent imputed to the powers above; an ignorance curable not by knowledge wholly, if at all, but by love. The lack of love is the one darkness and blindness. As soon as they turn away from evil motions to love and loyalty and patience and trust—the dog virtues—men, too, find out their mistake and the true nature of the gods begins to come in sight. But because men are not gods yet, but only stumbling along through the sand and thorns of their own nature toward God, and because they are so easily drawn away toward the dirt and dark, they too often give their four-footed friend compelling reason for moroseness and suspicion. They need to school themselves better in the deity rôle, so that they may send on the pulsation from above toward the lower places of the earth that are so loyally waiting for the adoption—to wit, the redemption of the body.

We may, perhaps, take a hint from Caleb not to lay up too much against our race or against any single specimen of it. The man who cuffed him (God made him, let him pass for a man) perhaps loves his wife and children; perhaps has a dog or a horse on whom he bestows a surly good-will according to his light. There is a germ of love in him struggling to get beyond the tether of property exclusiveness and become intrinsic. If he can be kind to his own dog he is in the way, so he will commit himself to it, of being kind to all dogs, and to men and to the world in which he is unwittingly undergoing education. If he can get out of that mesh of self, out of that cramping prison-house of his own claims, and let good-will have free course and be its own reason for existing—well, dogs' nature, too, will have less reason to outrage its healthy instincts, and the world itself will become a different place. The problem is to get the channels and sluiceways open for that elemental tide of love which is the deepest and realest thing in the world, so that in the far-off divine event there may be no clog or stricture.

A big problem? Yes; there is no denying that. The

Reality above took upon Himself no easy task when he endowed a multitudinous creation with such tremendous possibilities and then set it growing to make the possible real. We may well be thankful that so small a part of the task relatively falls on us of the human species. And perhaps if we will let ourselves learn from beings like my lowly teacher (there are many of them as good as he), who are all the while teaching as though they taught not, to accept the rôle that they tacitly accord us, with due appreciation of their dumb virtues, a livable theology may not seem so very hard a problem after all.

# OLD-TIME NAVAL OFFICIALS[1]

*By* CAPTAIN A. T. MAHAN

*Captain Mahan, author of* The Influence of Sea Power upon History *(1890), which was the foundation of modern naval policy, and of other books only less influential, was born in 1840, died in 1914, and spent his life in the service of the United States. This "familiar essay" was first published in* Harper's *for October, 1917.*

BY LUCK, I, FOR THE FIRST TIME in my life, have found a plausible derivation for midshipman.[2] It would appear that in the days immediately after the flood the vessels were very high at the two ends, between which there was a deep "waist," giving no ready means of passing from one to the other. To meet this difficulty there were employed a class of men, usually young and alert, who from their station were called midship-men, to carry messages which were not subject for the trumpet shout. If this explanation holds water, it, like fore-castle, and after-guard, and knight-heads, gives another instance of survival of nomenclature from conditions which have long ceased.

Whatever the origin of his title, it well expressed the anomalous and undefined position of the midshipman. He belonged, so to say, to both ends of the ship, as well as to the middle, and his duties and privileges alike fell within the broad saying, already quoted, that what was nobody's business was a midshipman's. When appointed as such, in later days, he came in "with the hayseed in his hair," and went out fit for a lieutenant's charge; but from first to last, whatever his personal progress, he continued, as a mid-



2 Acknowledgment is here due to Mr. Thomas G. Ford, once a professor at the Naval Academy, cordially remembered by the midshipmen who knew him there in the fifties. His article is in the issue of the *Naval Institute Proceedings* for June, 1906, which has just reached me. He attributes his information to the late Admiral Preble, almost the only American officer within my time who has had the instincts of an archæologist.

shipman, a handy-billy. He might be told, as Basil Hall's first captain did his midshipmen, that they might keep watch or not as they pleased—that is, that the ship had no use for them; or he might be sent in charge of a prize, as Farragut was, when twelve years old, doubtless with an old seaman as nurse, but still in full command. Anywhere from the bottom of the hold to the truck—top of the masts—he could be sent and was sent; every boat that went ashore had a midshipman, who must answer for her safety, and see that none got away of a dozen men, whose one thought was to jump the boat and have a run on shore. Betweentimes he passed hours at the masthead in expiation of the faults he had committed, or ought to have committed, to afford a just scapegoat for his senior's wrath. As Marryat said, it made little difference; if he did not think of something he had not been told, he was asked what his head was for; if he did something off his own bat, the question arose what business he had to think. In either case he went to the masthead. Of course, at a certain age, one "turns to mirth all things of earth, as only boyhood can"; and the contemporary records of the steerage brim over with unforced jollity, like that notable hero of Marryat's, "who was never quite happy except when he was d—d miserable."

Such undefined standing and employments taught men their business, but provided no remedy for the miscellaneous social origin of midshipmen. In the beginning of things they were probably selected from the smart young men of the crew; often also from the middle-aged; in any event, from before the mast. Even in much later days men passed backward and forward from midshipment to lower ratings; Nelson is an instance in point. When a man became a lieutenant he was something fixed and recognized, professionally and socially. He might fall below his station, but he had his chance. In the British navy many most distinguished officers came from anywhere—through the hawseholes, as the expression ran; and a proud boast it should have been at a time when every Frenchman in his position had to be of noble blood. What was all very well for captains and lieutenants, once those ranks were reached, was not so easy for midshipmen. We know in every walk of life the woes of those whose position is doubtful or challenged; and what was said to his crew by Sir Peter Parker, an active frigate captain, who was killed in the Chesapeake in 1812, "I'll have you touch your hat to a midshipman's jacket hung up to dry,"—curiously reminiscent of William Tell and Gessler's cap,—not improbably testifies to equivocalness even at that late date. Seamen are singularly observant and tenacious of their officers in such matters. I have known one reproved for disrespect say, sullenly, "I have always been accustomed to sail with gentlemen." In the instance the comment was just, though not permissible. Deference might be conceded to the midshipman's jacket, but it could not cover defects of a certain order. The midshipman's berth, as attested by contemporary sketches, was peopled by all sorts in age, fitness, and manners. In one of the many tales I devoured in youth, a middle-aged shellback of a master's mate, come in from before the mast, says with an oath to an aristocratic midshipman, "Isn't my blood as red as yours?" Still, even in the British navy, with its fine democratic record, the social rank was more regarded than the military. John Byng, Esquire, Admiral of the Blue, would thus be of higher consideration as esquire than as admiral.

In the practice cruises the social question did not arise. Independently of the democratic tendency of all boys' schools, where each individual finds his level by natural selection, the Naval Academy has been successful in assimilating its heterogeneous raw material and turning out a finished product of a good average social quality. Beyond this, social success or failure depends everywhere upon personal aptitudes which no training can bestow. But as officers, we were nondescript. There were too many of us; and for the mass the object was to acquire the knowledge of the seaman, not that of the officer. Yet, curiously enough, so at least it seemed to me, there was a disposition on the part of some to be jealous of any supposed infringement of our prerogative to be treated as "a bit of an officer." Ashore or afloat, we made our own beds, or lashed our own hammocks, swept our own rooms, tended our clothes, and blacked our boots; at manœuvres, we manned the gear side by side with the crew; our drills were those of the men before the mast, at sails and guns; all parts of a seaman's work, except cleaning the ship, were required and willingly done; but there was a comical rebellion on one occasion when ordered to pull—row—a boat ashore for some purpose, and almost a mutiny when one lieutenant directed us to go barefooted while decks were being scrubbed, a practice which, besides saving your shoe leather, is both healthy, cleanly, and, in warm weather, exceedingly comforting. Some asserted that the lieutenant in question, who afterward commanded one of the Confederate commerce-destroyers, and from his initials (Jas. I.) was known to us as Jasseye, had done this because he had very pretty feet which he liked to show bare, and we must do the same; much as Germans are said to train their mustaches with the Emperor's. At all events, there was great wrath, which I suppose I should have shared had I not preferred bare feet; not for as sound reasons as the lieutenant's. With so many details regulated, if not enforced —from the length of our hair to the cut of our trousers— it did seem hypercritical to object to going shoeless for an hour. But who is consistent? The uncertainty of our position kept the chip on the shoulder.

At the time of graduation I had a narrow escape from the cutting short of my career, resembling that which a man has from a railway accident by missing the train. To a certain extent the members of classes were favored in forming groups of friends, and choosing the ship to which they should be sent. Two of my intimates and myself applied for the sloop-of-war *Levant*, destined for the Pacific by way of Cape Horn; our motive being partly the class of vessel, supposed by us to favor professional opportunity, and partly the friendship existing between one of us and the master of the *Levant*, a graduate of two or three years before, who had just completed his examinations for promotion. Luckily for us, and particularly for me, as the only one of the three who in after-years survived middle age, the frigate *Congress* was fitting out, and her requirements for officers could not be disregarded. The *Levant* sailed, reached the Pacific, and disappeared—one of the mysteries of the deep.

We very young men had the impression that small vessels were better calculated to advance us professionally because, having fewer officers, deck duty might be devolved on us, either to ease the regular watch officers or in case of a disability. This prepossession extended particularly to brigs, a class then still existent. This was a pretty wild imagining, for I can hardly conceive any one entrusting such a vessel to a raw midshipman. It is scarcely an exaggeration to say they were all canvas and no hull; beautiful as a dream, but dangerous, except to the experienced. As it was, an unusual proportion of them came to grief. Our views were doubtless largely, if unconsciously, affected by the pleasing idea of prospective early importance as deck officers. The more solid opinion of our seniors was that we would do better to pause a while on the bottom step, under closer supervision; while as for vessel, the order, dignity, and scale of performance in big ships were more educative, more formative of military character, which, and not seamanship, is the leading element of professional value. "Keep them at sea," said Lord St. Vincent, "and they can't help becoming seamen; but attention is needed to make them learn their business with the guns." I have already mentioned that at the outbreak of the War of Secession it was this acquirement that decided the authorities to give seniority to the very young lieutenants over the volunteers from the merchant service, very many of whom had larger experience and—though by no means all of them—consequent skill as seamen.

The *Congress* was a magnificent ship of her period. The adjective is not too strong. Having been built about 1840, she represented the culmination of the sail era, which, judged by her, reached then the splendid maturity that in itself, to the prophetic eye, presages decay and vanishment. In her just but strong proportions, in her lines, fine yet not delicate, she "seemed to dare," and did dare, "the elements to strife"; while for "her peopled deck," when her five hundred and odd men swarmed up for an evolution, or to get their hammocks for the night, it was peopled to the square foot, despite her size. On her forecastle, and to the fore and main masts each, were stationed sixty men, full half of them prime seamen, not only in skill but in age and physique; ninety each for the starboard watch, and ninety for the port, not to count the mizzentopmen, afterguard, and marines, more than as many more. I have always remembered the effect upon me of this huge mass of human beings, when gathered once to wear ship in a heavy gale, the height of one of those furious pamperos which issue from the prairies (pampas) of Buenos Ayres. The ship having only fore and main topsails, close reefed, the officers were not summoned, beyond those of the watch; the handling of the yards required only the brute force of muscle, under which, even in such conditions, they were as toys in the hands of that superb ship's company. I had thus the chance to see things from the poop, a kind of bird's-eye view. As the ship fell off before the wind, and while the captain was waiting that smoother chance which from time to time offers to bring her up again on the other side with the least shock, she gathered, of course, accelerated way with the gale right aft; scudding, in fact. Unsteadied by wind on either side she rolled deeply, and the sight of the faces of those four hundred or more men, all turned up and aft, watching intently the officer of the deck for the next order, the braces stretched along taut in their hands for instant obedience, was singularly striking. Usually a midshipman had to be in the midst of such things, with no leisure for impressions, at least of an "impressionist" character. Those were the prerogatives of the "idlers," the surgeons, chaplain, and marine officers, who obtained thereby not only the benefit of the show, but material for discussion as to how well the thing had been done, or whether it ought to have been done at all. The midshipman's part at "all hands" was to be as much in the way as was necessary to see all needed gear manned, no skulkers, and as much out of the way as his personal stability required from the rush of the huge gangs of seamen, "running away" with a rope.

I never had the opportunity of viewing the ship from the outside, underway at sea, but she was beautiful to look at in port. Her spars, both masts and yards, lofty and yet square, were as true to proportions for perfection of appearance as was her hull; and the twenty-five guns she showed on each broadside, in two tiers, though they had abundance of working-room, were close enough together to suggest two strong rows of solid teeth, ready for instant use. Nothing could be more splendidly martial. But what old-timers they were, with the swell of their black muzzles, like the lips of a full-blooded negro! Thirty-two-pounders, all of them, except, on either side, five eight-inch shell guns, a small tribute to progress. The rest threw solid shot for the most part. Imposing as they certainly looked, and heavier though they were than most of those with which the world's famous sea-fights have been fought, they were already antediluvian. A few years later I saw a long range of them enjoying their last repose on the skids in a navy-yard, and a bystander, with equal truth and irreverence, called them pop-guns.

Like the ship and her equipment, the officers and crew, by training and methods, were still of the olden time in tone and ideals, a condition, of course, fostered at the moment by the style of vessel; yet with that curious adaptability characteristic of the profession, which enabled them to fall readily into the use of the new types of every kind evolved by the War of Secession. Concerning some of these, a naval professional humorist observed that they could be worshipped without idolatry, for they were like nothing in heaven or on earth or in the waters under the earth. Adored or not, they were handled to purpose. By a paradoxical combination the seaman of those days was at once most conservative in temperament and versatile in capacity. There was, however, among the officers an open vision toward the future. I well remember "Joe" Smith enlarging to me on the merits of Cowper Coles's projected turret ship, much talked about in the British press in 1860, a full year or more before Ericsson, under the exigency of existing war, obtained from us a hearing for the *Monitor*. Coles's turrets, being then a novel project, were likened, explanatorily, to a railway turntable, a very illustrative definition, and Smith was already convinced of the value of the design, which was proved in Hampton Roads the day after he himself fell gloriously on the deck of the *Congress*. There is a double tragedy in his missing by this brief space the open demonstration of a system to which he so early gave his adherence; and it is another tragedy, which most Americans, except naval officers, will have forgotten, that Coles himself found his grave in the ship, the *Captain,* ultimately built through his urgency upon this turret principle. This happened in 1870.

In 1859 the United States government was coquetting with the title "Admiral," which was supposed to have some insidious connection with monarchical institutions. Even so sensible and thoughtful a man as our sailmaker, who was a devout disciple and constant reader of Horace Greeley, with the advanced political tendencies of the *Tribune*, said to me: "Call them admirals! Never! They will be wanting to be dukes next." We had hit, heretofore, on a compromise, quite accordant with the transition decade of 1850-1860, and styled them flag-officers; concerning which it might be said that all admirals are flag-officers, but all flag-officers were not admirals.

Our flag-officer was a veteran of 1812. He was known familiarly in the navy by the epithet Buckey; I never saw it spelled, but the pronunciation was given. Report ran that he thus called every one, promiscuously; but, although I was his aide for near six months, I only heard him use it once or twice. Possibly he was breaking a bad habit.

Judging by my experience, which, I believe, was no worse than the average, the life of an aide is literally that of a dog; it was chiefly following round, or else lying in a boat at a landing, just as a dog waits outside for his master, to all hours of the night, till your superior comes down from his dinner out, or from the theatre. A coachman has a "cinch," to use our present-day slang, for he has only his own behavior to look to, while the aide has to see that the dozen bargemen also behave, don't skip off the wharf for a drink, and then forget the way back to the boat. If one or two do, no matter how good his dinner may have been, the remarks of the flag-officer are apt to be "such," not to speak of subsequent interviews with the first lieutenant. I trace to those days the horror, which has never left me, of keeping servants waiting. Flag-officers apparently never heard that punctuality is the politeness of kings.

The flag-officer, though not a man of particular distinction, possessed strongly that kind of individuality which among seamen of the days before steam, when the world was less small and less frequented, was more common than it is today. We now cluster so that, like shot in a barrel, we are rounded and polished by mere attrition; but formerly characteristics had more chance to emphasize themselves, and throw out angles, as, I believe, they still do in long polar seclusions. Withal, there came from him from time to time whiffs of a past naval atmosphere, like that from a drawer where lavender has been. Going ashore one day with him for a constitutional, he caught sight of my necktie, which my fond mother had given me. It was black, yes, but with variations. "Humph!" he ejaculated; "don't wear a thing like that with me. You look like a privateersman." There spoke the rivalries of 1812. A great chum of his was the senior surgeon of the ship, a man near his own years. Going ashore together one day for a walk, the surgeon, crossing the deck, smudged his clothes with paint or coal-tar, the free application of which in unexpected places is one of the snares attending a well-appearing ship. "Never mind, doctor," said the flag-officer, consolingly, falling back, like Sancho Panza, on an ancient proverb, "remember, the two dirtiest things in the world are a clean ship and a clean soldier." Coal-tar and pipe-clay, to wit. Another trait was an extensive, though somewhat mild, profanity, which took no account of ladies' presence, although he was almost exaggeratedly deferential to them, as well as cordially courteous to all. His speech was, like his gait, tripping. I remember the arrival of the first steamer of a new French line in Rio. Steam mail service was there and then exceptional, most of our home letters came by sailing vessel, consequently this was an event, and brought the inevitable banquet. He was present; I also, as his aide, seated nearly opposite him with two or three other of our officers. He was called to respond to a toast. "Gentlemen and ladies!" he began. "No! Ladies and gentlemen;

ladies always first, d—n me." What more he said I do not recall, although we all loyally applauded him. Many years afterward, when he was old and feeble, an acquaintance of mine met him, and he began to tell of the tombstone of some person in whom he was interested. After various particulars, he startled his auditor with the general descriptive coruscation, "It was covered with angels and cherubs, and the h—ll knows what else."

It would be easily possible to overdraw the personal peculiarities of the seamen. I remember nothing corresponding at all to the extravagances instanced in my early reading of Colburn's, such as a frigate's watch—say, one hundred and fifty men—on liberty in Portsmouth, England, buying up all the gold-laced cocked hats in the place, and appearing with them at the theatre. Many, however, who have seen a homeward-bound ship leaving port, the lower rigging of her three masts crowded with seamen from deck to top, returning roundly the cheers given by all the ships-of-war present, foreign as well as national, as she passes, have witnessed also the time-honored ceremony of her crew throwing their hats overboard with the last cheer. This corresponded to the breaking of glasses after a favorite toast, or to the bursts of enthusiasm in a Spanish bull-ring, where Andalusian caps fly by dozens into the arena. There, however, the bullfighter returns them, with many bows; but those of the homeward-bounders become the inheritance of the boatmen of the port.

As midshipman of the watch, being stationed on the forecastle, my intimates among the crew were the staid seamen, approaching middle age, allotted there, where they had least going aloft. A forecastle intimate of mine was the boatswain, who, like most boatswains of that day, had served his time before the mast. As is the case with many self-made men he, on his small scale, was very conscious of the fact, and of his general consequent desert. A favorite saying with him was, "Thanks to my own industry, and my wife's economy, I am now well beforehand with the world." He served on board one steamer, the *San Jacinto*, and what had pleased him was that the yards could be squared and rigging hauled taut—his own special function—before entering port, so that in those respects the job had been done when the anchor dropped. One of his pet stories, frequently brought forward, concerned a schooner in which he had served in the earlier period, and will appeal to those who know how dear a fresh coat of paint is to a seaman's heart. She had just been decorated within and without, and was standing into a West-Indian port to show her fine feathers, when a sudden flaw of wind knocked her off and over, on to a rocky point. The first order given was, "Stand clear of the paint-work!" an instance of the ruling passion strong in *extremis*.

This boatswain afterward saw the last of the *Congress* when the *Merrimac*—or rather the *Virginia*, to give her her Confederate name—wasted time murdering a ship already dead, aground, and on fire. He often afterward spun me the yarn, for I liked the old man, and not infrequently went to see him in later days. He had borne good humoredly the testiness with which a youngster is at times prone to assert himself against what he fancies interference, and I had appreciated the rebuke. The *Congress* catastrophe was a very big and striking incident in the career of any man, and it both ministered to his self-esteem and provided the evening of his life with material for talk. Unhappily, I have to confess, as even Boswell at times did, I took no notes, and cannot reproduce that which to me is of absorbing interest, the individual impressions of a vivid catastrophe.

The boatswain was one of the four who in naval phrase were termed "warrant" officers, in distinction from the lieutenants and those above, who held their offices by "commission." The three others were gunner, carpenter, and sailmaker, names which sufficiently indicate their several functions. In the hierarchical classification of the navy, as then established by long tradition, the midshipmen, although on their way to a commission, were warrant-officers also, and in consequence, though they had a separate mess, they had the same smoking-place, the effect of which in establishing a community of social intercourse every smoker will recognize.

At first thought it seems somewhat singular that the six lieutenants of the ship presented no such aggregate of idiosyncrasies as did the four warrant-officers. It was not by any means because we did not know them well and mingle among them with comparative frequency. *Mid*shipmen, we travelled from one side to the other; here at home, there guests, but to both admitted freely. But, come to think of it more widely, the distinction I here note must have had a foundation in conditions. Marryat, who lived the naval life as no other sea-author, has a full gallery of captains and lieutenants, each differing from the other; but his greatest success in portrayal, the characters that take hold of the memory, are his warrant-officers, boatswains, gunners, and carpenters. There have been particular, eccentric commissioned officers, of whom quaint stories have descended, but in early days originality was a classmark of those of whom I am speaking.

Thus the several lieutenants of our frigate call for no special characterization. If egotism, the most amusing of traits where it is not offensive, existed among them to any unusual degree, it was modified and concealed by the acquired exterior of social usage. Their interests also were wider. With them talk was less of self and personal experience, and more upon subjects of general interest, professional or external; the outlook was wider. But while all this tended to make them more instructive, and in so far more useful companions, it also took from the salt of individuality somewhat of its pungency. It did not fall to them, either, to become afterward especially conspicuous in the nearing War of Secession. They were good seamen and gallant men; knew their duty and did it; but either opportunity failed them or they failed opportunity; from my knowledge of them, probably the former.

# THE UNCHANGING GIRL[1]

By Edward S. Martin

*Edward S. Martin, one of the shrewdest commentators upon use and wont in our day, has for many years conducted the pungent editorial page of* Life, *and of late years has succeeded to the "Easy Chair" of* Harper's Magazine, *once held by Howells. He was born in 1856. This essay was first published in* Harper's *for December, 1913.*

WE KEEP HEARING THAT THE world has changed so much; is changing so fast; and especially for girls. People wonder whether anywhere there are back-waters where children are being brought up as they used to be. The suggestion is abroad—very disquieting to a good many people—that everything in the world, including the institutions and the human beings, is about to be different from what it has been, and that the change is now in full course and going fast. Old-fashioned people are getting rattled, and begin to inspect one another, with the kind of attention that one pays to menagerie animals, as examples of a species about to become extinct.

Still, for the moment, it is permitted to deprecate these anxieties. Things do move, to be sure, but there are still considerations that may keep up hope in folks who have agreeable memories of the world as it lately was, and prefer that it should not do a lightning change into a brand-new place peopled with complete strangers. We hear of the great change in children: how differently nowadays they are taught, clothed, trained, by methods unfamiliar to most of their elders, to ends that seem hypothetical and untried. And especially the girls. We are constantly invited to predict what the girls are going to be and do and what is going to happen to the world in consequence. The old-fashioned girls got married and—well—here we are! But these new-fashioned girls that are just about to be—can our old-fashioned world be altered sufficiently to suit them? Can the venerable institution of marriage have enough tucks let out in it to be a loose enough garment for their audacious requirements? Can man be trained to be wise enough or of a sufficient submissiveness for them to marry? And when they are done, will wary young men dare to love them?

Of course, if the girls are going to be different it's a serious thing, unless the boys and all the rest of creation are nicely adjusted to the change in them. Either a sufficient proportion of the girls must match the rest of the terrestrial institution, or the institution must match the girls. Otherwise things can't go on.

I understand Mr. Cram, who built that handsome new church on Fifth Avenue, says in his book on the ruined abbeys of Great Britain that it was the monks who lived in those abbeys who really put the foundation under England and gave her such a start in the right course that she has not entirely left it yet. And the monks were celibates. Perhaps out of the contemporary ferment we shall have a crop of celibates, and especially of free and independent single ladies, who shall do a great work for our world and mightily improve it. That is a conceivable consequence of the extinction of old-fashioned children, and of girls becoming different, and of course nobody who looks about will disparage the powers of celibate ladies in the improvement of mankind.

Such as we are, however, and with all our prejudices against the notion that we are detrimental products of civilization, we lean toward the older-fashioned women to whom we owe our being, and hope, half piously and half in self-extenuation, that the likeness of them is not about to pass from earth. To back that hope let us seek such reassurances as there may be. And there are some. It looks on the surface as though old-fashioned children had followed the pterodactyls and dinosauruses out of life in the direction of geology, but surface appearances often fool us. Childhood is conservative. It has back of it endless generations of mankind, and processes of development akin to the processes by which the egg develops into the living creature. Such processes are cousins to instinct, and are stubborn affairs that do not readily yield to fashion or new conditions of life. A new baby now is no wise different from what new babies have been for time immemorial. The younger children are, the more likeness we find in them to what children were. And perhaps, so far as concerns young children, the changes in raising are more superficial than we are apt to think. Mother Goose is still a mighty popular author. Robinson Crusoe and Man Friday, Sindbad and Morgiana and Aladdin and their fellows, and Jack the Giant-killer, and all the fairies, and a lot of other old familiars keep ever moving into the new cerebral apartments of the rising generation. And the Bible, for all that people say the young don't know it, is still the best seller and more read than any other book.

As for games, they come and go and change, but the good ones have great vitality. I doubt if cat's-cradle has disappeared or ever will. Battledore and shuttlecock has probably bowed gracefully to lawn-tennis and awaits revival on a back seat, but in tennis the essentials of it are preserved. There are always novelties in the toy-shops, but the old stand-bys, the hoops and balls and marbles and skipping-ropes and blocks and dolls, are always there in force.

And the old-time interest in appearance continues without perceptible abatement. No less attention than formerly is paid to the hair of little girls, and no less pains taken to make them "look nice." Girls don't make samplers any more, but they still crochet and still knit and embroider. I know not whether little boys still occupy themselves sometimes with a cork with a hole through it, and four pins stuck in the upper rim, and contrive with that once familiar apparatus to weave colored worsteds into a wonderful tail which, curled up flat and with due stitches, made a lamp-mat. That was a good trick. I doubt if it is taught in the public schools, but a little modern boy looking for entertainment on a rainy afternoon or a winter evening would probably take kindly to it.

Pantalets are gone, and a good riddance, and delightful bare brown legs of young children have emerged from them. Not even in the remotest back-water is there any longer a crinoline, which survives only on the stage in middle-of-the-nineteenth-century dramas. A bride, though, is still a bride, and glad to wear her grandmother's wedding veil, if there is one, and, though crinoline has passed away, skirts have not quite gone yet, but are like the Sibyl's books in that diminution in quantity does not seem to make them cheaper or less interesting, or less necessary to provide and consider. There is no perceptible abatement yet in the interest of mothers in dressing their children. Clothes are just as important as they ever were; rather better than they used to be and quite as pretty, and, on the whole, more sensible; though as to sense, the fashions change and often seem to leave it out.

Babies, then, being just the same as formerly, except that the great advance in medicine, surgery, sanitation, and such matters has improved their chances of growing up, and young children now being not so different as might be supposed from what young children used to be, one naturally wonders at what age the great changes in life (which are understood to be proceeding in this generation) begin to touch the girls and make them different. I inquired about that of an expert man who has to do with the training of the young, and always has a lot of them convenient for observation during their pupilage. "When," said I, "do the modern girls begin to feel the influence of their times and begin to be different from their grandmothers at their age?" He deliberated. "At about forty."

"Then you don't see any change in young girls and young women? You've known them by the hundred, intimately and over long periods of time, studied them more than anything else for nearly half a lifetime, and you say the new girls are just the same as the old?"

"Yes; just the same. The fashions change, but the girls don't. Sports have changed a little; studies have changed; but the girls haven't. They are still the same girls, and do things very much as they always did, albeit they do different things now from what their grandmothers did. Their grandmothers, also, in their day did different things from what *their* grandmothers did. The conditions of life change; employments change; education follows new fashions; new opportunities offer, old ones dwindle in importance; the girls as they come along take up the newer fashions in all things. That makes them look different, and people think they are changed, and are going to change still more, and that there is going to be the New Woman who is to be something that woman never was before. But that's a mistake. The girls don't change. They are just the same they always were, and they will keep on being so."

"And the New Woman?"

"Why, bless you! the New Woman is just the old woman in a new bonnet, adjusted more or less to enormous changes in the physical and mental apparatus of the world, learned in new branches, a reader of newspapers and many books full of undigested suggestion, unedifying quotation, and very doubtful assertion. She used to ride on a pillion; now she rides in a motor-car, and often drives it herself. Of course she goes faster than she did. So does all the world. She keeps her place in an advancing line—that's all. Her relation to life has not changed, but it would have changed unless she had kept up with the times. We men are not the duplicates of our grandfathers. Where would we be, where find companions, if our contemporary women were just their grandmothers over again? They are their grandmothers modernized, as they should be, as they must be; and so fitted to sustain the same relations to life in this century as their grandmothers did to the last.

"Don't worry about the New Woman. Of course there are individual women now, as there always have been, who have strong impulses and the strength to follow them, and are pioneers for good or bad, and attain to starry crowns or come tremendous croppers. But the average, the standard, woman is not new and is not going to be. She is the same woman as heretofore, a conservative force like church or constitution or anything that has come down from old times, but she moves with the procession as she ought to."

I give you the impressions of this observer for what they are worth. Perhaps on another day they would have been different impressions. I find that my own are a good deal affected by the season and the weather, and on good days I am sure the girls will stay by us, and on bad ones I am apprehensive that they will bolt. No doubt they also have different moods about it, and at times give up mankind entirely, and are all for the independent life, and again relent and feel that there are better ways to warm cold hands than to sit on them. In all these matters that concern human relations we have to allow for the ebb and flow of feelings, and I think that just now we should also allow for the enormous contemporary development of the apparatus of vociferation. Time was when the still, small voice had a say. Now it is apt to be drowned out by the vast din of words in type. Think of the steady clatter of the printing-presses —thousands of them—printing from whirling rolls of paper, and not, as formerly, on one sheet at a time! Think of the presses and of the minds that feed them; what sort of minds they are—how wise, how far furnished with truths to impart, how far "speeded up" because the rollers are turning and must be fed! How far do modern newspapers reflect modern life, and how far are our impressions of modern life merely the reflections of modern newspapers? I could almost believe that the whole contemporary unrest of women is an extravaganza put out on the great stage of the world by newspapers and magazines, and that presently the curtain will drop on it and we shall forget that it ever was. I could almost believe that, but not quite; but it is true enough that, thanks to cheap paper, rotary presses, and cheap postage, shrill voices carry vastly farther than they did, and individual disturbance is able to assume the tones of a convulsion of nature.

Probably the old-fashioned child, if we allowed her a few hours of preparation in a department store, would find herself less a stranger in our contemporary world than we think. When I started out of my own haughty front door this very afternoon two of the three nine-year-old young ladies who were occupying my proud brown-stone doorstep arose to let me pass. The third also started to rise, but I restrained her. She had a baby in her lap, as did one of the others. None of them resides with me. I think they reside hard by on Third Avenue, but they find my front steps more commodious than their own, and the air of our block better for their babies. They and their sisters come daily, after school-hours, when the weather is propitious, and it is a relief and a protection to have them, because while they are there the boys, who are much more destructive, cannot occupy our steps. They seem entirely old-fashioned. Maybe it is because they do not yet read the papers very much. Some of them are even polite and seem to attend when I beg them not to scatter apple-skins on our steps; and one bright-eyed taller girl, with whom yesterday I discussed the prevailing habit of keeping game-scores on our basement wall in colored chalks, was very encouraging in her responsiveness.

These children are old-fashioned under difficulties, for they have no really suitable place to play (though there are worse playgrounds than an asphalt pavement) and no animals except babies to play with. We should all be better, I think, and more contented if we associated more with animals. They are perfectly old-fashioned; they do not read the newspapers and they do not want to vote. They have other delightful virtues which Walt Whitman has enumerated. They think so much better of us than we are that it is an encouragement. They give so much to us in proportion to what they get that it shames our poor generosities. I respect considerably the idea that God made them to be, not exactly an example to us, but a suggestion.

> "Not one is dissatisfied, not one is demented with the mania for owning things.
>
> "Not one is respectable or unhappy over the whole earth."

I suppose they will continue to live in our changing world in spite of machinery, and we will have the benefit of their society. We have the habit of eating some of them, which is a very painful thought, but insures their continuance. Think what could be said in the newspapers of our terrible habit of killing and eating the kind and seemly animals, if it could be brought into politics or it paid anybody to take it up. Mr. Bernard Shaw disapproves of it, I believe, but it is not a topic on which as yet he has enlarged very much. Think how easy it would be to demonstrate the machinations of the wicked Meat Trust to rivet the animal diet on society, just as the armament-makers are supposed to machinate to keep up war! But since we seem to be carnivorous we keep right on eating meat, and I suppose a good many of our other habits will keep right along in spite of enormous inksheds of remonstrance and expostulation, because we are so contrived.

We are all old-fashioned; fashioned long, long ago, with inbred needs so imperative that the satisfaction of them in some degree is the very price of life. People talk and write about men and women as though they were so much putty, that could be pinched into any new shape that was promised in a successful "platform" and voted by a reform legislature. Not much!

Men and women were not made by hands nor made of putty. They are very tough, old-fashioned products, who have in them what was put there and must work it out according to laws which it is their business to discover. They cannot be repealed, those laws; they cannot be evaded; there is no escape from them; no recall of them by ever so large a vote; nothing to do but to discover and obey them.

And those great laws of life are our final defense against all ill-considered novelties. The novelties may make an immense din; they may cause a vast deal of temporary trouble, and "temporary" may be a word centuries long in the great affairs of human life. But only as novelties are truer to the great laws than the measures and customs they supplant can they prosper and endure. Innovators can never upset the world. They did not make it. They can make a mess of things for a time; they can contribute to ends which they could not imagine, but in the long run the Great Mind has its way, and the lesser ones come to blight or honor according as they go that way or not.

Does it sound procrustean, this idea of mankind turned loose on the earth inevitably subject to immutable laws which it only partially comprehends? Does it seem like a story of rats in a trap? Perhaps so to the desperate and the blind in spirit. But as one comes to better knowledge of the great laws of life his conception of them changes, and he sees them more and more, not as cruel restraints, but as defenses of the glorious liberties of men, by obedience to which, and not otherwise, we may climb to all the heights there are; heights far beyond our present ken, and where as yet no human footprints seem to lead.

I suppose that is why the minds of men who have got what they would of the material things, and tried most of the ordinary experiments in the pursuit of joy, turn so often in the end to knowledge as the thing above all others to be desired, and the search for which is most useful to promote.

There are two great branches of knowledge: that which works to make the earth a fit abode for man, and that which works to make man fit to live in his abode. In both of them current progress seems amazingly rapid, and the progress in one helps progress in the other. But at any given time progress in one branch may outrun the record in the other, and things for a time may go lopsided in consequence. The case just now seems to be the one where material development has outrun spiritual and political development, and there is a scramble to bring the inhabitants of earth abreast of their new opportunities and to fit them for the fuller life and broader liberties which lie ready to all hands that are fit to grasp them. In that scramble there are bound to be many false starts, much doubting of sound principles, much experiment with unsound ones. People pull apart who ought to pull together; people pull together who belong apart. But all the time the great movement is forward; a great charge of humanity up the heights; a charge in which many will fall and many be trampled on, but in which great numbers and great courage and devotion press on to attainment, and surely will attain much, for there is no great check in sight.

But that great, motley host is no army of new recruits. In it is all the best human substance that ever has been; all the courage and the wisdom of the centuries; the courage to drive on, the wisdom to direct and often to restrain. We must not tremble at modern life, for it is the same old life we have always known and read about, but traveling now on a new bit of road. If in its current development the powers of advancement seem to have outrun the powers of regulation, that is only a passing appearance, for they are geared together and both are equally a part of our inheritance.

And as the special need of the time is for development of that branch of knowledge which works to make men fit to live on earth, the great activity of women is the more readily understandable, for it is in that great province that their more important domain lies, and in that that their more important abilities are indispensable. New duties come to them of course; new thoughts assail and new decisions await them, but no new fashion can last that will swerve them from womanhood or leave the world unmothered.

# THE FRIENDLY ROCKS

*By* John Burroughs

*John Burroughs, naturalist and leader of the school of American nature writers through almost half a century, was born in 1837 and died in 1921. This essay was first published in* Harper's *for November, 1913.*

I FIND THERE IS ENOUGH OF the troglodyte in most persons to make them love the rocks, and the caves and ledges that the air and the rains have carved out of them. The rocks are not so close akin to us as the soil; they are one more remove from us, but they lie back of all, and are the final source of all. I do not suppose they attract us on this account, but on quite other grounds. Rocks do not recommend the land to the tiller of the soil, but they recommend it to those who reap a harvest of another sort—the artist, the poet, the walker, the student and lover of all primitive open-air things.

Time, geologic time, looks out at us from the rocks as from no other objects in the landscape. Geologic time! How the striking of the great clock, whose hours are millions of years, reverberates out of the abyss of the past! Mountains fall, and the foundations of the earth shift, as it beats out the moments of terrestrial history. Rocks have literally come down to us from a fore-world. The youth of the earth is in the soil and in the trees and verdure that springs from it; its age is in the rocks; in the great stone book of the geologic strata its history is written.

The rocks have a history; gray and weather-worn, they are veterans of many battles; they have most of them marched in the ranks of vast stone brigades during the ice age; they have been torn from the hills, recruited from the mountain-tops, and marshaled on the plains and in the valleys, and, now the elemental war is over, there they lie waging a gentle but incessant warfare with time, and slowly, oh, so slowly, yielding to its attacks! I say they lie there, but some of them are still in motion, creeping down the slopes, or out from the clay banks, nudged and urged along by the frosts and the rains and the sun. It is hard even for the rocks to keep still in this world of motion, but it takes the hour-hand of many years to mark their progress. What in my childhood we called "the old pennyroyal rock," because pennyroyal always grew beside it, has, in time, crept out of the bank by the roadside three or four feet. When a rock, loosened from its ties in the hills, once becomes a wanderer, it is restless ever after, and stirs in its sleep. Heat and cold expand and contract it, and make it creep down an incline. Hitch your rock to a sunbeam and come back in a hundred years and see how much it has moved. I know a great platform of a rock weighing hundreds of tons, and large enough to built a house upon, that has slid down the hill from the ledges above, and that is pushing a roll of turf before it as a boat pushes a wave, but stand there till you are gray and you see no motion; return in a century, and you will doubtless find that the great rock-raft has progressed a few inches. What a sense of leisure such things give us hurrying mortals!

One of my favorite pastimes from boyhood up, when in my home country in the Catskills, has been to prowl about under the ledges of the dark gray shelving rocks that jut out from the sides of the hills and mountains, often forming a roof over one's head many feet in extent, and now and then sheltering a cool, sweet spring, and more often sheltering the exquisite moss-covered nest of the phœbe-bird. As a boy these ledges appealed to the wild and adventurous. The primitive cave-dweller in me, which is barely skin deep in most boys, found something congenial there; the air smelled good, it seemed fresher and more primitive than the outside air, it was the breath of the rocks and of the everlasting hills; the home feeling which I had amid such scenes doubtless dated back to the time when our rude forebears were cave-dwellers in very earnest. The little niches and miniature recesses in the rocks at the side were so pretty and suggestive, and would have been so useful to a real troglodyte. Of a hot summer Sunday one found the coolness of the heart of the hills in these rocky cells, and in winter one found the air tempered by warmth from the same source. To get down on one's hands and knees and creep through an opening in the rocks where bears and Indians have doubtless crept, or to kindle a fire where one fancies prehistoric fires have burned, or to eat black birch and wintergreens, or a lunch of wild strawberries and bread where Indians have probably often supped on roots or game —what more welcome to a boy than that!

As a man I love still to loiter about these open doors of the hills, playing the geologist and the naturalist, or half playing them, and half dreaming in the spirit of my youthful days.

Phœbe-birds' nests may be found any day under these rocks, but on one of my recent visits to them I found an unusual nest on the face of the rocks, such as I had never before seen. At the first glance, from its mossy exterior, I took it for a phœbe's nest, but close inspection showed it to be a mouse's nest—the most delicate and artistic bit of mouse architecture I ever saw—a regular mouse palace; dome-shaped, covered with long moss that grew where the water had issued from the rocks a few yards away, and set upon a little shelf as if it grew there. There was a hole on one side that led to the soft and warm interior, but when my forefinger called, the tiny aristocrat was not in. Whether he or she belonged to the tribe of the white-footed mouse, or to that of the jumping mouse, I could not tell. Was the device of the mossy exterior learned from the phœbe? Of course not; both had been to the same great school of Dame Nature.

Through the eyes of the geologist I see what the agents of erosion have done, how the tooth of time has eaten out the layers of the soft old red sandstone, and left the harder layers of the superposed Catskill rock to project, unsupported, many feet. I see these soft red layers running through under the mountains from valley to valley, level as a floor, and lending themselves to the formation of the beautiful waterfalls that are found here and there on the trout brooks of that region. To one such waterfall, a mile or more from the old schoolhouse, we used to go, when I was a boy, for our slate-pencils, looking for the softer green streaks in the crumbling slaty sandstone, and trying them on our teeth to see whether or not they were likely to scratch our precious slates. In imagination I follow this slaty layer through under the mountains and see where it is cut into by other waterfalls that I know, ten, twenty, thirty miles away. At those falls the water usually makes a sheer leap the whole distance, twenty, thirty, or fifty feet, as the case may be, the harder rock at the top always holding out while the softer layers retreat beneath it, forming in this respect, miniature Niagaras. When near one of these falls I seldom miss the opportunity to climb the side of the gorge under the overhanging rock, and inspect its undersurface, and feel it with my hand. The elements have here separated the leaves of the great stone book and one may read some of the history written there. When I pass my hand over the bottom side of the superincumbent rock I know I am passing it over the contours, the little depressions and unevennesses of surface, of the mud of the old lake or inland-sea bottom, upon which the material of the harder rock was laid down more than fifty millions of years ago.

One thing that arrests one's attention in such a place is the abruptness of the change from one species of rock to another, as marked and sudden as a change in a piece of masonry from brick to stone, or from stone to iron. The two meet but do not mingle. Nature seems suddenly to have turned over a new leaf, and to have begun a new chapter in her great stone book. What happened? There is no evidence in this region of crustal disturbance since the original plateau out of which the mountains were carved was first lifted up in the Paleozoic times, when the earth was in her teens. But some quiet day the peaceful waters became suddenly charged with new material and the streams or rivers from some unknown land in the vicinity poured it into the old Devonian lakes where it hardened into rock. As these streaks of soft red sandstone alternate with the hard, laminated Catskill, well up the mountain-sides, with a sharp dividing line between them, this sudden change occurred many times during the Devonian age. During one geologic day the earth-building forces brought one kind of material, and the next day material of quite another kind, and this alternation without any change of character seems to have kept up for millions of years. How curious, how interesting! Both from near-by land surfaces, and yet so different from each other! How difficult to form any mental picture of the condition of things in those remote geologic ages! It is as if one day it had snowed something like brick-dust to a depth of many feet, and the next day it had snowed a dark gray dust of an entirely different character, and that this alternation of storms had kept up for ages. Long before we reach the tops of the mountains, or at about a thousand feet above the river valley, the red, soft strata cease, and the hard, dark, cross-bedded gray rock continues to the top.

In the higher peaks of the southern Catskills another kind of rock begins to appear before the summit is reached—a conglomerate. The storm of dark snow has turned to a snow of white hail. As you go up you seem to be climbing into a shower of quartz pebbles. Presently you begin to see here and there a pebble imbedded in the rocks; then as you go on you see more of them, and still more; it is like the first sprinkle of rain that precedes the shower, till long before you reach the summit the regular downpour begins, the rocks become solid masses of pebbles imbedded in a gray, hard matrix; there are many hundreds of feet of them. On the top the soil is mainly sand and coarse gravel from the disintegrated rock.

The streams at the foot of the mountains abound in fragments of this pudding-stone, or conglomerate, and in the hard, liberated quartz pebbles. These pebbles were rolled on an ancient seabeach incalculable ages ago.

Of course the Catskills were under water when this conglomerate was laid down upon them. The coal age was near at hand, and the conglomerate akin to this of the tops of the Catskills underlies the coal measures. The Catskill plateau was lifted up before Carboniferous times began, so that there is no coal in this region. We should have to look overhead for it instead of underfoot. When the Catskill plateau rose above the waters, Pennsylvania and most of the continent to the west was under the sea, receiving additional deposits, thousands of feet thick in many places, and in due time supporting a vegetation that gave us our vast deposits of coal.

The geologic tornado that brought this hailstorm of quartz pebbles, so marked in the conglomerate that caps the highest Catskills, seems to have been a general storm over a large part of the Northern Hemisphere, as this conglomerate underlies the coal measures, both in this country and in Europe.

An earlier storm of quartz pebbles occurred in Silurian times, which formed the Oneida conglomerate in central New York, and the Shawangunk range in southern New York. This latter range is a vast windrow made up of small pebbles varying in size from peas to large beans, cemented together by quartz sand. It is several hundred feet thick and runs southwest through Pennsylvania into Virginia, affording another proof of the abundance of quartz rock in those early geologic ages. Dana thinks they give us an idea of the seashore work of that period.

According to the published views of a natural philosopher and seer on the Pacific coast, this rain of rock material from the heavens is no myth. He believes that the earth in its early history was surrounded by a series of numerous concentric rings of floating cosmic matter, like the rings of Saturn, and that from time to time these rings collapsed and their material fell to earth, helping to make up the vast series of stratified rocks. This theory certainly simplifies some of the problems of the geologist. My Catskills did not have to go down under the sea to get this coat of mail of quartz pebbles, or these alternate layers of red and gray sandstone, and the question of the abrupt ending and beginning of the different series is easily solved; as is also the larger question of where all the diverse material of our enormous system of stratified rock, reckoned by some geologists to be not less than twenty miles thick in North America, came from. In some parts of Scotland, the old red sandstone, according to Geikie, is twenty thousand feet thick. This theory of the California seer gives us all this material, and gives it in the original packages. I wish I could believe it true, and be thankful that there are no more rings to collapse.

In South America Darwin saw hills and mountains of pure quartz. Not far from Buenos Ayres they formed tablelands, or mesas, without cleavage or stratification. On the Falkland Islands he found the hills of quartz and the valleys filled with "streams of stone"—huge fragments of quartz-rock, varying in size from a few feet in diameter "to ten, or even more than twenty, times as much." Darwin thinks that these streams of quartz stones may have had their origin in streams of white lava that had flowed from many parts of the mountains into the valleys, and then when solidified were rent by some enormous convulsion into myriads of fragments. Some such titanic force of nature must have been the stone-crusher that converted vast hills of quartz into the fragments that make up the Shawangunk Mountains, the Oneida conglomerate, and the conglomerate on the tops of the Catskills.

In our Northern States there are two classes of rocks, the place rocks and the wanderers, or drift boulders. The boulders are in some ways the more interesting; they have a story to tell which the place rock has not; they have drifted about upon a sea of change, slow and unwilling voyagers from the North many tens of thousands of years ago; now they lie here in the fields and on the hills, shipwrecked mariners, in some cases hundreds of miles from home.

"The shadow of a great rock in a weary land" is pretty sure to be the shadow of a drift boulder. The rock about which, and on which, we played as children was doubtless a drift boulder; the rocks beneath which the woodchucks and the foxes burrow are drift boulders; the rock under the spreading maples where the picknickers eat their lunch is a drift boulder; the rock that makes the deep pool in the trout-stream of your boyhood is a drift boulder; the rocks which you helped your father pry up from the fields and haul to their place for the "rock bottom" of the stone wall, in the old days on the farm, were all drift boulders.

The rocks that give the eyebrows to the faces of the hills are place rocks—the cropping out of the original strata. The place rock gives the contour to the landscape; it forms the ledges and cliffs; it thrusts a huge rocky fist up through the turf here and there, or it exposes a broad, smooth surface where you may see the grooves and scratches of the great ice-sheet, tens of thousands of years old. The marks of the old ice-plane upon the rocks weather out very slowly. When they are covered with a few inches of soil they are as distinct as those we saw in Alaska under the edges of the retreating glaciers.

One day on the crest of a hill above my lodge on the home farm in the Catskills, I used my spade to remove five or six inches of soil from the upper layer of rock in order to prove to some doubting friends that a page of history was written here that they had never suspected. I quickly disclosed the lines and grooves, nearly as sharp as if made but yesterday, and as straight as if drawn by a rule, running from northeast to southwest. Across the valley, a third of a mile away, I uncovered other rock surfaces on the same level, that showed a continuation of the same lines. The great jack-plane had been shoved across the valley and over the mountain-tops and had taken off rocky shavings of unknown thickness.

The drift boulders are not found beyond the southern limit of the great ice sheet—an irregular line starting a little south of New York and running westward to the Rocky Mountains, but in southern California I saw huge granite boulders that looked singularly like New England drift boulders. They cover the hill called Rubidoux at Riverside. I overheard a tourist explaining to his companions how the old glaciers had brought them there, apparently ignorant of the fact that they were far beyond the southern limit of the old ice-sheet. It is quite evident that they were harder masses that had weathered out of the place rock and had slowly tumbled about and crept down the hill under the expansive power of the sun's rays. But I saw one drift boulder in southern California that was a puzzle; it was a water-worn mass of metamorphic rock, nearly as high as my head, at the end of a valley several miles in among the hills, with no kindred rocks or stones near it. It was evidently far from home, but what its means of transportation had been I could only conjecture.

Amid the flock of gray and brown boulders that dot my native fields there is here and there a black sheep—a rough-coated rock much darker than the rest, which the farmers call fire-stone, mainly, I suppose, because they do not break or explode in the fire. They are a kind of conglomerate, probably what the geologists call breccia, made up of the consolidated smaller fragments of older crushed rocks. The materials of which they are composed are of unequal hardness, so that they weather very rough, presenting a surface deeply pitted and worm-eaten, that does not offer an inviting seat. They wear a darker coat of moss and lichens than the other rocks, and seem like interlopers in the family of field boulders. But they really belong here; they have weathered out of the place strata. Here and there one may find their dark, worm-eaten fronts in the out-cropping ledges. They were probably formed of the coarser material—a miscellaneous assortment of small, thin, water-worn fragments of rocks and mud and coarse sand—that accumulated about the mouths of the streams and rivers which flowed into the old Devonian lakes and seas. They are not made up of thin sheets like the other rocks, and seem as if made at a single cast. They are as rough-coated as alligators, and do not, to me, look as friendly as their brother rocks. They stand the fire better than other stone. The huge stone arch in my father's sugar-bush, in which the great iron kettles were hung, was largely built of these stones. I think the early settlers used them to line the open fire-places in their stone chimneys. Along the Hudson they used slate, which is also nearly fire-proof.

I know a huge iron-stone rock lying at the foot of a hill from beneath which issues one of the coldest and sweetest springs in the neighborhood. How the haymakers love to go there to drink, and the grazing cattle also! Of course the relation of the rock to the spring is accidental. The rocks help make the history of the fields, especially the natural history. The woodchucks burrow beneath them, and trees and plants take root beside them. The delightful pools they often form in a trout stream every angler remembers. Their immobility makes the water dissolve and excavate the soil around and beneath them and afford lairs for the big trout.

All through the Southwest the great book of geologic Revelation lies open to the traveler in an astonishing manner. Its massive but torn and crumpled leaves of limestone, sandstone, and basalt lie spread out before him all through Colorado, New Mexico, and Arizona, and he may read snatches of the long geologic record from the flying train.

I myself need not go so far to see what time can do with the rocks. On the Shawangunk range of mountains in my own State are scenes that suggest a rocky Apocalypse. It is as if the trumpet of the last day had sounded here in some past geologic time. The vast rock stratum of coarse conglomerate, hundreds of feet thick, has trembled and separated into vast blacks, often showing a straight, smooth cleavage like the side of a cathedral. As a matter of fact, I suppose there was no voice of the thunder or of earthquake that wrought this ruin, but the still, small voice of heat and cold and rain and snow. There is no wild turmoil or look of decrepitude, but a look of repose and tranquillity. The enormous four-square fragments of the mountain stand a few feet apart, as if carefully quarried for a tower to reach the skies. In classic simplicity and strength, in harmony and majesty of outline, in dignity and serenity of aspect, I do not know their equal.

What a diverse family is this of the stratified rocks! Never did the members of the human family—Caucasian, Negro, Jew, Jap, Indian, Eskimo, Mongolian—differ more from one another than do the successive geological formations. White and black, hard and soft, coarse and fine, red and gray, yet all in the same line of descent—all dating back to the same old Adam rock of the Azoic period. Time and circumstance, conditions of water and air, of sea and land, seem to have made the difference. As the races of men were modified and stamped by their environment, so the diverse family of rocks reflects the influence of both local and general conditions. When analyzed, their constituents do not differ so much. As in the different races of men we find the same old flesh and blood and bones, so in the rocks we find the same quartz, sand, and compounds of lime and iron and potash and magnesia and feldspar, yet in quantity and character what a world of difference! How differently they are bedded, how differently they weather, how differently they submit to the hammer and chisel of the mason and the stone-cutter! Some rocks seem feminine, smooth, fine-grained, fragile, the product of deep, still waters; others are more masculine, coarse, tough, the product of waters more or less turbid or shallow.

It is remarkable, the purity of the strain of the different breed of rocks; about as little crossing or mingling among the different systems as there is among the different species of animals. Considering the blind warring and chaos of the elements out of which they came, one can but wonder at the homogeneity of the different kinds. They are usually as uniform as if their production had been carefully watched over by some expert in the business, which is true. This expert is water. Was there ever such a sorter and sifter! See the vast clay banks, as uniform in quality and texture as a snow-bank, slowly built up in the privacy of deep, still rivers or lakes during hundreds or thousands of years, implying a kind of secrecy and seclusion of nature. Mountains of granite have been ground down or disintegrated, and the clay washed out and carried by the currents till they were impounded in some lake or basin, and then slowly dropped. The great clay banks and sand banks of the Hudson River valley doubtless date from the primary rocks of the Adirondack region. Much of the quartz sand is still in the soil of that region, and much of it is piled up along the river-banks, but most of the clay has gone down-stream and been finally deposited in the great river terraces that are now being uncovered and worked by the brick-makers. Flowing water drops its coarser material first, the sand next, and the mud and silt last. Hence, the coarser-grained rocks and conglomerates are built up in shallow water near shore, the sandstones in deeper water, and the slates and argillaceous rocks in deeper still. The limestone rocks, which are of animal origin, also imply deep seas during periods that embrace hundreds and thousands of centuries. It is, then, the long ages of peace and tranquillity in the processes of the earth-building forces that have contributed to the homogeneity of the different systems of secondary rocks. What peace must have brooded over that great inland sea when those vast beds of Indiana limestone and sandstone were being laid down! A depth of thousands of feet of each without a flaw. Vast stretches of Cambrian and Silurian and Devonian time were apparently as free from violent movements and warrings of the elements as in our own day.

It would seem to require as distinctly an evolutionary process to derive our sedimentary rocks from the original igneous rocks as to derive the vertebrate from the invertebrate, or the mammal from the reptile. Of course it could not be done by a mechanical process alone. It has been largely a chemical process, and, no doubt, to a certain extent, a vital process also. The making of a loaf of bread is, up to a certain point, a mechanical process, then higher and finer processes set in. And all the cake and pastry and loaves in the bake-shop do not differ from the original bin of wheat any more than the great family of secondary rocks differs from the unmilled harvest of the earth's original crust. And the increase in bulk seems to have been quite as great as that from the kernel to the loaf or the roll. Little doubt that the bulk of the material of the sedimentary rocks came through the process of erosion and deposition from the original igneous rocks, but how has it expanded and augmented during the process! It seems to have swelled almost as the inorganic swells in passing into the organic.

# THE HARVEST OF THE WILD PLACES

*By* WALTER PRICHARD EATON

---

*Walter Prichard Eaton, dramatic critic and student and essayist of nature, was born in 1878. This essay was first published in* Harper's *for November, 1914.*

OVER THE HILL BEHIND OUR house, and then a mile through the swamp, we come out into a pasture clearing set on a slope. The slope is to the south, with many an undulation and outcropping ledge, with here and there a group of young hemlocks, here and there an old apple-tree bristling with suckers, or a spiky seedling from the parent pippin, cropped into a dwarf cone like an inverted top; and almost in the center of the pasture a hollow where a spring makes an emerald patch in the grass, and an emerald ribbon follows the outlet brook into the woods. On its southern edge, the clearing meets the forest, with little bays running into the pines, or sallies of young birch coming out to prospect in the sunlight. The pasture grass is cropped by occasional sheep and a cow or two which wander through the woods from a distant farm. They like it especially in hot weather, for its spring and its clumps of hemlock, under which they gather in the dense shade and look out at you blankly. But, despite the cattle, it is a wild spot—an abandoned clearing going back to forest; part of a farm where man once reaped his hard-won harvests, and now reaps no more.

Yet it is harvested daily by the four-footed and flying creatures of the wilderness, and the human cultivation once expended upon it has made it the richer farm for them. They toil not, neither do they sow, yet they live well on a varied if vegetarian diet. They reap as the fancy strikes them in man's abandoned clearing.

There is so much to see in our pasture, so much to infer! It is so quiet, so delicately melancholy with its suggestion of a vanished race of New England pioneers, so lovely with its woods and spring, such a busy restaurant for the birds by day, with music furnished by the patrons, and by night a restaurant, too, always open, with no police restrictions, though we be not here to see. To take morning reckoning of last night's visitors, especially by their tracks in the snow, is one of the lesser but unfailing delights of woodcraft.

Birds are busy creatures, for all they find so much time to sing, and they pay a great deal more attention to their stomachs than the poets ever mention. You will come closer to the facts in those government bulletins which report the finding of two thousand mosquitoes in the stomach of a single martin, and similar interesting discoveries, than in the poet's pages. I don't know that I have ever seen it computed how many raspberries a catbird can eat, but I know it is more than I care to spare from the vines in my own garden, where a pair of catbirds who nest each year in a red-osier dogwood beneath my study window love to feed. Out in our abandoned clearing, however, I do not begrudge them the berries, which grow in a corner where the vanished farmer made his last cutting of timber. Many a time I have lain on the ground up the slope in fruiting season and watched a catbird darting back and forth to these vines, as if his appetite were insatiable, his trim gun-metal body taking the sun on head or wing-tip. Presently I would get up and stroll over to gather some berries for myself. You would have thought a band of human pickers had been there, to see all the whitish, thimble-shaped hulls hanging denuded from their stems. Even as I would put out my hand for a red fruit there would come from the thicket close by a mew of protest and an angry flutter of wings. Though, in my own experience, the catbirds are most addicted to raspberries, the thrushes, orioles, robins, flickers, and cedar wax-wings also eat them, and doubtless other birds besides.

But there are many other harvest products in and about our pasture besides the raspberries. Even the weeds yield their store, and in autumn, or better still in winter, when the weed tops stand up dry and stiff above a light covering of snow, you may see the Canadian or tree sparrows (so called, perhaps, because they spend most of their lives on the ground!) hopping up to peck at the seeds, or occasionally one more wise shaking the seeds down and picking them up from the snow. In our own farms and gardens, indeed, we may see the same thing occurring, and often beneath a weed top find on light snow the dust of seed shells and innumerable tiny tracks. There is nothing more beautiful than the weed tops above a deep snow by country roadside or forest edge. Consider a group of wild-carrot tops (Queen Anne's lace), dried and turned up into fretted cups to hold each its thimbleful of snow, or a clump of withered goldenrod blooms, as perfect in shape as they were when the frost struck them down, but a brownish gray now instead of gold. Above all, look for the pods of the milkweed, three or more on a single tall stalk, a lovely yellowish brown inside, a delicate mouse-gray on the tongue, which curls over like the hood of a Jack-in-the-pulpit! The milkweed pods, above the deep snows of winter, with the full sun upon them, are like petrified orchards. Grass tops are lovely, too, rising through the dazzle, and cattails in the swamp, and many a more humble weed. And every one that bears seeds is harvest for the birds and mice, as well as the most delicate of etchings—a few gracefully stiff lines, a puff of withered bloom, against the dazzling ground plate of snow. Tiny foot marks, with the line of the tail between, make roads amid all the weeds of our pasture after winter has come. We may call it an abandoned clearing, but it was busy enough last night!

Richer food than the weeds, however, is provided near our

pasture by the black-cherry-tree close to the old fence just over the ridge toward a desolate cellar-hole. It is the lush time of summer when this tree is in fruit, the time when the baby birds are getting their growth, when the mother robins are anxiously busy. Man may have forsaken this clearing, but if we take our stand quietly under the cherry-tree, and wait a few moments till the frightened birds are reassured, we find ourselves in the midst of almost feverish avian activity. Robins dart into the tree incessantly, making a considerable noise about it, too. Now and then a big flicker comes winging into the branches. There is the gorgeous flash of an oriole, and sometimes, perhaps, the brilliance of a rose-breasted grosbeak or a tanager. Only the robins so haunt our domestic cherry-trees (can you not remember how, as a boy, you were startled, when robbing a neighbor's tree, by the rush of wings almost against your face?); and I have been told that even in an orchard, if a wild cherry is planted amid the cultivated sorts, the red-breasted trespassers will choose it in preference. Perhaps they find the small fruit better for their young. I have seen a mother robin in our garden try twelve successive times to stuff a large red cherry down the throat of her offspring, and give up the task only when the fruit was entirely battered off the stone. The wild cherry-trees, of course, are undesirable to the gardener because they harbor so many insect pests, especially tent caterpillars, but if these pests were kept down by spraying, a few wild trees ought to be a considerable protection on the edge of a cherry orchard.

Along such a fence as that where the cherry-tree stands might well be several cedars. The cedar is not a common tree with us, to be sure, but it grows plentifully twenty miles south in Connecticut. There the pastures are studded with dark sentinels, and many an old fence post is companioned by a sturdy tree or two. When the blue cedar berries are ripe in the autumn the late visitors among the birds, such as cedar wax-wings, robins, jays, and perhaps bluebirds and ruffed grouse (partridges), find them a ready food, and find, as well, warm protection from early snow-storms in the thick foliage. The young cedars, too, make excellent nesting-places for the smaller sparrows in early summer. The foliage is so dense and upstanding about the trunk that such a nest is practically invisible, and one existed in our yard last year, only breast-high beside a frequented garden path, for many weeks before we discovered it.

The lively goldfinch is brother to the butterflies in our forsaken pasture in thistle-time. There are but few thistles, and they are clustered amid wild sun-flowers in a fork of an old logging road by the edge of the second growth—a pretty color scheme of pink and gold. It seems almost as if the finches realized their own harmony with this bit of wild gardening, for they wing into the bed, seeking thistle-down for their nests, and starting up a swarm of tiny brown butterflies which had been invisible before. This garden-patch, too, is murmurous with bees on a warm summer morning. Later the finch returns to the sunflowers for their seeds, and later still you may see the chickadees darting quickly and cheerily out of the pines on the same errand.

Pine buds are still another form of food the pasture affords, and the English pheasants which have overrun our Berkshire woods in the last decade are the feeders. The pheasant is a walking bird, treading with one foot directly behind the other in a perfectly straight line, and he will often tramp for miles without leaving the ground. I have myself tracked one in light snow for more than two, and found him at the end in a nest of leaves. Unlike the partridge (perhaps because they are protected fifty-two weeks in the year), the pheasants like to feed in open spaces, and they particularly affect our pasture because many little seedling pines have begun to creep out from the forest edge and climb the slope, especially around the spring. Only the other day, walking softly on snow-shoes, we came out of the woods into the open dazzle, and saw four brown pheasants close to the spring, waddling on the snow. They did not fly up till we were within fifty feet of them. The snow was two feet deep, and it had thus raised their feeding level. Their tracks were everywhere about the seedling pines, and the juicy little terminal buds, which had been out of reach before the storm, were nipped off by the hundred. Snow which made food scarcer for other birds made it easier for them to obtain. Perhaps that is one reason they are multiplying so fast. Many of their tracks led down to the spring, which was still open in the center—a black hole in the expanse of snow. Evidently they had gone down to drink or bathe.

This same deep snow and accompanying cold brought down to New England and New York from the north flocks upon flocks of the rare pine grosbeaks, large, beautiful birds which move silently save for occasional little soft notes, almost like the pleasant squeaking of a tiny hinge. They grew very tame as winter progressed, and, from a discovery of the wild barberry bushes in the woods and abandoned clearings, moved in to feed upon the barberry hedges lining the drives of summer estates, and then actually to the bushes in front of occupied houses. On one of our walks we found a barberry bush surrounded apparently by blood-stains on the snow, but sitting on a topmost spray was the cause. A young grosbeak, not yet arrived at the dignity of red plumage, his bosom feathers puffed out by the cold wind, held a barberry in his bill, and was working it back and forth, sideways, rolling off the skin, evidently to get at the seeds and pulp. Presently he dropped the skin on the snow, emitted a gentle squeak or two, hopped to a new spray, and quite unmindful of us, began on another. The snow had no terrors for him so long as that bush held out.

The major harvest of our pasture is undoubtedly the apple

crop, and the major harvesters are the deer. The apples are small and bitter—or else tasteless—now. Encouraged by the optimism of Thoreau, I have bitten into many hundreds of wild apples since I first read his immortal pæan in their praise, but I have yet to discover a second Baldwin, or even an equal of the poorest variety in our orchard crop. At any rate, I no longer pick the apples in this pasture. No one picks them. They fall to the ground on an autumn night, and no one hears the soft, startling thud in the silence of the forgotten clearing. But the squirrels and the deer know where they are. More than once, in autumn, we have come out into the pasture in time to see a squirrel leaping across the open spaces toward the shelter of the pines with an apple in his mouth, and we have often seen one pick an apple from its stem, run down to the ground to get it, and then climb back with it to a crotch and eat at it. Sometimes they spit out the pulp, apparently aiming to get at the seeds, especially after the fruit is over-ripe. Sometimes they appear to swallow it. In old fence-holes frequented by chipmunks and squirrels you will often find apple-seeds. On the other hand, you will often find apples partially eaten on the ground beneath the trees, but not bitten through to the core, unmistakably by squirrels. The rabbits, also, eat the apples in winter. They will even come into our garden close to the village street, and eat the rotten apples on the frozen compost heap. It is there the cat hunts them, stalking behind the hedge. One of the delights of a walk to our pasture is the soft, sneaking approach through the woods, and the surprised uprush of pheasants from the ground when we are discovered, or, at the sudden appearance of a white tennis-ball, bounding away from under the apple-trees. The pips and stalks of wild roses and the new wood of raspberry vines are food for the rabbits, nor are they at all averse to domestic roses and cultivated raspberry stalks, as I know to my sorrow. They are out in almost all weathers, and the alder thicket below the pasture, on the swamp edge, is in winter a perfect net-work of their regularly traveled roads leading out to the feeding-grounds. The dog goes quite mad on this crisscross of trails.

The old apple-trees of our clearing, studded with suckers and spikes, are also a favorite roosting-place for the pheasants. The pheasants evidently eat the terminal buds. The pine grosbeaks, too, discovered the apple-trees last winter, carefully rejecting the skin of the fruit, as they did the skin of the berries. Many people, I find, who attempted to attract the grosbeaks around their dwellings discovered that apples were one of the few tempting baits. These birds have not yet learned, like the chickadees and nuthatches, the ways of civilization; they will not touch suet nor crumbs—nor even sunflower seeds. But apples will tempt them always.

The deer come to the wild apple-trees most frequently at night. Wherever there is an abandoned clearing or secluded orchard near their ranges, they will find it out, and in the morning after a snowfall, or more likely the second day after, you will find their hoof-marks all about the trees, and plentiful signs where they have pawed up the snow and nozzled out the frozen fruit beneath. If I were the particular sort of "sportsman" who shoots tame deer in Massachusetts during our open week in November, I know a certain old apple-tree far back from the road in a nearly deserted township where I should build a blind and sit comfortably down to wait for the slaughter. But that is hardly the way in which I wish to hunt them. It is almost inconceivable to me, indeed, that the law should give any opportunity for the destruction of these beautiful and harmless creatures, the last of the larger four-footed wild things to roam our Eastern woods. Those who hunt them are few, if damnably destructive; those who would rejoice to see our forests peopled with the loveliest of wild creatures are legion. Yet the kill-lust of the few rules in our legislatures. The traditions of barbarism die hard!

As for me, I much prefer to track the deer back from the apple-tree in our clearing, where he has been pawing up the snow, into the woods, following his rambles to see what else he ate that day—not a difficult task when the snow is fresh. It is obvious that he has nibbled at young hemlocks, apparently pulling off the tips as he passed along, much as a horse will do when you are driving him idly down a country lane. But the ground-hemlock, or American yew, is not thus lightly passed over. When the deer find a clump of this evergreen rising above the snow, they fall upon it eagerly, and sometimes eat it down almost to ground-level. It is a staple of their diet. Another staple seems to be sumac. More than once I have come upon a deer along some back road, feeding close to the boundary wall, and investigation has disclosed that he was eating sumac fruit. In winter, when you pick up a deer track in the woods and have time and patience to follow, it will frequently lead you to some sumac hedge by a pasture wall or back road. Before it gets there, to be sure, it may take you into the deep forest for ground-hemlock, and over a frozen swamp to a spot where there are water-holes protected from frost between the peaty hummocks, or even over a mountain almost too steep and slippery for your feet. But ultimately in our New England country the deer will probably swing back toward a sumac patch, even if it brings him close to a village, and leave the signs of his feeding on the broken stems. To start a doe with her fawns by a sumac hedge, to see her clear a stone wall at a single leap with no running start, to see the fawns with white tails like rabbits go cavorting after her with all the grace of animated saw-horses, is one of the prettiest sights in nature.

As you are tracking your deer through the woods, you will come upon many other signs of wild harvesting. Perhaps you may be sitting under a pine-tree, when suddenly a cone scale will fall on your head. Listen, and you will hear the sound of crackling far above you. Creep out away from the tree, and look up. It may take you several seconds to find him, but presently you will spot a red squirrel sitting in a crotch, tearing busily at a cone held in his fore paws, to shred it down to the edible part. Perhaps if you are very quiet you may see him descend the trunk, spring out to the ground when he gets three or four feet from the bottom, and leap across the snow toward an old stump, or some other tree which contains his hole. Occasionally, even, he will disappear into the snow, working through a tunnel he has built to some hiding-place. There will be scarce a stump in the pine woods without its litter of cone scales on the snow about it, and scarce a tree without tracks leading close to it, and tracks leading away from it which start three, four, or even five feet out. The pine and purple finches feed on the cones, also, as well as the rare pine grosbeaks, and the crossbills. If you ever get a chance to observe a crossbill at work shredding a cone you will no longer consider his odd bill poorly adapted to its purpose. It never slips, but holds like a vise while the hidden neck muscles under those brick-red feathers do the work. This is the bird which an old German legend says got its twisted bill from trying to pull the nails from the Saviour's hands when he hung upon the cross, and its red feathers from the sacred blood.

But hark! the dog has flushed a partridge! It goes whirring off through the woods, with its uncanny facility in dodging obstructions. There is little difficulty in finding the spot whence it rose. On a southward-sloping bank, in a shaft of sunlight, the snow has almost melted away, and with a little scratching the bird has uncovered some partridge-berries, or eye-berries, as we boys used to call the fruit of the *Mitchella repens,* that dainty little evergreen trailer which bears its fragrant, waxy flowers in June, and later its bright red berries, on the forest floor of our American woods. How glossy the leaves look now, and how brilliant the berries, as they lie on the dark, exposed mold, amid the snow and the scattered fragments of dead leaves scratched away by the bird! They are pleasant to the human taste, also, though without the pungency of checkerberries.

The partridges are growing scarce in our Berkshire thickets. Certain game-keepers say it is because the English pheasants have driven them to the mountain-tops, but I have my doubts of this. We have thousands of pheasants, to be sure, and as they are protected the year through, they are extremely fearless, walking up to our very door-yards after grain. But there is a fatal open season on partridges, and where they are hunted they are shy and scarce. Ascend the Crawford Bridle Path up Mount Washington, however, where they are apparently not molested, and before you break out of the woods on Clinton you will often come upon whole coveys of them beside the path, so tame that they will almost let you touch them with your hand, as they will in the Canadian wilds. I have stood in the path and watched a male bird, with three or four females about him, scratching in the moss not six feet from me, and have talked aloud with my companion while the partridges continued feeding, quite indifferent to us, and keeping up a soft, hen-like *coot, coot* of their own, a lovely little woodland sound.

The fact that the English pheasants are not necessarily inimical to partridges, at any rate, is attested by the experience of a breeder in Lenox, who found both birds nesting on terms of perfect peace in the thickets of his carefully posted and patrolled estate. These beautiful birds could, he believes, hold their own with the pheasants if given the same protection. What a pity the chance, at least, is not afforded them! No surprise in the woods is more startingly sudden and nerve-tingling than the uprush of an unsuspected partridge and his booming flight along an alley of sunlight ahead.

Why must it for ever be a temptation to pull a trigger? Alas! man has got but little beyond the instincts of his remote ancestors!

The partridge feeds on strawberries, as well as on the berry which bears his name, on checkerberries, false Solomon's seal, apple buds, pine buds, and even on wild grapes. Sometimes the grouse will sit in a tall tree almost like hens at roost, and perhaps you may see them in the early morning, or late twilight after frosts. They are more at ease than hens, however, and negotiate a change of perch with far more grace and much less audible excitement.

We have no quail in Berkshire County, which is one of our serious failings. When I was a boy in eastern Massachusetts, a half-witted French Canadian was often my companion in the open, because he could sit down in a field by the edge of the woods, motion me to silence, and then whistle "Bob White" till sometimes a whole flock of quail would be gathered on the ground about us, almost like the penguins about Captain Scott's phonograph on the Ross Barrier. I can still remember the odd thrill of that experience, and my awe of the half-witted youth who had so little kinship with the rest of us boys, so much with the birds. But our Berkshire winters are too severe for the ground-dwelling quail, and we have too many foxes, as well—and doubtless, in times past, too many hunters.

Foxes are not generally accredited with vegetarian instincts. You never see their tracks, as you see those of the rabbits, around a young oak-tree shoot which has been nibbled down to the tough stem. But Æsop evidently thought otherwise when he wrote his fable of the sour grapes, and there is plenty of testimony that Æsop was right. Foxes do eat wild grapes, as many observers have testified, climbing a considerable way to get them; and probably at times they eat berries and perhaps apples. I have found their tracks, at any rate, beneath apple-trees. I have also been confidently assured that they eat the persimmons in Virginia; that the "ol' houn' dawgs" know how good this fruit is, too, and if you wish to find the very best tree, take a "dawg" with you.

Mr. Woodchuck, on the other hand, doesn't eat at all, after September. He hibernates, coming out on Candlemas Day to see his shadow and make an annual "weather story" for the newspapers. Up in our pasture one winter the ground-hog who lives there had to tunnel up through two feet of snow to get his outlook. The six-inch bore by which he emerged was yellowed by the dirt on his body, and he packed a hard, dirty track across the snow for ten feet to a bore leading down to the back entrance of his dwelling. Evidently he took some exercise between the two doors. But there was not a single track leading away in any direction.

The wood-mice—or deer-mice—eat apples, surely, and many other things, including maple seeds. They also harvest hazel and beech nuts in great quantities, and they are not at all averse, as I can unfortunately testify, to Spanish iris bulbs. They nest not only in the woods, but in our gardens, preferably under a pile of pea brush, or the straw protection on the flower-beds, and often I have found their tracks in the snow all about the weed stalks, and the dust of trampled seeds, as if they had shaken down their food by climbing the stems.

The mention of maple-seeds brings us around, by a process of suggestion plain enough to the Yankee, to spring. When the sap runs in the maple-trees, when the melting snow steams in the sugar-grove, and makes a haze that is permeated with the aroma of wood-smoke and boiling syrup, spring indeed is on the way. It is then that the yellow-bellied woodpecker, or sapsucker, comes into prominence, if not into repute. He makes one or two holes in a tree—deep holes, sufficient to induce a good run of sap—and then goes to another tree, and another, and still another. When his taps are all running, he starts back and makes the rounds, drinking insatiably, and also, some say, feeding on the insects which stick to the wet bark around his bores. Mr. Burroughs denies this, and on the occasions when I have driven a bird away from his bores I have never yet found anything but clean sap and bark in the hole. He taps the yellow birches, also, for they have a very considerable flow of sap in spring, which, in an unboiled state, tastes nearly as sweet as maple. Later he favors apple-trees.

The squirrels, likewise, are sap-drinkers at this season. If you will break the twig of a sugar-maple in spring you will soon find a crystal drop depending from the abrasion. The squirrels know this, and they either nip several twigs off or bite deeply into the larger shoots, and then go back over their tracks, drinking the sweet sap drops. I have seen them do it in the maple at my own door, as well as in the woods. Our investigation of that deer's diet has taken us far afield from our abandoned pasture, over the snow, through the woods, even into our own gardens. Let us return once more to the sunny slope where the stray sheep wander and the finches dart and dip above the nodding thistle-tops. The small wild apples are already forming in the trees, for future harvest. The little trickle of water which runs away from the spring, over a ribbon of emerald grass into the woods, tempts our feet for another brief excursion, till we stand on the edge of a swamp and see amid the weeds the winding canals of the muskrats, where they swim in their search for lily-roots. As we retrace our steps a squirrel chatters at us amid the pines, and when, a moment later, we break into the clearing once more, a startled cock pheasant rises from his feeding and skims away, his long tail-feathers streaming out behind like the rudder of a monoplane. The summer afternoon is very still, yet a hundred sounds are audible— the chime of crickets, the hum of bees, the croak of a frog in the spring, the sweet cheeps and liquid songs of the birds, the murmur of a lazy wind in the pines. How delicate, how peaceful, these sounds are! How unprovocative of tiring thought or senseless worry is this pasture solitude! Here the beasts of the wood and birds of the air find nourishment and go happily about their woodland harvesting. The declining sun bathes all the slope in "the golden light of afternoon," and pushes its beams down the forest aisles to play tag with the shadows. We lie quiet beside the spring, and see a rabbit hop across one of these aisles, his tail flashing white, and make for the shelter of a young pine thicket. A catbird mews by the raspberries. Out of the deep wood rings the elfin clarion of a thrush. It is a little world of little creatures, toiling happily for their bread; and yet the soul feels for them all a curious kinship, here in this silent pasture where the shadows lengthen and the rising sea-surf murmurs in the pines. To shoot the least and smallest would be to break with murderous hands the bonds which link nature into unity. The drumming partridge, the thrush who in shadowed thicket sounds his liquid call, the poet with his verse—how much of star-dust is in each? It is only the rash man who attempts the answer with a gun.

# PAGAN PERSONALITIES[1]

*By* William Beebe

*William Beebe, born in 1877, widely known as a dauntless explorer of the natural world and as author of a standard work on pheasants, is equally distinguished as a stylist most felicitous in fitting experience with words. This essay was first published in* Harper's *in May, 1916.*

IT WAS EARLY ONE MORNING when I first saw the white outlines of the beach at Hambantotta, Ceylon. This is an obscure little port. It is beautiful, but it has acquired no distinction in the eyes of the world. On this particular morning, however, it was a place of great importance to me. I had traveled half-way around the world to study pheasants in their native environment, and it was close by Hambantotta that I was to begin this work. From this point I was to make my brief excursions into the Ceylon jungle. Therefore, the moment when I first saw this sandy, sloping coast was a moment of great gravity and significance, for that moment marked the real beginning of my trip—the unofficial but real beginning.

It was a little after dawn that a dark, low cloud along the horizon resolved itself slowly into a beach, distant trees, and low-roofed huts. There was something almost magical about this. The East, perfect in every detail, alien and exotic beyond measure, appeared to rise out of the sea and move silently and gently toward us as if in welcome. Aladdin himself might have summoned such an island, such a sunlit and desolate coast, from the darkest depths of the green water. It was hard to realize that nothing extraordinary was under way—that it was a commonplace and casual happening for the sun to rise and disclose a small fishing village engaged in the necessary business of making a living, while the morning mist, like a broken white cloud, still hung over the tops of the palm-trees.

It was the necessity for landing which brought back some of the realities of life. For this appeared at best a somewhat treacherous proceeding if photographic plates, guns, ammunition, and all the perishable paraphernalia of an expedition were taken into consideration. Because it was necessary to lower these into a native outrigger canoe, which was nothing more than the hollow trunk of a tree, kept stable and upright by means of a log fastened to the boat proper by two long bamboo poles.

Considered from a purely artistic standpoint these outriggers are eminently satisfactory. They are graceful in contour, and when the single square sail is spread before the wind it shows a deep golden tan against the blue water. But either to sit or to stand in such a canoe is an achievement in itself. They are too narrow to afford even a semblance of security, and the curved space underfoot provides a most precarious foothold. These, however, are minor difficulties when compared with the problem of getting into port. To succeed in this one must depend largely upon the generosity of nature, for it is impossible to make a scientific landing; instead, one achieves the vicinity of the surf and waits, silent and expectant, for the auspicious breaker destined to wash one up on the beach. Afterward it is a comparatively simple matter to haul the vessel and one's luggage to relatively dry land.

This, in itself, is a fitting introduction to the East. The outriggers, constructed so simply from the material at hand, the fishermen's almost childlike faith in the providential breakers, demonstrate clearly the psychology of the people and show the tremendous influence which the country itself has had upon their development. They build their huts close to the sea, and are true to their traditions and ideals, with little or no thought for to-morrow, but a great faith in the possibilities of to-day. In all of my dealings with these people I found them much alike—contented with their monotonous lives and governed by simple desires.

My first night at Hambantotta, after I was officially installed at the dâk bungalow, I had dinner with the government agent. He was an Englishman who had lived for many years on the island. This experience and his judgment were of inestimable value to me. This first evening was remarkable in many ways. It showed above all else the manifold differences between the East and the West—yet it showed how the two were closely allied, were brought together so that they moved in perfect unity toward a given end.

To begin with, if I had been dining with him in London, he would not have found it necessary to send two men with lanterns so that the way to his home would be properly lighted. Yet this was fitting enough in Ceylon, for on either side the darkness seemed as solid and impassable as a stone wall; the flickering yellow flames showed black trees and a heavy tropical undergrowth.

I found my host waiting for me, perspiring and in full evening dress. The dinner itself was formal, and perfectly served by barefooted men-servants wearing white sarongs and a loose upper garment of the same coarse cloth. These servants came and went like ghosts in the long, shadowy room, and I have never forgotten their gentle, dignified bearing. They had an air of detachment, of unreality, which was in some mysterious way enhanced by their curious headdress; for it is the custom for the men of this caste to twist the hair in a loose psyche knot at the back of the head, and to wear above this knot a tall, circular comb. In certain lights this transparent comb looks like a broken halo—a halo fixed at a somewhat humorous angle, although this does not detract from the kindliness of their faces nor rob their manner of its natural distinction.

It was late in the evening when my host dismissed the

servants and told me some of the reasons for maintaining with such careful detail the conventions of his own country. He said that it was absolutely necessary to dress for dinner at least twice during each week, for the moral effect on himself as well as on the members of his native household. It is imperative to keep up certain standards of conduct, to make evident constantly the laws of caste which operate in such a relation between an English master and a Singhalese servant. It is fatal for a white man to allow the slightest infringement upon these unwritten codes, else he loses the respect of the natives, and the foreign government which he represents becomes accordingly less powerful. If he makes any concessions to local conventions he is no longer considered a superior being from a superior country, but a native, an equal, and to be treated as such.

This was a new side-light upon conditions. It showed clearly how little an outsider can know of such practical administration. I wondered if the people over in England who had made the laws for Ceylon knew with what infinite tact and patience, with what painstaking vigilance, they were being daily inforced and reinforced on the island.

But I had come to study pheasants, not politics. I had little time for speculation, and none in which to hazard any conclusions; so I went back to the bungalow and put things in order for the next day's trip. This dâk was cool, fairly well lighted, a little musty from disuse. All during the night lizards kept up a commotion on the porch roof above my head; they were as noisy and as indefatigable as they were overgrown. Later, I shot one that measured eighteen inches, and he was being pursued at the time by one much larger. These roofs support also a fair number of snakes; these are always welcomed and comfortably lodged because they catch rats and mice. According to this, one at least can choose the preferable pests.

It was my intention to discover more of Hambantotta,

to learn something of the people, but a certain species of pheasant summoned me very shortly to Welligatta. However, this village was but eight miles distant, and I found the general conditions much the same, except that here the natives were in a little lower stage of development, and came oftener to my bungalow to be treated for the diseases which ran rife in the small community. Antiseptics and mercury were needed in most of the cases; for many there was nothing to do but give a little morphine. And even then little could be accomplished, for, despite all threats and warnings, every pill and powder would be swallowed the instant it was received, the theory being that the greater the amount of medicine consumed the quicker the cure.

The living conditions in this section were very primitive, and the dress equally so. The children wore one or more necklaces, and the men and women were dressed in a draped skirt; while the Veddahs, an inland, isolated tribe, were yet a step lower in the scale. Their clothing was scanty and nondescript, and they were close to absolute savagery. They were unsophisticated, slow in thought and speech, and incurious. It was very hard to discover anything of their ways of life; they were taciturn, and their habits, religion, and superstitions were all enveloped in mystery. However, they were good trackers and understood all the secrets of the jungle. But when I left Ceylon I knew no more of them than when I had come. Somewhere, well within the wilderness, they built their homes, prayed to their gods, and taught their children to live according to the laws of the tribe. But they chose to be let alone in this, to succeed or to fail unmolested. Therefore all of the doors were barred against outsiders.

Some months later, in Darjeeling, I engaged thirty-two Tibetan coolies who were to carry the baggage and paraphernalia of the expedition over the Himalayan trails. Six of these luggage coolies were women, but women as strong and fit to cope with hardship as the men who worked shoulder to shoulder with them. I could not help but compare these people with Veddahs of Ceylon, for these mountain coolies were boisterous, good-natured, jolly, indefatigable, frank and outspoken beyond measure. At the end of a long day's trek, when both my horse and I were thoroughly tired, I have seen several of these Tibetan women, who had kept up with me since early morning, race with one another the last hundred yards to the dâk bungalow, and make some sort of a game out of unfastening the heavy loads from their backs and heaping them up on the porch.

It may have been that the climate played a part in this. The heat of the low countries is depressing, just as the sharp cold of the hills is a stimulant. Certainly there is little in the lives of these Tibetans to make them happy. They live in eternal winter, where the snow-covered mountains look down on range upon range of white hills, and their transient homes are filthy and infested with vermin. But they are immune to suffering and privation; their excess of jubilance and joy in living spills over in the midst of the hardest labor. They laugh at everything, good or bad. They seem to have acquired some rough, instinctive philosophy which gives a bright color to the world.

One day when I was tragopan-hunting I came across one of their settlements, where eight persons and thirty-three hybrid yaks were gathered together in the semblance of a village. A single shed-like building was perched on a small, grassy platform which jutted out from the thousand-foot slope of a great Himalayan mountain, a precipitous slope dotted here and there with rhododendron-trees in full scarlet bloom. It was a sudden rift in a driving, vaporous cloud which revealed this isolated dwelling, and, when closing, shut it as quickly from view. This seemed in some way to emphasize how hopelessly these human beings were set apart from the world, to show how every outside influence must die out before it could reach them, to bring out with merciless detail the completeness of their segregation.

When I climbed down to the shed I found the people stolid, unwashed—the women hardly to be distinguished from the men. They were all of them dressed in layer upon layer of tattered, dirty cloth, and stood silent, close together, as if afraid. But after I had been with them an hour the mental and physical differences in the separate individualities became apparent. One small boy, clad in the rags of his ancestors, was the superior being among men. He stepped forward of his own accord and made friendly advances, volunteering the information that his name was Yat-ki. His small, dark face with its Mongolian eyes and typical low, broad forehead was alight with eagerness and curiosity.

This young Tibetan readily understood the business which had brought me to the mountains, and pointed out a distant gully where pheasants thrived in abundance. Also he offered his services as guide should I have need of one. He asked about my camera, and when he learned that it was my ambition to point it at the yaks, drove several up to me. In all of this he conducted himself with the greatest gravity and courtesy. The other members of his clan were stupid, with that impregnable stupidity which far transcends the reputed stupidity of animals. When I was leaving and asked for the symmetrical copper jar from which I had been served with yak milk, it was Yat-ki who engineered the bargaining which ensued. And when I had climbed back up the slope and turned to look down at the plateau, I saw him standing far out on the ledge, waving both hands in farewell. He seemed smaller than when he had stood beside me, younger, even a little helpless, with the snow whirling up around him like luminous spray from the depths of the blue valley which lay so far below. He could not have been more than twelve years old, but he was centuries older than his people in sympathy, in tact, in imagination. I hope that since that day the gods of his Tibetan clan have dealt kindly with him.

It seems that in every village, in every community, there is one person more gifted, more developed, than those around him. This is more apparent, perhaps, among savages or primitive tribes because their communal and personal affairs are not complex, and it is easier to know all the thoughts and motives which lie below the surface. Yat-ki, twelve years old, was a most dramatic example of this innate superiority. And many months later I came in contact with another such individual, equally fine and equally set apart from the world of affairs which might have found some use for his talents.

It was when I was camped along the western boundary of Yunnan, a district which had come into bad repute because of the border-line disturbances—intermittent scrimmages in which, every few weeks a considerable number of natives were killed or made slaves. Therefore, this camp was a little more elaborate than was customary; first, because I had with me six additional men, a body-guard of six Ghurkas which the English government had insisted should go with the expedition through this district; and secondly, because it was necessary to pitch the tents where they could be easily defended should this become necessary. For some time marauding bands of Chinese and mongrel tribes had been further complicating the situation along the frontier, so that the entire country was in a state of unrest and upheaval. As a matter of fact we were never seriously molested beyond some minor skirmishes with Mongolian robbers fleeing inland for safety. Once, at night, they shot down on our sentry with poisoned arrows, but these did no damage beyond striking the walls of the tent and knocking down whatever happened to be hanging up there.

This might have been due to the advantageous position of our camp, because for safety the tents had been placed on the summit of a small cleared knoll, while those of the servants and the Ghurkas straggled down one side of the hill. The valley which we overlooked was of great extent, and when the morning clouds would drift down from the Yunnan mountains it would be filled to the brim with blue vapor that, moving before a light wind, would take a thousand inconceivable forms and shadowy outlines, each and every one of which reflected and intensified the brilliant sunshine like a mirror. Across this valley, facing us from the opposite slope, was the village Sin-Ma-How. The dozen thatched huts were set back in among the thick trees and at one side an icy mountain torrent showed white against the green background.

It was in this village that I found the superior man who, like Yat-ki, had gone so far ahead of his people. He was the head-man officially of this Chinese-Kachin tribe, and I believe that he was a full-blooded Chinaman. He was a man well toward middle-age, a strong, lovable personality, dramatic, keen, who would have taken a high place among the people of his lawful country if life had but placed him among them. Instead, he spent his days with low-caste savages whose existence was so cheerless and uninspired that there must have been times when he was overcome with bitterness and despair, for even the huts which these people built were the most pitiful structures, ill-thatched, inhabited equally by vermin, pigs, and humanity. They were windowless and always filled with foul air, thick with smoke. These natives were in all ways of an exceedingly low order, and I found in them but one spark which redeemed them from utter degradation. This was the fervent devotion of each individual to his particular household god. No matter how poor the home, regardless of the fact that nothing more than a heap of rags in a corner formed the bed, and that one single pot sufficed for all the cooking, there was always a tiny shrine built in worship of the mysterious spirit whose privilege it was to superintend the fortunes of the family. This shrine was sacred and held in such high regard that even to have touched it would have been a desecration.

At every point where we pitched camp along the Yunnan border the natives would for the first few days watch us with doubt and suspicion, but little by little they would become assured that our presence among them portended no danger. Then they would straightway become less shy and more friendly. At the beginning only the most intrepid souls would brave the mysteries and terrors of our camp, but after a time the general atmosphere of distrust would be dispelled and our headquarters became increasingly popular.

There were times, however, when the native diffidence could not be fully overcome, and this was true of the Lishao women above all others. It was not that they were incurious, because they found the tents and every part of the equipment of such engrossing interest that they would stand for hours watching everything that took place, absorbed in every detail. But they showed in no way whatsoever the impression which these new objects made upon their minds, beyond the fact that they sometimes whispered together, said a few low words without gesturing or without change of expression.

The conventions of dress were well established in this tribe. These women wore loose waists, high-necked, with long sleeves as well as long, full skirts. They wore also high leggings made of dark cloth, and a flowing headdress which fell like a cape over their shoulders. These costumes must have required a great amount of labor in the making, for the material was not only hand-woven, but many times richly decorated with borders of shells and colored beads. Their belts were made wholly from such ivory-toned shells, linked together in some regular design, and supporting at either side two long braided tassels which hung almost to the knees. These were sometimes weighted with copper ornaments for copper is held in high favor by the Lishao women. They wear numberless necklaces of it—slender hoops of beaten wire strung around their necks and over their shoulders in such profusion that they are like a shining breastplate.

The children also give evidence of this tribal passion for ornamentation. A baby, only old enough to be carried in the cloth cradle on his mother's back, must have his beaded cap with its shells and silk dependent tassels. This is brightly colored, with high lights of copper, and does not fail to give him a ceremonious and imperial air, even when asleep.

It was in this same region at our nightly camp-fires of great rhododendron logs that we came to know more intimately one of the most appealing of our retainers. When the embers glowed brilliantly in the utter blackness of night we drew close, for we were camped near a high pass in northern Burma, and the icy breath from the Tibetan snows siphoned down with the mist at nightfall. Twice on similar evenings we had started at the sight of a tall form looming suddenly, ghostly, from the darkness. The apparition made us reach for our weapons, for more than once poisoned arrows had rattled against our canvas, sent from the cross-bow of some Chinese renegade. But we now knew our regular evening visitor would be only Angad Singh, the Sikh orderly, come obviously for the following days' commands, actually in the hope of a chance to talk for a few moments at the sahib's fire.

Angad Singh was a true Sikh and wore the five k's of his caste—the uncut hair, the short trousers, the iron bangle, the steel dagger, and the comb. And he was handsome, like most of his two million fellows, as the Greeks gods were handsome, and his manners were those of a courtier. But Angad Singh had a temperate daring which set him apart. Sustained by the thin veil of asking for orders, he stood by our camp-fire each evening, grave, respectful, attentive. I asked after the horses one by one, and ascertained that the worn girth had been mended, and I promised punishment for the syce who had driven the extra pack-mule over the aconite meadows, without harm, to be sure, but with a carelessness not to be condoned.

Then each evening, I spoke of some subject casually, very casually, for any more direct speech would touch our difference in caste, and we should both become conscious, and the delightfully slender daring of Angad Singh would be ended forever. It was always a subject of my own country and always of war, for the Sikh is first a warrior, and next native, orderly, syce, or what not. And his eyes would glisten, and in the flickering light I would see him sway restlessly, as a tethered elephant sways when the wind blows from swampy jungle. I spoke once of the great war between the North and South, and of the battle waged at Gettysburg. After a respectful pause the question came eagerly, "At this great battle, O Sahib, at the Burg of Getty's, this Pickett Sahib, did he not charge with elephants?" And I considered gravely, and finally confessed that there were no elephants in that encounter. Ashamed to admit that our American armies were destitute of elephants, I hinted that the jungle was too thick for their use. And Angad Singh shook his head sympathetically.

In the great Punjab and Northwest Provinces the Sikhs form a marvelous body of men. In numbers they equal the Norwegians. Their caste is high, their laws strict. They may not touch wine nor tobacco. They are not born to the title Singh, or lion, but acquire it by baptism, the water of which is called amrit, or nectar. The Sikhs form the backbone of the English native army and constabulary in India. When, as master, you win the respect and affection of a Sikh servant, you need fear neither poison nor steel in so much as it is humanly possible for him to protect you. At first it is sometimes difficult to keep the line quite distinct, to preserve the balance and distance of your relationship.

For his gentle courtesy and dignity is natural and very charming, and in appearance they are the most aristocratic, handsome race of living men. As one looks deep into their clear eyes one longs for a hint of their true ancestry. It seems altogether reasonable that their forefathers were the remnants of Alexander's Grecian army, many of whom settled in the northern provinces. And the kinship of face, of morals, makes of them companions beyond all other native tribes.

I could not fail to compare the Lishao women, the Kachins, and the Burmese, with the native Dyaks of Borneo, who also came within the range of the expedition. It was an irresistible comparison which sprang up full-fledged without any conscious thought on the matter. Throughout the entire trip I was so much taken up with the pheasant work in hand that I was not always able to cope with the problems which the various tribes presented in themselves. But this was a contrast which could not be escaped, for the simple reason that these two people were so singularly unlike. It was an innate and a profound difference, and it showed in countless outward details, even in the most trivial matters of speech and deportment.

For the Dyaks are simple, outspoken, wholly savage—that is, savage in the best meaning of the word. They have not been open to outside influences, or have resisted whatever pressure has been brought to bear. And they are undeveloped, uncivilized, loyal to the ideals which served the generations before them. These things have combined to make them both splendid and naïve; and this naïveté, this unsophistication, is only the more remarkable when placed side by side with their great mental quickness and receptivity, for they never fail to appraise a situation or a personality at an instant's notice; and they are resourceful, tactful, and courteous in dealing with whatever events may ensue. These are the head-hunters of Borneo.

However, they act always on impulse, from instinct. They have no civilized ideals and conventions. They have their own laws of conduct and morality as well as their customs. It is their custom, after having killed an enemy to cut off his head, then to take it home and cure it by a certain process, after which it is entitled to a place of honor among the human heads which depend in a circle from the ceiling of any reputable Dyak dwelling. This appears to them both a legitimate and a well-advised ceremony, and is accordingly held in high respect by the tribe.

I have no doubt that the Dyak mind considers the taking of heads an honorable practice. I do not know how they justify it, or what motives lie behind the deed, but I know that as a people the Dyaks are honest and straightforward in all that they do. Unlike the Lishaos, they were friendly and curious, invaluable hunters and trappers. They did not understand the purpose of the expedition and were at times sorely troubled by the scientific mysteries they were encountering for the first time. They thought it supremely illogical to follow a pheasant for hours with the greatest possible patience and discretion, only to refuse to shoot it once it was within easy range. They considered it a waste of energy to pack so many bugs and pheasants and flowers in big boxes and nail them up securely. But whatever their personal opinion in such matters, it did not at any time interfere with their work. They were good subordinates, and generous in their judgment of others.

This was especially true of the thirteen Dyak paddlers who were with me on all of the canoe trips through Borneo. These trips were long, and the men had to work hard day and night. Such association as this and such conditions will bring out all that is good and bad in any character, but these Dyaks had little to fear from such revelations. They were unfailingly trustworthy and loyal. There were numberless times when the fate of the expedition was wholly in their hands, when they determined whether or not it should survive and reach fulfilment.

There were dire hours when they fought for our safety all during the night, for the rivers were treacherous, and the canoe carried a full cargo. Sometimes the heavy tropical downpour, which begins at dusk and does not stop until dawn, would churn the water into a white froth, covering the whole surface of it with broken eddies of muddy foam. In the bluish twilight these appeared singularly menacing as they creamed up along the sides of the boat—they moved so silently and swiftly before the wind. But it was at midnight that the storm would make a black avalanche out of the river; in the darkness great tree-trunks would rush past, and it would seem that nothing could save the canoe from being cut in two. Then I would look out from the compartment amidships, and a flash of lightning would show me a row of heads, like a moving cordon, surrounding the boat. I would see a hand and an arm lifted out of the water to fend off some debris bearing down upon us, or the moving light would show me one of my men signaling to assure me that all was well. And yet in the early morning they would be ready to take up the day's work, ready to tramp for miles through the jungle, to build causeways for landing and loading, to make camp or to break it at an instant's notice.

It was this corps of paddlers whom I learned to know well and to understand, but at every Dyak village where we stopped we were welcomed with the greatest courtesy and respect. There was but one tribal house that we passed which did not make some advance and offer some friendly salutation. This communal dwelling of hostile Dyaks was built at the foot of a steep hill so that low trees overhung the roof and gave the whole structure a curiously peaceful and sequestered air. This was purely accidental and fictitious, but it was so convincing that to run away from it appeared a wholly unnecessary precaution. However, we had little to gain by seeking them out, and much to lose, so we passed them by within a discreet radius, as we had been told to do.

However, the unaffected pleasure which the other tribes showed at our coming was compensation. It seemed, each time, as if they could not offer sufficient evidence of hospitality. They would arrange an orderly programme of events in honor of our arrival, and the chiefs and high dignitaries would wear their most precious decorations as a token of esteem. I remember with great vividness the day when we landed at the home of Narok, one of the younger men of my crew who had earned considerable distinction among his people as a dancer. On this particular day two men had gone ahead in a fast canoe to give word that a war-canoe manned by thirteen paddlers, and carrying various gifts as well as a white man, would appear in the early evening at an appointed time. Therefore, at dusk, when our boat grated against the pebbly beach bordering the jungle where Narok lived, a crowd of men, women, and children, and a still greater host of mongrel dogs, rushed down to greet us. These men and women were like very polite boys and girls at some great celebration. I do not believe that they had ever seen but one white person, and certainly every article included in my equipment, even down to the pots and pans, as well as the last minute detail of my clothing, filled them with unparalleled curiosity. I even think that secretly they were a little amused at such manifestations of an alien culture. But they made no sign to show it. Instead, those of the proper caste came forward silently and gravely to greet us.

This Dyak greeting holds true to the old, primitive ideal that a guest must be welcomed with a gift. This gift is a very modest one, but it is also very valuable. It is an egg. Throughout the whole country, if you find favor in the eyes of a tribe, you are formally presented with an egg on the day of your arrival in their village. And in the heart of

Borneo, where food is in the nature of things a more or less undetermined quantity, the possession of an egg is a matter of profound gratitude. Particularly a fresh egg, because at times the Dyaks show a marked preference for high game and preserved eggs—an instinctive, almost racial, preference not easily acquired by a more sophisticated taste. There is always the chance, however, that the gift egg will be a good egg. So the presents of Narok's tribesmen found great favor with us when they were ceremoniously pressed into our left hands, and in exchange we offered our small supply of scissors, mirrors, beads, and flat chocolate wafers wrapped in tin-foil. These wafers did not fail to bring forth sounds of delight, but at the same time they did not fail to provoke a great indecision in the minds of those who had fallen suddenly heir to them, because nobody could bring himself to destroy the beautiful, smooth, shining contour of his silver disk, regardless of the chocolate within. It was remarkable to see how momentous this question was to them; to see the real emotion brought out by these scraps of cheap, bright foil that had been of so little value to the civilized people who had produced them.

When the ceremony of landing was fully and properly achieved, Narok and his chief led us to his tribal house, where one by one, we climbed the steep, notched pole that was the sole roadway between a high veranda and the earth, some ten feet or more below. This veranda gave directly upon a low-roofed corridor which ran the full length of the dwelling. At intervals resinous fires burned in shallow bowls before two long rows of barred doors. Behind these doors the individual members of the tribe lived out the daily routine of their lives in some small semblance of seclusion. I would have liked to have the privilege of opening one of these doors, to have seen the personal possessions gathered together in the room itself, but instead I was conducted to a seat of honor in the direct center of the long corridor, where I sat down on some spotlessly clean mats and awaited the programme which was to honor our coming. Directly above me, suspended from the roof by slender strips of bamboo fiber, hung a circle of dried heads, each one equally distant from its neighbor. White, wooden eyes had been placed in the eye-sockets of these heads—white eyes unnaturally large and distended. They seemed to be staring at something which was hidden in the dark shadows of the inner roof.

Narok danced for us that night, and others danced with him, or alone, according to the spirit of the story which they interpreted. For music there were the Dyak tom-toms, extraordinarily low and resonant, perfect primitive instruments for the expression of primitive emotions. Their rhythmic beat, minor and inevitable, seemed to embody every savage ideal, every secret thought and feeling of those people who were ranged so close around me in that dim corridor where the heads of their enemies watched above them with their white, blind eyes.

It was late—for the moon had dropped down below the topmost branches of the trees—when we went back down to the canoe, which was no more than a long, black shadow in the little harbor. The men took up their paddles and pushed off, because we had a good distance to cover before morning, but I stood amidships and watched the lights of Narok's house become smaller and smaller until they were no more than pin-points of flame in the darkness. I remembered the Dyak women who had come down to the beach to welcome us—remembered the frankness, the utter unsophistication of their attitude toward life—and compared them with those tribes who had learned more complex ways of living. For some reason the simplicity of these Dyaks seemed of greater value.

I thought, too, of all the many people who, knowingly or unknowingly, had furthered the progress of the expedition which had brought me to their countries. I thought of Ceylon and the white, curved beach at Hambantotta; of the Singhalese fishermen and their great, unwavering faith in the kindness of the sea. I remembered the Veddahs who had worked so zealously for the success of a trip whose purpose was so obscure and meaningless to them, and I thought that the money paid to them was a very small recompense for the service they had done. This brought home sharply that real tragedy of any expedition—the fact that people must take some place in the work for a little while, then the ordinary course of their lives. One cannot return and find that course unchanged; life moves swiftly and inevitably, with no sentimental repetition of its successes or its failures. And as if in proof of this, I looked back and saw the lights in Narok's house go out suddenly—all of them at once, as if a gust of wind had blown them out, while the sudden darkness there seemed to spread slowly, cover the trees, then close down like a black curtain over the purple stretch of river behind us.

# THE ANCIENT BARRIER OF THE PYRENEES[1]

*By* Hilaire Belloc

*Hilaire Belloc, perhaps the most competent writer upon travel and the road in our times, literary critic and apologist for Catholicism, was born in 1870. This essay was first published in* Harper's *in March, 1915.*

WHEN A MAN GOES SOUTHWARD through the Gauls—and best of all on foot—he goes through one district after another which, though varying from garden to pastures, from pastures to deserted upland moors and back to gardens again, pass from one into the other with little of abrupt transition. The forests he passes through, though ancient, are orderly. Even the dead volcanoes of the central knot are guardians rather than lords of the flats below them; and as he comes down their farther slopes to the sheet of vineyards along the southern rivers he has everywhere found the many landscapes of his journey maintaining a certain scale, moderate and apt to the high civilization of France. He has seen nothing awful; he has been arrested by nothing tremendous in nature; he will rather remember the works of man; for France (save for the marshy gate to the northeast) is everywhere inclosed by mountains or sea, and within that inclosure is a habitation for men.

But at last from some swell of land, not high, rising from the valley of the Garonne or of the Adour, or from that great Domitian Way which was the earliest triumph of Rome outside her Italian boundaries, he will perceive the sunlit sky in the south to be distinguished by a high and not uneven line, faint but continuously discernible throughout all the stretch of the horizon; and all below this line is of a graver, mistier tint of blue. This broad, faint belt, lifted high and seemingly separate from the world, he may take for a very distant and singularly changeless bank of cloud; it has the even texture and the distance of a cloud in still air, and it comes too much against heaven for him to think of it at first (after so many hundred miles of undulating fields) as being anything but of the sky. But that line does not move; and as he still goes southward through the day it still stands unchanging between him and the sun. It is lost only to the left and to the right in infinities of distance. It is so little broken by darker shadows against its universal gray that if it is not the bank of cloud it seemed, it must be a giant's wall rising sheer up out of France. That line is the Pyrenees.

I saw it thus when first I went out ten years ago with the intention of discovery. I had then, in seeing what so many millions have seen in just this sudden fashion, an experience as novel as a landfall, as fresh as the finding of an unknown world. And there is something about this ordered, even, and unchanging height which, though I have repeated that experience now very often and in varied seasons, forbids it ever to lose its original appeal. I could almost say that everything I have known grows stale except good verse and the Pyrenees.

This great rampart runs unbroken from the sea to the sea for two hundred and fifty miles. So even is it that no break or saddle cuts it—as the Alps are cut continually, as the Carpathians everywhere. The paths and tracks by which men painfully surmount it, numerous enough, rise up with the mountain slopes into the sky. When a man wanders into the heart of the chain he must climb on to the ridge of it and there find no more than a notch or neck but slightly bitten below the higher ridge on every side. Save for the broad Cerdagne, chiseled widely southward out of the mass from the summit, every way over the Pyrenees is by a little nick in their heights, not one by a gulf marring their continuity.

So much for the main matter of this range. It is, what so many other ranges have with less justice been called, a *wall*. It contains and it forbids. I wish I could put here in written words what perhaps the modern camera skilfully used might do for me, and what surely some great landscape-painter should long ago have done for this amazing thing—I mean the sense of command, of an ordered halt, and of a sheer limit which it imposes.

Nowhere in the world does a barrier so completely isolate one province of a civilization from its peers. Europe, from its most ancient origins one thing, and forged into an active unity by the energies of Rome, has had cut off from her by these mountains that Iberian part in which is preserved (less corrupted than perhaps in any other department of the West) the old stock and the enduring virtues of our race. For the Spanish peasant of the bare upland plateaus is a sort of unchanging model showing us whence we came and by what qualities we may be preserved.

These mountains, then, which make such a wall between the Spaniards and the North, are a matter of the liveliest interest; and the causes of shape and structure which have given them this strange power to isolate a single people from the rest are worthy of much more care than historians or travelers have given to them. To understand the scenery of the Pyrenees and to seize its meaning in culture, as well as its splendor to the eye, is half to understand the story of Europe.

That they have been more neglected than the other great ranges of the Continent is due to that very power of isolation which they possess; nor need we fear that the increasing study of them and their greater frequentation which has come in quite recent years will mar their sublimity; for that very character of theirs which makes them so different from all the other mountain masses of Europe will, as I shall presently show, preserve them from vulgarity. No host of men could spoil the Pyrenees.

Before I speak of the physical forms which thus mark them out and which have given them their peculiar effect throughout the Christian centuries, I would register some examples of what their effect has been. They kept separate and vigorous for over three hundred years a special national church in which the chief features of our faith took root. There is in the creed a famous clause upon the full divinity of Christ, which fought its way for admission into Christian formula—the first use of that clause in the chanting of the ritual sprang from Toledo. It was the Pyrenees which set a term to the attempted Mohammedan conquest of Christendom a thousand years ago. The valleys of the Pyrenees were *foci* where the energy of Europe concentrated in the perpetual and repeated charges of raids of Northern men, mounted and armed, beating back Islam. The mule-tracks and the huddled hamlets of those valleys first saw knighthood, and they were the school of war in which Europe re-arose in the Dark Ages until she awoke at last to the Crusades. In those valleys the greatest of our epics was forged, the first of our true Parliaments met—commons, lords, and priests at Jaca under a king who was king of nothing as yet beyond the narrow Torrent Gorge of the Aragon. It was the Pyrenees that kept the Iberian Peninsula apart during the spiritual storm of the sixteenth century. It was the Pyrenees that, more than any other natural feature, or than any other inanimate thing, interrupted the scheme of Napoleon.

To-day we assist at the beginning of a transformation. New roads are piercing where for so many centuries no wheels could pass. High on that Aragon torrent I heard year after year the blasting of the tunnel that will re-open such a scheme of ways as had been lost since the Romans. Something is passing that has hitherto been capital in all our fortunes, and something the departure of which may change Europe in the future much more than those engineers or their masters dream.

The Pyrenees, thus distinguished as a wall of walls among mountains, rise as you come close upon their edges from the north in a clear spring.

Where other mountains have foothills, the first heights of the Pyrenees stand up sharply, as a rule, from thick, flat, river meadows running parallel to them at their feet; the bastion outermost heights lift abruptly, half as tall as the greater peaks behind; and all along the file of giants stand in good dressing like ranks upon parade above the plains.

I have so seen them in a summer evening when the sun at his setting had crept round northward of their line. His light shone level, and the reddened headlands so exactly set seemed like the too-strict shores of an inaccessible country that falls to a calm and deep sea from awful inland regions.

But as you come near to this seemingly unbroken face you perceive that other strong feature in the chain which I have seen nowhere else, unless it be in their nearest parallel, the California Sierras. This feature may, I think, be called the valley gates.

Here and there in the Alps (and even in the Apennines) you will find something of the kind. Two great cliffs will form the edges of a gap that cuts right down to the plain and admits a valley floor, through the front, into the rear of the mountains. Such is the once-famous entry to the Grésivaudan which leads up to Grenoble, the portal through which Hannibal passed (as I believe) when he challenged the Alps and forced the barriers of Italy. But in the Pyrenees this sight is not a rare nor an exceptional one. It is the introduction to each of the great valleys; and you come on each so definitely and at so precise a moment—

there is so clear a mark *before* which you are still in the plains, *after* which you have been taken by the mountains —that you seem to be meeting a person and to be asking for a name.

In or near such gates (I am talking of the northern Gallic escarpment of the range) you will find in valley after valley a further natural feature peculiar to the Pyrenees, arresting the eye and provoking the historical curiosity of every man that comes on it for the first time. This natural feature consists in an isolated rock or rocky hill standing well out from the great mountains upon either side, and, if it be fortified by men, blocking the issue from the valley—indeed, from a time beyond all records, men have fortified these holders of the gates. The whole region of Foix, with its glory of the later Middle Ages and of the Renaissance, takes its name from such a rock where for centuries the castle stood defending the issue of the gold-rolling river—"Aurigera"—the Ariége. Boldly out in front of the main pass where the Romans built their great road through the heart of the mountains you have Oloron so standing. Right in the narrow entry of the gorges that lead to Gavarnie you have the rock of Lourdes. And so it is all up and down the chain. What guess the geologians may have made at this formation I do not know. Nor is it of any great value, for they will change their guess three or four times in the next fifty years. But I know what it is in landscape: as perplexing and sharp a thing as there is in Europe—that there should be in valley after valley this fortified rock forbidding an entry to the hills, and, round about each, perfectly flat meadows, so that each stands individual and alone.

When a man has entered one of these gates and passed one of these ancient fortresses, he will, after following the road through the gorge which is the issue of the torrent, come, behind the gates of the valley, into yet another feature of the Pyrenees, a feature as characteristic of them as the two I have already mentioned. This third feature of their scenery is the broadening out of the valley into what looks like, and may have been in remote ages, the level floor of a lake. These inclosed arenas upon which the steep slopes, wooded and cascading one above the other, look down from every side, are not only typical of Pyrenean scenery, but, like most things in the Pyrenees, are typical also of their history and of their part in the formation of Europe. For these inclosed and hidden fertile places within the hills, nourishing each its five or seven villages, have maintained probably through the Roman time, certainly through the Middle Ages (and, what is more remarkable, furtively in our own day), a sort of independent democracy.

One, indeed, the Valley of Andorra, with its ramifications, can assert its independence upon the map and in the language of diplomacy. This blessed little republic (when it is touched at last, its peril may well be a symbol of impending evil for Europe) is suspended politically between France and Spain. It makes its own laws, or rather observes its own customs, and portrays all that was ever said for or against political freedom. It is the happiest community of men I have ever known.

But apart from this fortunate, and secluded place, every one of those defended and cut-off groups of villages in the amphitheatres of the hills has, in spite of modern central governments, a life of its own. It observes its own customs in land tenure, it voluntarily subserves a life not guaranteed by the great capital of the state, but by a local loyalty. So it is with the finest of them all, of which Bedous is the capital, and there, I think, the quiet traveler will best observe the unconquerable spirit of these heights. The French Republic, the Empire before it, and before that the Monarchy, have called the circle of Bedous for now four hundred years a mere division of French land. But live within it only for a few days and you will find that it has maintained its soul. The young men are conscript for the army; the children go to schools where their teachers are named from Paris; the priest in the village church came, until quite lately, like an official from any distance, and would move again to any distance farther. But all this false homogeneity —suitable to the plains, not suitable to the hills—does not seem to have diminished in the least the corporate social tradition of that valley.

It is the same with that Spanish unity (Spanish by exception, for it stands to the north of the hills), the Val d'Aran. For the Val d'Aran, quite cut off from its own government not to be reached by any Spanish vehicle (there is no road from it into Spain), lives its own life like a little nation. The same force which made the Swiss cantons works still with splendid vigor in the Pyrenees. Further, I will believe that it is more natural and stronger in those hills.

In the limits of the valleys where the torrent is now no more than a thread, where the ridge of the main range stands up before one at last in a line of serrated rock or of high snow-flaked grass against the sky, there must be noted in these mountains one special sort of human mold, discoverable, indeed, in every mountain range, but here vivid and apart. This is what I may call "The Hamlet at the Foot of the Pass." Modern travel has slightly degraded these, for they stand where the peaks above them are most awful and they command the entry to the wildest land. But they are still, and I think will always be, things apart. Gavarnie is the only one I know to have been hurt, and even Gavarnie may return to sanity and quietness under those cliffs of silence. But for the rest, I can recall twenty such hamlets, sometimes but a cluster of twenty houses, sometimes a true village with a church, which guard the last descent to the ridge and the passage into Spain. Gabas is one, Urdos another, Campan a third, Serrat a fourth. These last vestiges of men have this in common: a huddling close together as of sheep in a storm (for the snow oppresses them most of the year), a great sadness in demeanor and in song—they have their own songs—and lastly a fidelity to their homes, a patriotism of the roof, more enduring than that of the lower levels. There are villages in the Pyrenees that emigrate, but (paradoxically, perhaps, and strangely) it is not these higher villages that emigrate; and while you find men complaining, nearer the plains, that the plains are better worth seeking, in the higher valley you find nothing but regret that ever a man should leave his land.

But all this deals with the Gallic escarpment of the Pyrenees: well watered, dense with forests of pine and of beech and enormously lofty in the mists, with perpendicular after perpendicular of limestone reaching up into the hidden sky.

Cross the watershed and get to the southern slope, toward the sun with the entry into Spain, and you find another business in the mountains. It is not for nothing that those farther torrents debouching into once conquered land and into the Ebro Plain that the Mohammedan ravaged so long (filling the wells, cutting the trees—it is still parched to-day) played a part in history different from their twins of the north.

The Pyrenees in the south show their changed country in their soil and sparse trees and very ancient, roughly built roofs.

I will dare to be so fantastic as to say that the outlines of the hills betray a new fate. Nor will even modern men think this so fantastic, after all, perhaps, when they remember that rocks standing up to the southern sun will suffer different accidents of erosion from those that look northward and nourish sheltered and shaded streams.

There are standing up, then, southward, such abrupt hills, with such names as "The Enchanted," "The Accursed," "The Stony," "The Peaks of Hell." They are savage, they contain no regular secluded valleys as does the slope to the north; rather they stand out like ramparts, ridges parallel one with the other, defending Gaul against the irruption of Africa through Spain.

Here are not forests, but groves or woods made of trees standing singly and landscapes of bare earth. Here the torrents also lose their lucidity and become, as the Aragon or the Gallego, tawny like the tawny soil around; and their names—like those two names, Gallego and Aragon—are the names of the Reconquest and of the chief adventure of Christendom. For down their banks Christendom did what fools think cannot be done at all, and what has been done so rarely in the history of the world. The men that drank of these rivers set their will against the stream of things and unmade the Mohammedan conquest of Spain.

There is a place where the whole spirit of that enormous thing is fixed in landscape. That place is Riglos. Here the Gallego torrent, escaping from the last flanking walls that stand out, parallel with and defending the Pyrenees, comes at last upon the plain. The torrent cuts through cliffs bright red in color, enormous in height, a visionary entry into Spain, and these cliffs have by the process of years' frost upon frost for centuries become cut into great isolated pillars which men call the "The Chimneys of Riglos." They can be seen from very far away in the brown plains, standing up thus crimson and in shape like the turrets and bastions of some incredibly high castle: a stronghold for Atlas and his sons. By this gap, also, the little railway that now runs no farther than Jaca issues from the hills. By this gap will run in a few years the new great railroad of Europe which they are making, and which will directly connect, for the first time since the Roman roads fell out of use, Madrid and Paris. The tunnel is already pierced under that same Col which carried the old main Roman road, and, I know not in how many months more, the new highway will begin to change the travel of Europe.

All that country, from Huesca at the foot of the hills upon the plain to Jaca on the high torrent of Aragon, and for a day's ride around, is crammed with history. That torrent Aragon gave its name to the great kingdom because, from its gorge men rode out fighting for three hundred years, and only after those three hundred years had they at last recovered their Christian earth now parched and treeless to the limits of the Ebro. It is perhaps that countryside in Europe which could tell most of our medieval origins and of how our assemblies, our ranks, and our romance arose. But it is very silent, its record is confused and slight. Only its legends are enormous.

The Pyrenees upon this southern edge of them show well why they have been such a barrier, and why they have so molded history. For not only do these separate walls of theirs run out flanking the main chain, abrupt and steep ridges, for all the world like huge earthworks, but (save by few passages) they entice one, before one comes to the main crest, to attempt impassable gorges that lead up to no traverse, but run athwart one's way. Of these the hugest, a cañon more awful than any that I have seen, more impressive even than those of Western America (for though those are of greater depth, they are broader), is that which runs south of the Marboré, cut through quite naked cliffs from heights that take a man a day to climb.

It is not until one has attempted such a northward journey into the green lands of the Garonne from the deserts of the Ebro, and attempted it on foot, that one sees either the miraculous contrast between the Gauls and the hard Iberian land, or the obstacle, equally miraculous, which the Pyrenees afford.

Water is no small part of this obstacle. For it is not plentiful or limpid here upon the southern side as upon the north. A man must know his way if he is to be certain of camping by water before night. Of roads there are none save the four or five, in two hundred and forty miles of country, which lead to the very rare permanent crossings of the hills. I think one may best express the difficulty of that land by this example: news there is three days old. The communication of Europe to these remote groups of huts is not directly from across the hills, but round them, and Madrid hears of what is doing in Tolouse half a week before the mountaineers can learn it, though they are by four-fifths nearer to the north.

Those who know Spain well say that of all her isolated parts Estremadura is the most alone: that there the noise of the world comes last, and that there men live their lives most as they will without the impress of any foreign fashion. But I think that the Five Towns east of the Basque boundary, or all that broken land between the Valley of Esterri and the Gallego, or even the Catalan tumble of hills to the south, run Estremadura close for this. The Pyrenean chain that shelters them from the northern wind shelters them also from every influence of change.

The Pyrenees will endure not only in their heights and forests, but the simplicity of their villages, their political customs, and all their being. They were saved from too early a discovery at the hands of the vulgar in the days when the charlatans of art were ruining so much else that was beautiful in Europe fifty years ago. They have the advantage of a high differentiation—many different races and different dialects side by side: always an element of permanence. And on the physical side they have this strong guarantee: that they are too large to be overrun and wasted.

In the Alps narrow valleys, checked and contained by vast fields of snow and ice above, are soon peopled with fashion, and the area which men without roots have had given over to them to spoil is necessarily restricted. But in the Pyrenees you have region after region of mountain land, not one much less than sixty miles in breadth and all of them open to the ranging of a man on foot. The valleys are contained by no snow-fields, and the customs of the people and their contempt for the plains are as strong as oak. I do not think that by any accident of travel they can now be overcome or degraded.

# YOUR UNITED STATES

*By* Arnold Bennett

---

*Arnold Bennett, born in 1867, won reputation as an essayist before* The Old Wives' Tale *made his fame as a novelist. This essay, first published in* Harper's *in May of 1912, was a chapter in his book bearing this title. Time has not dulled its descriptive value.*

WHEN I FIRST LOOKED AT FIFTH Avenue by sunlight, in the tranquillity of Sunday morning, and when I last set eyes on it, in the ordinary peevish gloom of a busy sailing-day, I thought it was the proudest thoroughfare I had ever seen anywhere. The revisitation of certain European capitals has forced me to modify this judgment; but I still think that Fifth Avenue, if not unequaled, is unsurpassed.

One afternoon I was driving up Fifth Avenue in the company of an architectural expert who, with the incredible elastic good nature of American business men, had abandoned his affairs for half a day in order to go with me on a voyage of discovery, and he asked me, so as to get some basis of understanding or disagreement, what building in New York had pleased me most. I at once said the University Club—to my mind a masterpiece. He approved, and a great peace filled our automobile; in which peace we expanded. He asked me what building in the world made the strongest appeal to me, and I at once said the Strozzi Palace at Florence. Whereat he was decidedly sympathetic.

"Fifth Avenue," I said, "always reminds me of Florence and the Strozzi. . . . The cornices, you know."

He stopped the automobile under the Gorham store and displayed to me the finest cornice in New York, and told me how Stanford White had put up several experimental cornices there before arriving at finality. Indeed, a great cornice! I admit I was somewhat dashed by the information that most cornices in New York are made of cast iron; but only for a moment! What, after all, do I care what a cornice is made of, so long as it juts proudly out from the façade and helps the street to a splendid and formidable sky-line? I had neither read nor heard a word of the cornices of New York, and yet for me New York was first and last the city of effective cornices! (Which merely shows how eyes differ!) The cornice must remind you of Italy, and through Italy of the Renaissance. And it is not the boast of the United States to be a renaissance? I always felt that there was something obscurely symbolic in the New York cornice—symbolic of the necessary qualities of a renaissance, half cruel and half humane.

The critical European excusably expects a very great deal from Fifth Avenue, as being the principal shopping street in the richest community in the world. (I speak not of the residential blocks north of Fifth-ninth Street, whose beauty and interest fall perhaps far short of their pretensions.) And the critical European will not be disappointed, unless his foible is to be disappointed—as, in fact, occassionally happens. Except for the miserly splitting, here and there in the older edifices, of an inadequate ground floor into a mezzanine and a shallow box (a device employed more frankly and usefully with an outer flight of steps on the East Side), there is nothing mean in the whole street from the Plaza to Washington Square. A lot of utterly mediocre architecture there is, of course—the same applies inevitably to every long street in every capital—but the general effect is homogeneous and fine, and, above all, grandly generous. And the alternation of high and low buildings produces not infrequently the most agreeable architectural accidents: for example, seen from about Thirtieth Street, the pale-pillared, squat structure of the Knickerbocker Trust against a background of the lofty red of the Æolian Building. . . . And then, that great white store on the opposite pavement! The single shops, as well as the general stores and hotels on Fifth Avenue, are impressive in the lavish spaciousness of their disposition. Neither stores nor shops could have been conceived, or could be kept, by merchants without genuine imagination and faith.

And the glory of the thoroughfare inspires even those who only walk up and down it. It inspires particularly the mounted policeman as he reigns over a turbulent crossing. It inspires the women, and particularly the young women, as they pass in front of the windows, owning their contents in thought. I sat once with an old, white-haired, and serious gentleman, gazing through glass at Fifth Avenue, and I ventured to say to him, "There are fine women on Fifth Avenue." "By Jove!" he exclaimed, with deep conviction, and his eyes suddenly fired, "there are!" On the whole, I think that, in their carriages or on their feet, they know a little better how to do justice to a fine thoroughfare than the women of any other capital in my acquaintance. I have driven rapidly in a fast car, clinging to my hat and my hair against the New York wind, from one end of Fifth Avenue to the other, and what with the sunshine and the flags wildly waving in the sunshine, and the blue sky and the cornices jutting into it and the roofs scraping it, and the large whiteness of the stores, and the invitation of the signs, and the display of the windows, and the swift sinuousness of the other cars, and the proud opposing processions of American subjects—what with all this and with the supreme imperialism of the mounted policeman, I have been positively intoxicated!

And yet possibly the greatest moment in the life of Fifth Avenue is at dusk, when dusk falls at tea-time. The street lamps flicker into a steady, steely blue, and the windows of the hotels and restaurants throw a yellow radiance; all the shops—especially the jewelers' shops—become enchanted treasure-houses, whose interiors recede away behind their façades into infinity; and the endless files of innumerable vehicles, interlacing and swerving, put forth each a pair of glittering eyes. . . . Come suddenly upon it all, from the leafy fastnesses of Central Park, round the corner from the Plaza Hotel, and wait your turn until the arm of the policeman, whose blue coat is now whitened with dust, permits your restive chauffeur to plunge down into the main currents of the city. . . . You will have then the most grandiose impression that New York is, in fact, inhabited; and that even though the spectacular luxury of New York be nearly as much founded upon social injustice and poverty as any imperfect human civilization in Europe, it is a boon to be alive therein! . . . In half an hour, in three-quarters of an hour, the vitality is clean gone out of the street. The shops have let down their rich gathered curtains, the pavements are deserted, and the roadway is no longer perilous. And nothing save a fire will arouse Fifth Avenue till the next morning. Even on an election night the sole sign in Fifth Avenue of the disorder of politics will be a few long strips of tape-paper wreathing in the breeze on the asphalt under the lonely lamps.

It is not easy for a visiting stranger in New York to get away from Fifth Avenue. The street seems to hold him fast. There might almost as well be no other avenues; and certainly the word "Fifth" has lost all its numerical significence in current usage. A youthful musical student, upon being asked how many symphonies Beethoven had composed, replied four, and obstinately stuck to it that Beethoven had only composed four. Called upon to enumerate the four, he answered thus, the C minor, the Eroica, the Pastoral, and the Ninth. "Ninth" had lost its numerical significance for that student. A similar phenomenon of psychology has happened with the streets and avenues of New York. Europeans are apt to assume that to tack numbers instead of names on to the thoroughfares of a city is to impair their identities and individualities. Not a bit! The numbers grow into names. That is all. Such is the mysterious poetic force of the human mind! That curt word "Fifth" signifies as much to the New-Yorker as "Boulevard des Italiens" to the Parisian. As for the possibility of confusion, would any New Yorker ever confuse Fourteenth with Thirteenth or Fifteenth Street, or Twenty-third with Twenty-second or Twenty-fourth, or Forty-second with One Hundred and Forty-second, or One Hundred and Twenty-fifth with anything else whatever? Yes, when the Parisian confuses the Champs Elysées with the Avenue de l'Opéra! When the Parisian arrives at this stage—even then Fifth Avenue will not be confused with Sixth!

One day, in the unusual silence of an election morning, I absolutely determined to see something of the New York that lies beyond Fifth Avenue, and I slipped off westward along Thirty-fourth Street, feeling adventurous. The excursion was indeed an adventure. I came across Broadway and Sixth Avenue together! Sixth Avenue, with its barbaric paving, surely could not be under the same administration as Fifth! Between Sixth and Seventh I met a sinister but genial ruffian, proudly wearing the insignia of Tammany; and soon I met a lot more of them: jolly fellows, apparently, yet somehow conveying to me the suspicion that in a saloon shindy they might prove themselves my superiors. (I was told in New York, and by the best people in New York, that Tammany was a blot on the social system of the city. But I would not have it so. I would call it a part of the social system, just as much a part of the social system, and just as expressive of the national character, as the fine schools, the fine hospitals, the superlative business organizations, or Mr. George M. Cohan's Theatre. A civilization is indivisibly responsible for itself. It may not, on the Day of Judgment, or any other day, lessen its collective responsibility of baptizing certain portions of its organism as extraneous "blots" dropped thereon from without.) To continue—after Seventh Avenue the declension was frank. In the purlieus of the Five Towns themselves—compared with which Pittsburgh is seemingly Paradise—I have never trod such horrific sidewalks. I discovered huge freight-trains shunting all over Tenth and Eleventh Avenues, and frail flying bridges erected from sidewalk to sidewalk, for the convenience of a brave and hardy populace. I was surrounded in the street by menacing locomotives and crowds of Italians, and in front of me was a great Italian steamer. I felt as though Fifth Avenue was a three days' journey away, through a hostile country. And yet I had been walking only twenty minutes! I regained Fifth with relief, and had learned a lesson. In future, if asked how many avenues there are in New York I would insist that there are three: Lexington, Madison, and Fifth.

The chief characteristic of Broadway is its interminability. Everybody knows, roughly, where it begins, but I doubt if even the topographical experts of Albany knows just where it ends. It is a street that inspires respect rather than enthusiasm. In the daytime all the uptown portion of it—and as far downtown as Ninth Street—has a provincial aspect. If Fifth Avenue is metropolitan and exclusive, Broadway is not. Broadway lacks distinction, it lacks any sort of impressiveness, save in its first two miles, which do—especially the southern mile—strike you with a vague and uneasy awe. And it was here that I experienced my keenest disappointment in the United States.

I went through sundry disappointments. I had expected to be often asked how much I earned. I never was asked. I had expected to be often informed by casual acquaintances of their exact income. Nobody, save an interviewer or so and the president of a great trust, ever passed me even a hint as to the amount of his income. I had expected to find an inordinate amount of tippling in clubs and hotels. I found, on the contrary, a very marked sobriety. I had expected to receive many hard words and some insolence from paid servants, such as train-men, tram-men, lift-boys, and policemen. From this class, as from the others, I received nothing but politeness, except in one instance. That instance, by the way, was a barber in an important hotel, whom I had most respectfully requested to refrain from bumping my head about. "Why?" he demanded. "Because I've got a headache," I said. "Then why didn't you tell me at first?" he crushed me. "Did you expect me to be a thought-reader?" But, indeed, I could say a lot about American barbers. I had expected to have my tempting fob snatched. It was not snatched. I had expected to be asked, at the moment of landing, for my mature opinion of the United States, and again at intervals of about a quarter of an hour, day and night, throughout my stay. But I had been in America at least ten days before the question was put to me, even in jest. I had expected to be surrounded by boasting and impatient vanity concerning the achievements of the United States and the citizens thereof. I literally never heard a word of national boasting, nor observed the slightest impatience under criticism. . . . I say I had expected these things. I would be more correct to say that I *should* have expected them if I had had a rumor-believing mind: which I have not.

But I really did expect to witness an overwhelming violence of traffic and movement in lower Broadway and the renowned business streets in its vicinity. And I really was disappointed by the ordinariness of the scene, which could be well matched in half a dozen places in Europe, and beaten in one or two. If but once I had been shoved into the gutter by a heedless throng going furiously upon its financial ways, I should have been content. . . . The legendary "American rush" is to me a fable. Whether it ever existed I know not; but I certainly saw no trace of it, either in New York or Chicago. I dare say I ought to have gone to Seattle for it. My first sight of a stock-market roped off in the street was an acute disillusionment. In agitation it could not have competed with a sheep-market. In noise it was a muffled silence compared with the fine racket that enlivens the air outside the Paris Bourse. I saw also an ordinary day in the Stock Exchange. Faint excitations were afloat in certain corners, but I honestly deemed the affair tame. A vast litter of paper on the floor, a vast assemblage of hats pitched on the tops of telephone-boxes—these phenomena do not amount to a hustle. Earnest students of hustle should visit Paris or Milan. The fact probably is that the perfecting of mechanical contrivances in the United States has killed hustle as a diversion for the eyes and ears. The mechanical side of the Exchange was wonderful and delightful.

The sky-scrapers that cluster about the lower end of Broadway—their natural home—were as impressive as I could have desired, but not architectually. For they could only be felt, not seen. And even in situations where the sky-scraper is properly visible, it is, as a rule, to my mind, architecturally a failure. I regret for my own sake that I could not be more sympathetic toward the existing sky-scraper as an architectural entity, because I had assuredly no European prejudice against the sky-scraper as such. The objection of most people to the sky-scraper is merely that it is unusual—the instinctive objection of most people to everything that is original enough to violate tradition! I, on the contrary, as a convinced modernist, would applaud the unusualness of the sky-scraper. Nevertheless, I cannot possibly share the feelings of patriotic New-Yorkers who discover architectural grandeur in, say, the Flat Iron Building or the Metropolitan Life Insurance Building. To me they confuse the poetical idea of these buildings with the buildings themselves. I eagerly admit that the bold, prow-like notion of the Flat Iron cutting northward is a splendid notion, an inspiring notion; it thrills. But the building itself is ugly—nay, it is adverbially ugly; and no reading of poetry *into* it will make it otherwise.

Similarly, the Metropolitan Building is tremendous. It is a grand sight, but it is an ugly sight. The men who thought of it, who first conceived the notion of 't, were poets. They said, "We will cause to be constructed the highest building in the world; we will bring into existence the most amazing advertisement that an insurance company ever had." That is good; it is superb; it is a proof of heroic imagination. But the actual designers of the building did not rise to the height of it; and if any poetry is left in it, it is not their fault. Think what McKim might have accomplished on that site, and in those dimensions!

Certain architects, feeling the lack of imagination in the execution of these enormous buildings, have set their imagination to work, but in a perverse way and without candidly recognizing the conditions imposed upon them by the sky-scraper form: and the result here and there has been worse than dull; it has been distressing. But here and there, too, one sees the evidence of real understanding and taste. If every tenant of a sky-scraper demands—as I am informed he does—the same windows, and radiators under every window, then the architect had better begin by accepting that demand openly, with no fanciful or pseudo-imaginative pretense that things are not what they are. The Ashland Building, on Fourth Avenue, where the architectural imagination has exercised itself soberly, honestly, and obediently, appeared to me to be a satisfactory and agreeable sky-scraper; and it does not stand alone as the promise that a new style will ultimately be evolved.

In any case, a great deal of the poetry of New York is

due to the sky-scraper. At dusk the effect of the massed sky-scrapers illuminated from within, as seen from any high building up-town, is prodigiously beautiful, and it is unique in the cities of this world. The early night effect of the whole town, topped by the aforesaid Metropolitan tower, seen from the New Jersey shore, is stupendous, and resembles some enchanted city of the next world rather than of this. And the fact that a very prominent item in the perspective is a fiery representation of a frothing glass of beer inconceivably large—well, this fact too has its importance.

But in the sky-scrapers there is a deeper romanticism than that which disengages itself from them externally. You must enter them in order to appreciate them, in order to respond fully to their complex appeal. Outside, they often have the air of being nothing in particular; at best the façade is far too modest in its revelation of the interior. You can quite easily walk by a sky-scraper on Broadway without noticing it. But you cannot actually go into the least of them and not be impressed. You are in a palace. You are among marbles and porphyries. You breathe easily in vast and brilliant foyers that never see daylight. And then you come to those mysterious palisaded shafts with which the building and every other building in New York is secretly honeycombed, and the palisade is opened and an elevator snatches you up. I think of American cities as enormous agglomerations in whose inmost dark recesses innumerable elevators are constantly ascending and descending, like the angels of the ladder. . . .

The elevator ejects you. You are taken into dazzling daylight, into what is modestly called a business office; but it resembles in its grandeur no European business office, save such as may have been built by an American. You look forth from a window, and lo! New York and the Hudson are beneath you, and you are in the skies. And in the warmed stillness of the room you hear the wind raging and whistling, as you would have imagined it could only rage and whistle in the rigging of a three-master at sea. There are, however, a dozen more stories above this story. You walk from chamber to chamber, and in answer to inquiry learn that the rent of this one suite—among so many—is over thirty-six thousand dollars a year! And you reflect that, to the beholder in the street, all that is represented by one narrow row of windows, lost in a diminishing chess-board of windows. And you being to realize what a sky-scraper is, and the poetry of it.

More romantic even than the sky-scraper finished and occupied is the sky-scraper in process of construction. From no mean height, listening to the sweet drawl of the steam-drill, I have watched artisans like dwarfs at work still higher, among knitted steel, seen them balance themselves nonchalantly astride girders swinging in space, seen them throwing rivets to one another and never missing one; seen also a hugh crane collapse under an undue strain, and, crumpling like tinfoil, carelessly drop its load onto the populous sidewalk below. That particular mishap obviously raised the fear of death among a considerable number of people, but perhaps only for a moment. Anybody in America will tell you without a tremor (but with pride) that each story of a sky-scraper means a life sacrificed. Twenty stories—twenty men snuffed out; thirty stories—thirty men. A building of some sixty stories is now going up—sixty corpses, sixty funerals, sixty domestic hearths to be slowly rearranged, and the registrars alone know how many widows, orphans, and other loose by-products!

And this mortality, I believe, takes no account of the long battles that are sometimes fought, but never yet to a finish, in the steel webs of those upper floors when the labor-unions have a fit of objection more violently than usual to non-union labor. In one celebrated building, I heard, the non-unionists contracted an unfortunate habit of getting crippled; and three of them were indiscreet enough to put themselves under a falling girder that killed them, while two witnesses who were ready to give certain testimony in regard to the mishap vanished completely out of the world, and have never since been heard of. And so on. What more natural than that the employers should form a private association for bringing to a close these interesting hazards? You may see the leading spirit of the association. You may walk along the street with him. He knows he is shadowed, and he is quite cheerful about it. His revolver is always very ready for an emergency. Nobody seems to regard this state of affairs as odd enough for any prolonged comment. There it is! It is accepted. It is part of the American dailiness. Nobody, at any rate in the comfortable clubs, seems even to consider that the original cause of the warfare is aught but a homicidal cussedness on the part of the unions. . . . I say that these accidents and these guerrillas mysteriously and grimly proceeding in the skyey fabric of metal-ribbed constructions, do really form part of the poetry of life in America—or should it be the poetry of death? Assuredly they are a spectacular illustration of that sublime, romantic contempt for law and for human life which, to a European, is the most disconcerting factor in the social evolution of your States. I have sat and listened to tales from journalists and other learned connoisseurs till— But enough!

When I left New York and went to Washington I was congratulated on having quitted the false America for the real. When I came to Boston I received the sympathies of everybody in Boston on having been put off for so long with spurious imitations of America, and a sigh of happy relief went up that I had at length got into touch with a genuine American city. When, after a long pilgrimage, I attained Chicago, I was positively informed that Chicago alone was the gate of the United States, and that everything east of Chicago was negligible and even misleading. And when I entered Indianapolis I discovered that Chicago was a mushroom and a suburb of Warsaw, and that its pretension to represent the United States was grotesque, the authentic center of the United States being obviously Indianapolis. . . . The great towns love thus to affront one another, and their demeanor in the game resembles the gamboling of young tigers—it is half playful and half ferocious. For myself, I have to say that my heart was large enough to hold all I saw. While I admit that Indianapolis struck me as very characteristically American, I assert that the unreality of New York escaped me. It appeared to me that New York was quite a real city, and European geographies (apt to err, of course, in matters of detail) usually locate it in America.

Having regard to the healthy mutual jealousy of the great towns, I feel that I am carrying audacity to the point of foolhardiness when I state that the streets of every American city I saw reminded me on the whole rather strongly of the streets of all the others. What inhabitant of what city could forgive this? Yet I must state it. Much of what I have said of the streets of New York applies, in my superficial opinion, for instance, to the streets of Chicago. It is well known that to the Chinaman all Westerners look alike. No tourist on his first visit to a country so astonishing as the United States is very different from a Chinaman; the tourist should reconcile himself to that deep truth. It is desolating to think that a second visit will reveal to me the blindness, the distortions, and the wrong-headedness of my first. But even as a Chinaman I did notice subtle differences between New York and Chicago. As one who was brought up in a bleak and uncanny climate, where soft coal is in universal use, I at once felt more at home in Chicago than I could ever do in New York. The old instinct to wash the hands and change the collar every couple of hours instantly returned to me in Chicago, together with the old comforting conviction that a harsh climate is a climate healthy for body and spirit. And, because it is laden with soot, the air of Chicago is a great mystifier and beautifier. Atmospheric effects may be seen there that are unobtainable without the combustion of soft coal. Talk, for example, as much as you please about the electric sky-signs of Broadway—not all of them together will write as much poetry on the sky as the single word "Illinois" that hangs without a clue to its suspension in the murky dusk over Michigan Avenue. The visionary aspects of Chicago are incomparable.

Another difference, of quite another order, between New York and Chicago is that Chicago is self-conscious. New York is not; no metropolis ever is. You are aware of the self-consciousness of Chicago as soon as you are aware of its bitumen. The quality demands sympathy, and wins it by its wistfulness. Chicago is openly anxious about its soul. I liked that. I wish I could see a livelier anxiety concerning the municipal soul in certain cities of Europe.

Perhaps the least subtle difference between New York and Chicago springs from the fact that the handsomest part of New York is the center of New York, whereas the center of Chicago is disappointing. It does not impress. I was shown, in the center of Chicago, the first sky-scraper that the world had ever seen. I visited with admiration what was said to be the largest department store in the world. I visited with a natural rapture the largest book-store in the world. I was informed (but respectfully doubt) that Chicago is the greatest port in the world. I could easily credit, from the evidence of my own eyes, that it is the greatest railway center in the world. But still my imagination was not fired, as it has been fired again and again by far lesser and far less interesting places. Nobody could call Wabash Avenue spectacular, and nobody surely would assert that State Street is on a plane with the collective achievements of the city of which it is the principal thoroughfare. The truth is that Chicago lacks at present a rallying-point—some Place de la Concorde or Arc de Triomphe—something for its biggest streets to try to live up to. A convocation of elevated railroads is not enough. It seemed to me that Jackson Boulevard or Van Buren Street, with fine crescents abutting opposite Grant Park and Garfield Park, and a magnificent square at the intersection of Ashland Avenue, might ultimately be the chief sight and exemplar of Chicago. Why not? Should not the leading thoroughfare lead boldly to the lake instead of shunning it? I anticipate the time when the municipal soul of Chicago will have found in its streets as adequate expression as it has already found in its boulevards.

Perhaps if I had not made the "grand tour" of those boulevards, I might have been better satisfied with the streets of Chicago. The excursion, in an automobile, occupied something like half of a frosty day that ended in torrents of rain—apparently a typical autumn day in Chicago! Before it had proceeded very far I knew that there was a sufficient creative imagination on the shore of Lake Michigan to carry through any municipal enterprise, however vast, to a generous and final conclusion. The conception of those boulevards discloses a tremendous audacity and faith. And as you roll along the macadam, threading at intervals a wide-stretching park, you are overwhelmed—at least I was—by the completeness of the scheme's execution and the lavishness with which the system is in every detail maintained and kept up.

You stop to inspect a conservatory, and find yourself in a really marvelous landscape garden, set with statues, all under glass and heated, where the gaffers of Chicago are collected together to discuss interminably the exciting politics of a city anxious about its soul. And while listening to them with one ear, with the other you may catch the laconic tale of a park official's perilous and successful vendetta against the forces of graft.

And then you resume the circuit and accomplish many more smooth, curving, tree-lined miles, varied by a jolting section, or by the faint odor of the Stock-yards, or by a halt to allow the longest freight-train in the world to cross your path. You have sighted in the distance universities, institutions, even factories; you have passed through many inhabited portions of the endless boulevard, but you have not actually touched hands with the city since you left it at the beginning of the ride. Then at last, as darkness falls, you feel that you are coming to the city again, but from another point of the compass. You have rounded the circle of its millions. You need only think of the unkempt, shabby, and tangled outskirts of New York, or of any other capital city, to realize the miracles that Chicago has put among her assets. . . .

You descry lanes of water in the twilight, and learn that in order to prevent her drainage from going into the lake Chicago turned a river back in its course and compelled it to discharge ultimately into the Mississippi. That is the story. You feel that it is exactly what Chicago, alone among cities, would have the imagination and the courage to do. Some man must have risen from his bed one morning with the idea. "Why not make the water flow the other way?" And then gone, perhaps diffidently, to his fellows in charge of the city with the suggestive query, "Why not make the water flow the other way?" And been laughed at! Only the thing was done in the end! I seem to have heard that there was an epilogue to this story, relating how certain other great cities showed a narrow objection to Chicago draining herself in the direction of the Mississippi, and how Chicago, after all, succeeded in persuading those whom it was necessary to persuade that, whereas her drainage was unsuited to Lake Michigan, it would consort well with the current of the Mississippi.

And then, in the night and in the rain, you swerve round some corner into the straight, by Grant Park, in full sight of one of the most dazzling spectacles that Chicago or any other city can offer—Michigan Avenue on a wet evening. Each of the thousands of electric standards in Michigan Avenue is a cluster of six huge globes (and yet they will tell you in Paris that the Rue de la Paix is the best lit street in the world), and here and there is a red globe of warning. The two lines of light pour down their flame into the pool which is the roadway, and you travel continually toward an incandescent floor without ever quite reaching it, beneath mysterious words of fire hanging in the invisible sky! . . . The automobile stops. You get out, stiff, and murmur something inadequate about the length and splendor of those boulevards. "Oh," you are told, carelessly, "those are only the interior boulevards. . . . Nothing! You should see our exterior boulevards—not quite finished yet!"

# WHY IS A BOSTONIAN?[1]

*By* Harrison Rhodes

*Harrison Rhodes, born in 1871, has a rare faculty for characterizing a community. This essay, first published in* Harper's *for January, 1916, is one of a series upon American cities.*

THE AUTHOR OF THE "ROLLO Books," famous in that dim nineteenth century, wrote also the familiar "Lucy" and "Jonas Books," and another series less well known but invaluable to the American who is curious-minded as to the social history of his country. *Marco Paul's Adventures in Pursuit of Knowledge* (is the title not indicative of the pretty, harmless wit of those innocent days?) is the record of an early attempt to "see America first." Marco Paul, after showing his native city of New York to the excellent Forrester, at once his cousin and his tutor, visited in that relative's company, and in a hot and praiseworthy pursuit of knowledge, Vermont, the Springfield Armory, the forests of Maine, Boston, and the Erie Canal! Agreeable though all the volumes are, it is with the one upon the capital of Massachusetts that we are here concerned, and in especial with the chaper describing the visit of our travelers to the Bunker Hill Monument.

"Who fought the battle on Bunker Hill?" Marco Paul asked his cousin Forrester. And the author of the *Adventures*, who was, it is to be noted, a Bostonian, comments in this astonishing way upon the young hero's ignorance. "Marco Paul," he says, "was a New York boy and did not know much about the battle of Bunker Hill."

In 1843 the Revolution was not—one would now say—so very remote. The discovery is therefore the more significant that so long ago Boston was casting at New York the same reproach of being "un-American" over which recent writers upon our civilization have so often become philosophical. Even after more than three-quarters of a century this acidity of tone about poor Marco Paul seems, at the very outset, to warn off any New-Yorker preparing to comment upon Boston. Perhaps the only apology for recklessness is recklessness itself. But it can at least be hinted that nowadays few New-Yorkers are New-Yorkers; they are more commonly Ohioans.

Since the Bostonians' attitude toward New York has, by the accident of Marco Paul's *faux pas* upon Bunker Hill, already been introduced, it may be as well to go on, and to say that their feeling concerning the metropolis, varying in quality and in emotional force, is one of the most curious and distinguishing marks of our other cities. Philadelphia, for example, ignores New York. Boston, on the other hand, is over-acutely conscious of it, hates it, despises it, loves its fleshpots and its Great White Way, and is ashamed of itself for doing so. All this, be it clearly understood, is said in praise rather than dispraise of Boston. But the facts are as they are. New York is perpetually upon Boston's nerves. To a foreigner school-boy studying his atlas, Philadelphia would seem to be considerably nearer the mouth of the Hudson than Boston; spiritually, if one may put it that way, the New England capital is far closer at hand.

Until very recently it was possible to take a train from Boston to New York at a later hour than you could enter the subway and take a street-car for Cambridge—a fact which in the days before Harvard became a serious scholarly athletic college was often taken by belated and cheerful students of that institution as a sign direct from God. The development of what is known as the "brass-bed train" between the two cities is evidence of an almost exacerbated anxiety to make the night transit endurable to overwrought, quivering creatures returning to the shores of Massachusetts

Bay. New York's tango roofs and pleasure palaces are the constant familiar haunt of Bostonians, yet it is never certain that the visitors are quite at their ease there. Even for the larkish trip to New York they bring certain grave prejudices and scientific ideas as to hygiene, which look very odd when unpacked in Manhattan. A Bostonian lady who was enthusiastic over New York's dancing-in-public restaurants, asserting that at home it was difficult regularly to secure this excellent health-exercise, caused considerable confusion one New-Year's Eve in a place of entertainment where, for that evening, only champagne was being served to patrons, by insisting upon having "certified milk," which was, she stoutly maintained, the exact thing which could, without harming her, keep her going at three in the morning!

It is no bad thing to pass from the image of the blousy beauty of Manhattan to one of the more frugal, nipped loveliness of Boston. Of course, the New-Yorker might well feel terror on his arrival in Boston, especially if it is after nightfall, in that strange Back Bay station where the electric lamps seem to produce light without shedding it. He might reasonably fear that now justice is at last to be meted out to him. But when the first moment's panic is over he cannot but feel, as does doubtless the repatriate Bostonian, that the contrast is, for the time being at least, agreeable between what he has left and the cooler, grayer, more distinguished civilization to which he has come. More distinguished, in the accurate sense of that word, Boston is. While the national metropolis is at once vehement and vague, the New England capital is more measured, more clean-cut, more distinguished in the sense of having somehow so concentrated and clarified its special flavor that no one can for a moment doubt that—for better or worse—Boston is Boston. When the sharp east wind has cleared away the vapors of Broadway, New York becomes less an actuality than a nightmare, and the northern town and its inhabitants are perceived to be standing very firmly on their own feet.

These northern folk are passionately Bostonian—if they are passionately anything. It is pleasant for a moment to think of the lady living in Milton (a town of concentrated Bostonianism) who said of her son, whose career in the diplomatic service of his country had kept him in Paris for several years, that her only fear was that he should "get out of touch with Milton"! There was no confusion in her mind as to what is valuable in life. In this matter of values and belief in Boston the Society for the Preservation of New England Antiquities presented itself lately to great advantage, gallantly going to the courts to prevent the alien—generally French-Canadian—from changing his name by the ordinary legal processes to that of any of Boston's old, historic families. There is a something here that insists on being like the Gilbert and Sullivan operetta. And yet there is also something magnificent—in a democracy—in the fact that you can become Smith, but never—shall we say Homans?

The intentions of this article—though honorable—are not topographical, yet something must be said of the look of Boston, for it is indicative of the town's inner quality—as indeed to any one who has a feeling for the personality of places is always the look of streets and squares and parks. New York sprawls; Boston really composes itself around Beacon Hill, and falls away from the lovely, peaceful, red-brick quarter which surrounds the State House to the business district and the foreign North End on one side, and on the other to the Back Bay, the great South End, the huge, trailing suburbs that lie farther out, and finally the New England country of which it is the metropolis and the commercial and spiritual head. Somehow all through the town one gets hints of the great tributary province. There is a little old shop near the busy center where are displayed in the window slippery-elm and licorice sticks—does the sight not bring all New England's rocky fields and white villages immediately before your eyes?

The State House is to the eye as to the imagination the center of New England, and its gilded dome rising over the dark-green of the elms on the Common is typical of the unexuberant, distinguished beauty of this Northern Athens. There is probably quite as much gold upon the dome as would be necessary to decorate a New York bar-room. But in the former case there is no vulgar ostentation in its use. There is not even the kind of warm, barbaric lavishness which incrusts the Venetian St. Mark's with the precious metal. The Bostonian State House seems instead to proclaim that here in a shrewd, inclement climate and upon an arid, stony soil New England industry and thrift have won a living and even wealth, and that when the occasion reasonably and sanely demands it New England can be lavish, almost spendthrift. You get a sense everywhere in Boston that they spend money upon public enterprises like state houses, opera-houses, art museums, and so forth because there is a need to have such things and the money can be found, not because the money is there and there is a need to find some way to spend it—the latter being a much more characteristic American frame of mind. Reason rather than emotion guides New England expenditure, and the result is a cool and restrained distinction which the wanton cities of the South and West never quite attain.

The old Boston dwellings upon Beacon Hill have this look of tempered luxury to perfection. But what is more remarkable is the sobriety of domestic architecture in the newer districts, even in that decorous Commonwealth Avenue, in which the true Bostonian so fantastically asks the stranger to detect a note of the vulgarity of the *nouveau riche*. The Louises have never wrought much of their French mischief in the Back Bay. A certain indigenous ugliness of architecture is preferred, solid and roomy, suggesting comfort rather than slender, gilded elegance. There is not much foreign lace nonsense at the windows; instead sometimes only simple, colored silk curtains drawn back to admit the sun and allow its due hygienic effect. Where the outlook is toward the south, plants flourish in the Bostonian windows, and the passer-by instinctively feels that they actually grow there, and may even be watered by the ladies of the house instead of being merely a temporary installation by some expensive florist, to be lavishly and immediately replaced when neglect has withered them.

The Bostonian interior, too, has something of this frugal quality, and may be recognized even in houses in the Middle West where the influence of the summer upon the North Shore has chastened the exuberance of taste natural in those remoter regions. There is something extremely pleasant in these sunny, cleanly scoured, airy, rather scantily furnished rooms, with big expanses of polished floor and well-worn furniture. They seem a little old-fashioned now, but this is merely a proof that taste struck Boston in something like the '70's of the last century, a little before it hit our other towns.

There is, of course, a comic side to this frugality. One can imagine that in the early esthetic days the inexpensiveness of the jar of dried cattails was not without its appeal to the Bostonian decorator. No Bostonian thinks of spending his income; no New-Yorker thinks of spending merely his income: this is an exaggeration of something fundamentally true. The solid, piled-up, quiet wealth of Massachusetts is enormous—what the department-store experts call the "shopping power" of the regions within a forty-mile circle around the State House dome is some amazing proportion of the purchasing ability of the whole country. Yet Boston shops have never the air of inviting gay, wayward extravagance, the highest-priced ones are the least obtrusive, and the best always seem as if they could be instantly adapted to the sale of that traditional black silk of our grandmothers which could "stand alone."

Bostonian spending is the result of mature and deliberate thought. It is rarely vulgar, but it knows nothing of the spendthrift's *joie de vivre.* People in New York may dine at the Ritz from obscure motives of economy, a vague feeling that a holiday for the servants at home may make them more efficient at other times. In Boston they eat in restaurants, one somehow feels, only after fasting and prayer. The name given at once to the latest smart hotel, "The Costly-Pleasure," is significant. There is even something a little grim about the phrase; it is almost as if the costliness of pleasure repelled instead of allured, as it does in less serious towns. Young men in evening dress do not idly stroll forth into the Bostonian streets with their overcoats carelessly unbuttoned; it would give a false idea that a white-waistcoated Costly-Pleasure night-life is real Bostonianism. They hurry into motors and taxis and are about their business of dining and dancing seriously, almost half apologetically. There is, in short, very little bead on native Boston pleasure; it does not run to froth.

The job of being very young and very gay and very foolish is left to Harvard undergraduates. The proximity of a great supply of young men with hearty appetites and strong dancing legs has made Boston fashion dependent and complaisant. The boys, in consequence, do all the things which gay young men do in light magazine fiction. They go to parties with a self-confident indifference as to whether they have been invited or not. And there is a pretty story of some lads bringing suit-cases from Cambridge, in which they packed bottles of champagne, thus transferring supplies to the groves of Academe after the ball. It is no idle boast of the enthusiastic advocates of Harvard education that youth there is more prepared to deal with the great world than are the students of a country college. The crimson thread of Harvard is woven into the very fabric of Bostonian existence; yet though it is perpetually there, it always seems exotic.

The Bostonian opera—now temporarily suspended—was beautifully Bostonian; it presented in agreeable clearness the indigenous social quality. The decoration of the house was quiet gray and gold, and the garb of the audience had on the whole something of the same sobriety. To this effect the native frugality doubtless contributed; on opera nights the streets leading to the edifice were thronged with intrepid women equipped to give battle to extravagance for music's sake, with galoshes and woolen scarfs—in this rude Northern climate even "fascinators" must be woolen. If an Italian lady in evening dress could not afford a cab to the opera, she would quite simply stay at home—and yet we prate of the love of music nourished in those sunny climes! This tribute to ladies in fascinators is not to be taken as meaning that there were not more luxurious women—and plenty—in the stalls and boxes—lovely, carriage-borne creatures, expensively dressed and well jeweled, probably with the best old Brazilian stones; the point is that the total effect of the Bostonian audience was what it rarely is in opera-houses—subordinate to the stage.

The opening night was an incredible event. Banquet parties of the gayest Bostonians had gathered to dine at an hour when food would poison the fashionable people of other cities, and the crush of carriages was beyond everything ever known, not because more people were going to the opera than go in other cities, but because, for the first time in the history of opera, every one wanted to arrive on time. The intervals of the performance were devoted to a general promenade, in which many boxholders joined. Indeed, the attention paid to the occupants of boxes by the general audience was barely sufficient to induce female loveliness to display its charm in the traditional entr'acte manner—the ladies, if the truth be told, excited about the same amount of admiration as did the silver-gilt soda-water fountain which had been installed in the foyer. Here, it seemed to the irreverent outsider, the last word had been said. To have linked opera with the nut-sundae is to have, once for all, domesticated the gay, wayward institution and made it Boston's harmless, admirable own.

Light-minded comment, however, never discloses more than one side of a medal. The Bostonian opera showed, as a matter of fact, an admirable and sane sense of proportion. It was not the London, the Paris, or the New York opera. Why, pray, should it have been? It was opera of exactly the size and sumptuousness which it was likely that a town of Boston's extent and wealth could afford. It seemed something which could reasonably hope to exist, not the product of a spasmodic, hysterical effort such as occasionally brings fabulously paid singers to some of our smaller cities for a feverish May Festival or special operatic week. It was not a provincial enterprise, because it was not aping any metropolis. It was the opera of the capital of New England, and it stood firmly, like many other neighboring institutions, upon its own sturdy galoshed, Bostonian feet. It may, of course, always be open to question whether operatic art is not a too essentially artificial and emotional blend ever to please the Bostonian public as does the classically severe fare offered in Symphony Hall. But the Huntington Avenue opera was meant to stand or fall by the genuine music-loving support of its public. Even if the operatic dose was bitter, it was to be disguised by no "diamond horseshoe," by no soft Ionian ways. And who shall say that, though now suspended, the Boston opera has not had its nation-wide effect? Has not its gifted scene-painter already been chosen by New York to do the decoration for its leading summer "girl-show," and does he not thus continue to enliven Boston?

Culture has always seemed to the outsider a little rigorous in Boston. But as one looks over the whole field of American life one is inclined to say that desperate situations demand desperate remedies, and that to have caught culture in any trap, even just to have got it fighting in a corner, is an achievement.

This is not altogether a question of art, though art is no doubt one of the town's chief preoccupations. Still less is it a question of producing art. It is no great reproach to Boston that it is nowadays more a center of appreciation than creation. There is here no question of where the divine afflatus blows most fiercely. New York is the mart, and that is about all there is to be said upon an already threadbare subject.

Culture has, perhaps, more to do with education than with art. We study enough in America—that is, we go to schools and colleges—but somehow, it may as well be admitted frankly, we do not succeed in weaving our education into the very fabric of our daily social intercourse; we are not cultivated in the unobtrusive, easy way of the best Englishmen and Frenchmen. Now the newspaper humorists' best jokes hinge upon the alleged universality of Boston culture. And though the alien visitor may never find the infant who spouts Greek while brandishing his rattle, he will in simple justice admit that education has gone both far and deep in Boston, that slang is not the only dialect spoken, and that even among shop-girls and elevator-boys some traces of our original national speech are still to be detected.

Here, parenthetically, it may be said that what is meant by Bostonians speaking English is the words themselves rather than the intonation and pronunciation with which they are uttered. The "Boston accent" is of course famous and cannot but fail to give the keenest pleasure to even a child traveling thither. The point to be made here is that it does not, as the Bostonians appear to think, approximate to the

English accent of England any more than any other of our national accents. The total elision of the R and the amazing broad, flat A—as in "Park Street" and Harvard College" —give to Bostonian speech a magnificently indigenous tang, hint at juniper and spruce forests and rocky fields and pumpkins and Thanksgiving and pie; make you feel again how triumphantly New England is new, and not old, English. But its vocabulary is, on the whole, the best chosen of all the American dialects.

It is somewhat difficult to find in ordinary Bostonian speech the ten and twelve syllabled words of which it is popularly supposed to be exclusively composed. But the joke is so old that there must be something in it. As far back as Brook Farm it was alleged that they said, "Cut the pie from the center to the periphery," and asked, "Is the butter within your sphere of influence?" But this was humor, as New England as a wintergreen lozenge. It was a by-product of an unashamed passion for education which distinguished American antebellum days. Even in the Middle West, when James Garfield, later to be President, with his friends in the little fresh-water college of Hiram, indulged in "stilting," as they termed this humorous riding of the high-horses of the language, they were in the Bostonian tradition. "Stilting" has perhaps disappeared. But there are here and there indications of the survival of the English of a robuster period. The old lady who said that she didn't, after all, know that Bostonians were so "thundering pious," produced with the phrase all the effect of an Elizabethan oath. She made you feel that Bostonian culture was no mere thin affair of yesterday.

It should be acknowledged handsomely that there is a certain amenity of tone in the town which comes not so much from exuberant good nature as from a reasoned belief in life's higher interest. The policeman who in Commonwealth Avenue used to stop promenading strangers and urge them to turn and admire the sunset was extending the city's hospitality no less to nature's beauty than to the visitors. He was notably Bostonian in that he was ashamed neither of the sunset nor of his belief that pleasure was to be derived from its contemplation. His culture was genuinely a part of his existence, of his everyday life. And culture is unquestionably a more integral part of Boston's normal existence than of our other cities' lives. Only in Boston, to imagine a concrete and pleasing example, could a lady, if she were so inclined, be distinguished by a love for extreme *décolletage* and for early Buddhistic philosophy. There is, in Boston, nothing essentially inharmonious in such a combination.

In any case, variations from a standard type are not so severely penalized in Boston as in other parts of our country. Eccentricity is almost encouraged; to take but one example, old age is openly, almost brazenly, permitted. Just how they kill the old off in New York is not known, but they get rid of them somehow. Boston, on the contrary, has famous old people, especially old ladies, and the community's pride in them is not merely that they have been able so long to withstand the Boston climate. These veterans do not eat their evening meal up-stairs on a tray; instead, their visit to a dinner-table honors and enlivens the board. There is something extraordinarily exciting in meeting the lady whose witticisms were famous when you were almost a child and finding her still tossing them off so vigorously and gaily that you can with a clear conscience encourage your own children to grow up with the promise that when they are old enough to dine out they, too, shall be privileged to go to Boston and hear really good talk.

The New England capital cherishes affectionately links with the past. There was until lately for some favored people the possibility of going to tea in a faded, old-fashioned Boston drawing-room, from the windows of which you saw the sunset across the Charles River basin, and hearing wise, graceful, tender talk that made the literary past of England and America for almost three-quarters of a century seem like the pleasant gossip of to-day. The delight of such moments in the fading light was poignant—the tears would come into one's eyes at the realization that it was all too good to be true and also too good to last.

The respect for the person or the thing which has become "an institution" is always to be noted with interest in our American life. And for an evening newspaper—a vulgar and fly-blown thing elsewhere—to have a half-sacred character is possible only in Boston. The publication in question is not thought of as a mere private enterprise; it is integrally a part of the whole community's life, its policy and its grammar are both constant matters for the searchings of the New England conscience. It is even solemnly asserted—by those who should know—that more Bostonians die on Friday than on any other day because they thus make sure of being in the special Saturday night obituary notices! To pay, even in the date of death, such a tribute to the Bostonian tradition is magnificent.

But if one is to speak of institutions, there is of course Harvard College, without which it is impossible to imagine Boston and Boston culture. Changes in Cambridge are changes in Boston. For a ten or twenty year period there has been a determined and conscientious attempt across the Charles to break down the old barriers and traditions which kept Harvard from being democratic and efficient in the modern way. What has been accomplished in Cambridge is for the purposes of this article less important than what has been wrought in Boston. Undergraduates may take innovation lightly, but in the fastnesses of clubs upon Beacon Hill irate old gentlemen declare that Harvard is now nothing but a "slap-shoulder college," and younger philosophers of a more suavely cynical turn of mind deplore the out-Yaleing of Yale, and the rough, boyish virility, wholly unconnected with education, which, they maintain, now distinguishes Cambridge rather than New Haven. They tell you that "college spirit," with all its attendant vulgarities of tone, is rampant where the college elms once stood, and there are no longer any disloyal sons of Harvard. This is the pleasant, crabbed, characteristic way in which Boston tells you that, after all, it is moving with the times, and that if a big, regenerative movement as some believe is sweeping over the country, it will have Harvard men in the very first battle-line. Boston may bewail changes in the nation, but it knows they cannot happen without changes in Harvard. Centuries of history prove it.

These centuries of history are singularly alive in Boston. The reference is not to Faneuil Hall or the Old South Church or any of the historic spots about which our modern Marco Paulos from Michigan and Oregon know so much. What is meant is the amazing sense of a continuous social connection back to the very English roots of the New England tree.

An unwise stranger, sitting at ease in the Somerset Club one day of this very year of grace, ventured the observation, not deeply original or stimulating, that Boston was remarkable for the way in which the old Bostonian families had kept the money and the position and were still, as it were, in the saddle. The Bostonians looked at one another. They murmured a negative, and the faintest trace of embarrassment seemed to creep over the group. The confused stranger was so sure that his remark, if banal, was true that he thought they had not understood. He carefully explained again. The negative was now sharper and the embarrassment deeper.

"I don't think you quite understand—" began one of the Bostonians; and it is possible that the miserable stranger might have tried to explain still again had not his friend gone on:

"You see there are almost no Bostonians living here"—he paused for an instant—"almost all the Bostonian families went back home at the time of the Revolution. The inhabitants here now, with the exception of perhaps four families, are all Salem people!"

There is no way of commenting upon such an episode; there it is, in sheer Bostonian beauty, for such as are worthy of seeing its Bostonianism. The tormented un-Bostonian mind will possibly seek refuge in the thought of the club itself. (One does not say clubs, although it is just possible to maintain that there are two in Boston.) Its grave, suave distinction can only be savored by many visits and by quiet, meditative hours. But once you have felt its charm you will henceforth find the ordinary American organization more like a hotel or a railway station than like a club. To sign no checks, but instead to receive an unobtrusive and unitemized bill at the end of the month, is at once to gain the impression that you are being notably treated like a gentleman. The impression is deepened by genuine blue Canton ware, by waiters of a dignified and ancient kindliness which has elsewhere disappeared from American life, and by food excellent in that strange, tempered New England way—oysters from the club's own planted waters, and peppers and pepper sauces dated and labeled like vintage wines.

The right to belong to such a club is, as it were, beyond the power of the mere individual to acquire—it is something with or without which he is born. The club, indeed, has been described as an "Institution for the Congenitally Eminent." But within its doors you catch furtive hints of an inaccessible inner eminence—caused possibly by Bostonian instead of Salem descent—which makes even its exclusiveness seem common. There is a fabulous story of an eighth-degree Bostonian who referred lightly to his rare visits to this holy of club holies, of which he was, as it were automatically, a member, and said that it was "at times a pleasure to be *franchement canaille.*" In this wind-swept Northern clime the phrase in the French language somehow seems to accentuate the odd, bitter, cultivated venom of a description of the greatest Bostonian exclusiveness as "frankly of the gutter." Let Ohio and Oklahoma pause and think before they too quickly describe our American civilization as twentieth-century democracy.

Bostonian democracy is not the spontaneous product of naturally genial temperaments; it is rather a thing extorted from oneself by will and fierce conviction. But will, belief, and a conscience can make the Northern city burst into flames. In Boston least of anywhere in the North does the passion for human freedom which brought on our own Civil War seem a dead or forgotten thing. And even now the black brother—though modern thought judges him to be not quite a brother in the old sense—can still count on a helping hand and some belief in his future. It is well for the visitor to Boston to sit for a peaceful half-hour under the elms of the Common and think of New England's part in the national life. Geographically and spiritually New England is a little apart. It is a tight, small province, and it is a long way from there to Washington in ordinary times. It is in the crises that Boston becomes most intensely American; then you realize how far-flung is the battle-line of the New England conscience. One never quite forgets in Boston the great moments in our history when the country has kindled at New England's burning heart.

Modern workers, who believe that charity and good deeds begin at home, sometimes scoff at the Bostonian "long-distance philanthropy." And they cite you the story of the lady found wildly weeping because she had just heard how cruel they were to cats in Persia in the thirteenth century! She is indeed a shade fantastical, poor lady; but in the monotonous dead levels of American life we can be grateful to Boston for her.

Indeed, is not gratitude, after all, the chief feeling one has for Boston? Nipped and sour though the fruit sometimes may be of the tree which grows upon her thin soil in her bitter east wind, does not every descendant of the old American stock, and every one who has in his Americanization made the traditions of that stock his own, know that the core of that fruit is sound, and the cider that might be pressed from it the best of our native wines, if one may put it that way? The packed trains that carry Thanksgiving travelers to Boston seem somehow symbolic. The statistics are not at hand—when are statistics ever at hand when they are needed?—but it must be that these trains are more heavily freighted than those that go to any other of our great American cities. Whether we are from New England or not, Boston is for many of us, in a deeper sense, our "home town."

# WHEN THE CITY WAKES

*By* Simeon Strunsky

*Simeon Strunsky, born in 1879, is better known as the author of essays with a delicate, ironic edge than as an editorial writer which, first upon the* Evening Post *and then upon the* New York Times, *has been his vocation. His* Belshazzar Court *will be remembered as one of the best collections of recent American essays. This article was first published in* Harper's *in October, 1914.*

THE SUN HEAVES UP FROM ITS sleeping-place somewhere in the vicinity of Flatbush, an extremely early riser, like most suburban residents, and loses no time in setting out upward and westward to its place of business over Manhattan. But the sun is not the first-comer there. Its earliest rays surprise an army at work. Creatures of the night, they cower and dissolve in the oncoming of the light. The yellow glare of their oil-torches and the ghastly violet-blue of their vacuum tubes pale, flicker, and go out before the onrush of dawn.

It is amazing how a great city can snore with equanimity while entire regiments and squadrons carry on operations in the streets, quietly, but with no attempt at concealment, under the very eyes of the police, with whom, in fact they seem to have a complete understanding. No political revolutions in the name of good citizenship, no shifting of commissioners and inspectors and captains, can conceivably destroy the *entente cordiale* between the police and these workers in the dark. If anything, the patrolman will stop in his rounds to watch their manœuvers with an eye of amicable appraisal, and when they begin to scatter with the dawn from their places of congregation he speeds them on their way with a word of greeting.

And the great city sleeps, its pulse scarcely disturbed by

the feverish activity of the hosts of darkness. Or if the city catches a rumble of their movements and stirs in its slumber, it is only to turn over and go to sleep again. No hypnotic spell will account for this indifference of a city of five millions to the presence of an army in its gas-lit streets. It is merely habit. If here and there in the cubical hives where New York takes its rest an unquiet sleeper tosses in his bed and resents the disturbance, it is not to wish that these prowlers of the night were caught and sent to jail, but only to wish that they went about their business more discreetly—this great host of market-men, grocers, butchers, milkmen, push-cart engineers, and news-venders who have been engaged since soon after midnight on the enormous task of preparing the city's breakfast.

For this, of course, is the real night life of New York—the life that beats at rapid pace in the great water-front markets, in the newspaper press-rooms around Brooklyn Bridge, under the acetylene glare over excavations for the new subways, and in the thousands of bakeshops that line the avenues and streets.

This is the underworld of which we speak so little because it is a real underworld. It is not made up of subterranean galleries and shafts inhabited by a race engaged in sapping the upper world. It is a true underworld, on which the upper world of the daylight hours is grounded. The foundations of society run down into the night where the city's food, the city's ways of communication, and the city's news are being made ready and garnished for the full roar of the day's life.

Compared with these workers of the dark the operations of the house-breaker and his sister of the shadowy side-walks sink into significance. It is but a turn of the hand for the army of the laborious underworld to undo the mischief which the outlaws of the night have performed. Between one and five in the morning they create ten thousand times the wealth which it is in the power of the jailbird to destroy.

The subject fascinates me. We need urgently a vindication of the Night, and especially of night in the city. Occasionally, it is true, we pay lip service to Night as the kindly nurse that brings rest to the fevered brow and forgetfulness to the uneasy conscience. But at heart we think of the things of night as of things of evil. It would pay to set to work a commission of moralists, economic experts, and statisticians at striking a balance between the good and evil that are done in the night and the day. Personally I have no doubt at all as to which way the figures would point. It is only a question of how far the day is behind the night in its net contribution to the welfare of humanity. Against night in Greater New York you would have to debit, say, half a hundred burglaries and highway assaults, a handful of fires, a handful of joy-ride fatalities, much gambling and debauchery, and possibly some of the latest plays on Broadway. But as regards the moral laxities of the dark, it depends on what you call immorality. Greater harm to the fiber of the race may be wrought during the day by the intrigues of unscrupulous men, by factory fire-traps, by sweat-shops, by the manipulators of our political machines, than by all the gambling-houses and dives in the Tenderloin. After all, the get-rich-quick promoters, the jerry builders of tenements, the bank-looters, bosses, and ward heelers, suspend their labors at night.

No: the more you think of it the more you will be persuaded that night is primarily the time of the innocent industries, and for the most part the primitive industries, employing simple, innocent, primitive men—slow-speaking truck-farmers; brawny slaughterers in the abattoirs; stolid German bakers, apathetic milkmen. The milkman alone is enough to redeem the night from its undeserved evil reputation. A cart-load of pasteurized milk for nurslings at four o'clock in the morning represents more service to civilization than a truck-load of bullion on its way from Sub-treasury to the vaults of a national bank five hours later.

I am, of course, not thinking now of the early part of the night on Broadway, which is but the bedraggled fringe of day, but of the later half of night which is the fresh anticipation of the dawn. In the still coolness before daybreak the interests of the city come down to human essentials. The commodities dealt in are those that men bought and sold tens of thousands of years before they trafficked in safety-razors and Brazilian diamonds. The dealers of the night are concerned with bread, flesh, milk, butter, cheese, fruits, and the green offerings of the fields. Contact with these things cannot but keep the soul clean. Where is the specialist in nervous diseases who will first advise his patients to rise at three in the morning and walk a mile between the rows of wagons and stalls in Gansevoort or Wallabout Market and draw strength from the piles of sweet, green produce, dewy under the lamplight, and learn patience from the farmers' horses, and observe that even men in their chafferings can be subdued to the innocent medium in which they traffic?

To be sure there are the newspapermen. I have always assumed that it is primarily for them the churches in the lower part of the city offer special services for night workers. If any class of night workers stands in need of prayer it must be the men of my own profession, surely the least ingenious of all legitimate trades that are plied after midnight. But as I think of it, even among newspaper-men it is the comparatively unspoiled and harmless who work after midnight —members of the lobster squad left on emergency duty, cubs who have not lost all the freshness of the little towns in the Middle West and the South, the men on the typesetting-machines, the men sweating in the press-rooms, and the husky men who stagger under enormous bundles of newspapers to the railway stations and the elevated trains. Here, too, night has exercised its cleansing effect. The big men of the press, the shrewd directors of newspaper policy, the editorial pleaders of special causes, the city editors with insistence on the "punch" as against the mere fact, the Titans of the advertising columns, have all gone home before midnight. As I think of it, the only deleterious elements of the newspaper profession that work at 2 A.M. are the writers of the extra special afternoon editions for the next day. Let us hope that they take advantage of the churches' standing offer to special services and prayers for night workers.

When you stroll through the markets, between lines of wagons, stalls, crates, baskets, and squads of perspiring men, you need not force the imagination to call up the solid square miles of brick and stone barracks in which New York's five million, minus some thousands, are asleep, outside the glare of the arc-lights and kerosene-torches. You can tell Hercules from his foot and you can tell New York from the size of its maw, of which a single day's filling keeps these thousands of men at work. There it sleeps, the big, dark brute, and in another three hours it will yawn and sit up and blink its eyes and roar for its food.

The markets are only the foci of highest activity in the business of providing fodder for the creature. Walk out of the crush of Gansevoort Market and turn south through Washington Street and Greenwich Street and Hudson Street, a good mile and a half south through silent warehouses all crammed with food, a solid square mile of provender. The contents of these grim weather-beaten storehouses are open to appraisal by the mere sense of smell as you pass through successive strata of coffee and sugar and tea and spices and green vegetables and fruits. If you are sufficiently educated you may detect the individual species within the genus, discern where the pepper merges into cloves, and the heavy odor of banana into the acid aroma of the citrus. It seems almost indecent, this vast debauch of gluttony, this tenderloin district of the stomach, this great area given up to the most elemental of the appetites—until you once more recall the five million individual cells of the animal that will soon have to be fed.

The markets and the warehouses are not the belly of the city, as Zola has called them in his own Paris. The digestive processes of a great city are worked out later and in a million homes. The markets are the heart of the city, pumping the life fuel to themselves from across the rivers and the seas and pumping them out again by drayloads and cartloads through the streets. In the late afternoon of the day before, everywhere on the circumference of the city, you have come across the driblets and streamlets of nourishment which the markets suck to themselves. In Jersey, in Long Island, and in Westchester you encounter, toward nightfall, heavy farm-wagons of exactly the prairie-schooner type that you first met in the school histories, plodding on toward the ferries and the bridges, the drivers nodding over the reins, the horses philosophically conscious of the long hours as well as the long miles ahead of them. Taken one by one, these farmers' wagons moving at two miles an hour seem pitifully inadequate to the appetites and imperious demands of a metropolis. But they are only the unquestioning units in the great mobilization of the army of food providers. Their cubic contents and their rate of progress have been accurately estimated by the Von Moltkes of the provision-markets. At the appointed time they will drop into their appointed place, forming by companies and squadrons into hollow squares for the daily encounter with humanity's oldest and most indefatigable foe—hunger.

The markets on the water-front are the heart of the city's night life, but in all the five boroughs there are local centers of concentrated vitality—the milk-depots, the street-railway junctions, the car-barns. Where elevated or subway meets with cross-town and longitudinal surface lines you will find at three in the morning as active and garishly illuminated a civic center as many a city of the hinterland would boast of at nine o'clock in the evening. Groups of switchmen car-despatchers, conductors, motormen, and the casual onlooker whom New York supplies from its inexhaustible womb even at three in the morning, stand in the middle of the road and discuss the most wonderful mysteries—so it seems, at least, in the hush before dawn. And because the cars which they switch and side-track and despatch on their way depart empty of passengers and lose themselves in the shadows, their business, too, seems one of impressive mystery.

A car-conductor at three o'clock in the morning is the most delightful of people to meet. His hands are not yet grimy with the dirt of alien nickels and dimes. His temper is as yet unworn by the day's traffic. In the beneficent cool of the night his thwarted social instincts unfold. If you share the rear platform with him, which you will do as a rule, he will accept your fare with a deprecating smile, as money passes between gentlemen who stoop to the painful necessity but take no notice of it. Having registered your fare, he will engage you in conversation, and it is amazing how the harassed soul of the car-conductor is open to the ideas and forces that rule the great world. But if you are timid with car-conductors and take your way into the car after paying your fare, he will make a pretense of business with the motorman and, coming back, he will find a remark to draw you out of your surliness or your timidity. He may even sit down next to you, and after five minutes you will be cursing the mechanical necessity of the daylight life which takes this eminently human creature and turns him into a bundle of rasping hurry and incivility. If a visit to the markets is a good cure for neurosis, a trip down Amsterdam Avenue in a surface car at 3 A. M. is a splendid tonic for democracy.

And once more food. For the men who labor in the night, primarily for the city's breakfast, must themselves be fed.

Clustered around the markets and around the markets and around the railway-junctions and car-barns are the popular and brilliantly illuminated Delmonicos of the industrial underworld. What places of warm cheer they are, on a winter night, these long rows of Lunches, whose names are a perpetual lesson in the national geography! They all have tiled floors and white walls and spacious arm-chairs with a table extension, like the chairs in which we used to write examination papers at college. In the rear of the room is the counter supporting the great silver coffee-urn. The placards on the walls would tempt Lucullus. You wonder how the resources of an establishment operating on an average level of fifteen cents the meal can supply the promised bounty—sirloins and small steaks, and shell-fish out of season, and all the delicacies of the griddle and the casserole; only the prudent consumer will concentrate on the coffee and doughnuts. The rarities are to be had, if you insist, and who would quarrel with the quality of a sirloin steak selling for twenty cents, with bread, butter, and coffee, at three in the morning? But it is better to ask for coffee and doughnuts.

An affable humanism permeates one of these Lunches. The proprietor, the *chef,* the waiter, and cashier will come forward to meet you and exchange a word or two with you as he wipes up the arm-table. He will take your order and, going behind the counter, will deliver it to himself. If you are extravagant and ask for meats, he will disappear into some sort of cupboard which is a kitchen, and powerful, pungent odors will precede his reappearance. He will punch your check as a protection against malfeasance by the waiter, and he will ring up your payment on the cash-register as a protection against malfeasance on the part of the cashier. If your manners permit, he will come forward and watch you while you eat, not with the affected paternal mien of the head-waiter at the Ritz, but as a brother, a democrat, and a *chef* who has presided over your food from the first moment till the last and is qualified to take an intimate interest in its ultimate disposal. He is generous with the butter and as a rule he is indifferent to tips.

Can I do you justice, O friendly Lunchman of the Gay White Way in the vicinity of Broadway and Manhattan Street, where the enormous black iron arch of the Subway viaduct casts its shadow over all the cars that run west to Fort Lee Ferry and north to Fort George and south into the deserted regions of lower Broadway? Your napkins unquestionably were white once upon a time, and your apron is but so-so, but your heart is in the right place, and consequently your manners are perfect. On you, too, the night has exercised its cleansing effect, wiping out commercialism and leaving behind the instinct for service. You accept my money, but only that you may have the means to go on feeding the useful toilers of the night and occasional castaways like myself. The spirit of profit does not lurk under your flaring arc-lights. Where is the profit in sirloin steak, with bread, butter, and coffee, at twenty cents? You are not a trafficker in food, but a minister to human needs, almost as disinterested as the dogs of St. Bernard, of whom, if you don't mind my saying so, you strongly remind me, with your solid bulk and great shock of hair and the two days' beard and your strangely unmanicured fingers. You do not cater to the pampered palate of the rich, which lusts for strange plants and strange animals and strange liquids to devour. Your sizzling coffee is nectar in the veins of big men who run in on winter nights stamping their feet and their hands, hands stiff from the icy brake-handle and switching-lever—the simple, hearty toilers of the night. Occasionally your walls resound to the gaiety of young voices, and your arc-lights glow on the shimmer of linen and finery which put your regular customers somewhat out of countenance when a troop of young men and girls, after loitering wickedly at the dance, seek refuge with you while waiting for a car. They taste your coffee and nibble at your doughnuts for a lark. So they say. It is pretense. They do not nibble; they do not taste; they eat and drink with undeniable relish the rough, unfamiliar fare. After five hours' exercise on the dancing-floor and a ten minutes' wait on a wintry corner there is an electric spark in your coffee and Titan's food in your doughnuts. Motormen, draymen, young men and women in dancing pumps. What a line of customers is yours!

The gray of dawn overtakes the armies from the markets, the car-barns, and the excavation pits in full retreat toward the ferries, the bridges, and along the main arteries to the crowded sections where the early risers live. They scatter in every direction, weary, heavy-eyed, but with no sense of defeat in their souls. They throng to the ferries to lose themselves in the mysterious wilds of Jersey. Their cavalry and train rumble down empty Broadway to South Ferry. They pour eastward toward the bridges or to lose themselves in the cellars and ramshackle booths of the East Side. They plunge into the Subway and, stretched out at full length in the illuminated spaciousness of the Interborough's cars, they pass off into the sleep which falls alike upon the just and the unjust, contrary to general supposition. When the day breaks it finds their haunting-places deserted or given over to small brigades of sweepers and cleaners, who make ready for the other kinds of business that are carried on in the full glare of the sun.

Blessed are the meek! While waiting for the inheritance of the earth they are already in full possession of the glory of the sunrise, which we of the comfortable classes know only by hearsay. The tremulous milky gray of the firmament followed by the red flush of daylight is reserved in New York for the truck-farmer from the suburbs, the drayman, the food-venders, and the early factory hands. For them only is the beauty of New York, as it heaves up out of the shadows. The farmer who has disposed of his wares with expedition and is now on his way back to the Jersey shore, sees, when he looks back, the jagged silhouette of our towers and massed brick piles, like a host of negroid Titans plodding northward in retreat. Or if his way is by the municipal boats to Staten Island, he may look back and see a thin shaft of light, ethereal, tremulous, almost of faery, and that pillar of light will be Broadway cañon between its brick walls still clad in shadow. It is given only to the foreign-born ditchers and levelers of the crowded lower Bronx, as they trudge across the bridges over the Harlem, to see before them mighty iron spans flung forward into the shadows or to catch the mirrored sweep of magic arches lifting up out of the water to link themselves to arches overhead.

The beauty of New York rising to meet a new day is for these lowly workers, and for the unfortunates who stay out in the night not to work but to sleep, because night and the open are their refuge. When the curtain of night rises on Riverside and reveals Grant's tomb in misty vagueness at the end of a green vista, the sight is rarely for those who sleep in the expensive caravansaries along the Drive, and most often for the sleepers on the benches. It is the men who sleep on the benches in Morningside Park that are the first to wonder at the dark front of poplars holding desperate defense against the charging line of daylight, and over the poplars the huge, squat octagon of St. John's buttressed chapels; unless the sleepers on the benches are anticipated by the angel atop of St. John's greeting the dawn with his trumpet. Because night loiterers are excluded from Central Park, I suppose that all its awakening loveliness must go for naught. But if the first impingement of the sun on the massed verdure of the Park, on its lakes, its alpine views, its waterfalls, and the fresh, sweet meadows, does find a rare spectator, it must be again one of the homeless who has eluded police regulations to find a night's rest in the great green inclosure. Possibly there may be a poet or two wandering about in Central Park at dawn, but the poets are early risers only in the country. To them the city is only the monstrous, noisy machine of the full day. That on New York City, too, the sun rises in the morning, working its miracles of beauty, seems to have escaped the poets—or else they have escaped me.

As the sun continues to mount from Flatbush toward the East River bridges the demoralization of the hosts of night workers grows complete. Either they have disappeared or they straggle on through isolated streets as mere units, the flotsam of a beaten army. The full light strips them of their dignity. As late even as five o'clock the milkman in the quiet streets is a symbol and a mystery. By six o'clock he is a common purveyor. Contact with frowsy elevator-boys and gaping grocers' clerks has vulgarized him. His interests are no longer in food, but in commerce. Instead of communing with the night, he is busy with a memorandum-book and pencil.

Some time before, the acetylene flares over the excavation pits have gone out. The dazzling arc-lights in the Lunches are out. The street-cars, running on shorter schedules, have taken on their daylight screech and clangor. The conductor is fast sinking into daylight surliness. The huge bundles of newspapers which at night and in bulk have the merit of a really great commodity—the dignity almost of a bag of meal or a crate of eggs—are now resolved into units on the stationers' stands, and if the new day be Sunday the newsman is busy sorting out the twelve different sections of the Sunday paper and putting the comic section on top.

Nor can I think of anything in human affairs which must be more futile in the eyes of a Creator than a stationer sorting out comic supplements in the full glory of early sunrise. With its newspaper waiting for it, New York of the ordinary life is ready to get out of bed.

# THE DEATH OF JEAN[1]

*By* Mark Twain

*Samuel Clemens, known in literature as Mark Twain, was, like so many humorists, a master also of sorrow and pathos. In this personal record his power lifts the expression above the immediate sorrow. It was posthumously published in* Harper's *in January, 1911. He was born in 1835 and died in 1910.*

THE DEATH OF JEAN CLEMENS occurred early in the morning of December 24, 1909. Mr. Clemens was in great stress of mind when I first saw him, but a few hours later I found him writing steadily.

"I am setting it down," he said, "everything. It is a relief to me to write it. It furnishes me an excuse for thinking." At intervals during that day and the next I looked in, and usually found him writing. Then on the evening of the 26th, when he knew that Jean had been laid to rest in Elmira, he came to my room with the manuscript in his hand.

"I have finished it," he said; "read it. I can form no opinion of it myself. If you think it worthy, some day—at the proper time—it can end my autobiography. It is the final chapter."

Four months later—almost to the day—(April 21st) he was with Jean. It would seem, now, that the world may, with propriety, read these closing words.

Albert Bigelow Paine.

Stormfield, Christmas Eve, 11 a. m., 1909.

*Jean is dead!*

Has any one ever tried to put upon paper all the little happenings connected with a dear one—happenings of the twenty-four hours preceding the sudden and unexpected death of that dear one? Would a book contain them? would two books contain them? I think not. They pour into the mind in a flood. They are little things that have been always happening every day, and were always so unimportant and easily forgettable before—but now! Now, how different! how precious they are, how dear, how unforgettable, how pathetic, how sacred, how clothed with dignity!

Last night Jean, all flushed with splendid health, and I the same, from the wholesome effects of my Bermuda holiday, strolled hand in hand from the dinner table and sat down in the library and chatted, and planned, and discussed, cheerily and happily (and how unsuspectingly!) until nine —which is late for us—then went up-stairs, Jean's friendly German dog following. At my door Jean said, "I can't kiss you good night, father: I have a cold, and you could catch it." I bent and kissed her hand. She was moved—I saw it in her eyes—and she impulsively kissed my hand in return. Then with the usual gay "Sleep well, dear!" from both, we parted.

At half past seven this morning I woke, and heard voices outside my door. I said to myself, "Jean is starting on her usual horseback flight to the station for the mail." Then Katy* entered, stood quaking and gasping at my bedside a moment, then found her tongue:

*"Miss Jean is dead!"*

Possibly I know now what the soldier feels when a bullet crashes through his heart.

In her bath-room there she lay, the fair young creature, stretched upon the floor and covered with a sheet. And looking so placid, so natural, and as if asleep. We knew what had happened. She was an epileptic: she had been seized with a convulsion and heart failure in her bath.

* Katy Leary, who had been in the service of the Clemens family for twenty-nine years.

The doctor had to come several miles. His efforts, like our previous ones, failed to bring her back to life.

It is noon, now. How lovable she looks, how sweet and how tranquil! It is a noble face, and full of dignity; and that was a good heart that lies there so still.

In England, thirteen years ago, my wife and I were stabbed to the heart with a cablegram which said, "Susy was mercifully released to-day." I had to send a like shock to Clara, in Berlin, this morning. With the peremptory addition, "You must not come home." Clara and her husband sailed from here on the 11th of this month. How will Clara bear it? Jean, from her babyhood, was a worshipper of Clara.

Four days ago I came back from a month's holiday in Bermuda in perfected health; but by some accident the reporters failed to perceive this. Day before yesterday, letters and telegrams began to arrive from friends and strangers which indicated that I was supposed to be dangerously ill. Yesterday Jean begged me to explain my case through the Associated Press. I said it was not important enough; but she was distressed and said I must think of Clara. Clara would see the report in the German papers, and as she had been nursing her husband day and night for four months* and was worn out and feeble, the shock might be disastrous. There was reason in that; so I sent a humorous paragraph by telephone to the Associated Press denying the "charge" that I was "dying," and saying "I would not do such a thing at my time of life."

Jean was a little troubled, and did not like to see me treat the matter so lightly; but I said it was best to treat it so, for there was nothing serious about it. This morning I sent the sorrowful facts of this day's irremediable disaster to the Associated Press. Will both appear in this evening's papers?—the one so blithe, the other so tragic.

* Mr. Gabrilowitsch had been operated on for appendicitis.

I lost Susy thirteen years ago; I lost her mother—her incomparable mother!—five and a half years ago; Clara has gone away to live in Europe; and now I have lost Jean. How poor I am, who was once so rich! Seven months ago Mr. Rogers died—one of the best friends I ever had, and the nearest perfect, as man and gentleman, I have yet met among my race; within the last six weeks Gilder has passed away, and Laffan—old, old friends of mine. Jean lies yonder, I sit here; we are strangers under our own roof; we kissed hands good-by at this door last night—and it was forever, we never suspecting it. She lies there, and I sit here—writing, busying myself, to keep my heart from breaking. How dazzlingly the sunshine is flooding the hills around! It is like a mockery.

Seventy-four years old, twenty-four days ago. Seventy-four years old yesterday. Who can estimate my age to-day?

I have looked upon her again. I wonder I can bear it. She looks just as her mother looked when she lay dead in that Florentine villa so long ago. The sweet placidity of death! it is more beautiful than sleep.

I saw her mother buried. I said I would never endure that horror again; that I would never again look into the grave of any one dear to me. I have kept to that. They will take Jean from this house to-morrow, and bear her to Elmira, New York, where lie those of us that have been released, but I shall not follow.

Jean was on the dock when the ship came in, only four days ago. She was at the door, beaming a welcome, when I reached this house the next evening. We played cards, and she tried to teach me a new game called "Mark Twain." We sat chatting cheerily in the library last night, and she wouldn't let me look into the loggia, where she was making Christmas preparations. She said she would finish them in the morning, and then her little French friend would arrive from New York—the surprise would follow; the surprise she had been working over for days. While she was out for a moment I disloyally stole a look. The loggia floor was clothed with rugs and furnished with chairs and sofas; and the uncompleted surprise was there: in the form of a Christmas tree that was drenched with silver film in a most wonderful way; and on a table was a prodigal profusion of bright things which she was going to hang upon it to-day. What desecrating hand will ever banish that eloquent unfinished surprise from that place? Not mine, surely. All these little matters have happened in the last four days. "Little." Yes—*then.* But not now. Nothing she said or thought or did is little now. And all the lavish humor!—what is become of it? It is pathos, now. Pathos, and the thought of it brings tears.

All these little things happened such a few hours ago—and now she lies yonder. Lies yonder, and cares for nothing any more. Strange—marvellous—incredible! I have had this experience before; but it would still be incredible if I had had it a thousand times.

*"Miss Jean is dead!"*

That is what Katy said. When I heard the door open behind the bed's head without a preliminary knock, I supposed it was Jean coming to kiss me good morning, she being the only person who was used to entering without formalities.

And so—

I have been to Jean's parlor. Such a turmoil of Christmas presents for servants and friends! They are everywhere; tables, chairs, sofas, the floor—everything is occupied, and over-occupied. It is many and many a year since I have seen the like. In that ancient day Mrs. Clemens and I used to slip softly into the nursery at midnight on Christmas Eve and look the array of presents over. The children were little then. And now here is Jean's parlor looking just as that nursery used to look. The presents are not labelled—

the hands are forever idle that would have labelled them to-day. Jean's mother always worked herself down with her Christmas preparations. Jean did the same yesterday and the preceding days, and the fatigue has cost her her life. The fatigue caused the convulsion that attacked her this morning. She had had no attack for months.

Jean was so full of life and energy that she was constantly in danger of overtaxing her strength. Every morning she was in the saddle by half past seven, and off to the station for her mail. She examined the letters and I distributed them: some to her, some to Mr. Paine, the others to the stenographer and myself. She despatched her share and then mounted her horse again and went around superintending her farm and her poultry the rest of the day. Sometimes she played billiards with me after dinner, but she was usually too tired to play, and went early to bed.

Yesterday afternoon I told her about some plans I had been devising while absent in Bermuda, to lighten her burdens. We would get a housekeeper; also we would put her share of the secretary-work into Mr. Paine's hands.

No—she wasn't willing. She had been making plans herself. The matter ended in a compromise. I submitted. I always did. She wouldn't audit the bills and let Paine fill out the checks—she would continue to attend to that herself. Also, she would continue to be housekeeper, and let Katy assist. Also, she would continue to answer the letters of personal friends for me. Such was the compromise. Both of us called it by that name, though I was not able to see where any formidable change had been made.

However, Jean was pleased, and that was sufficient for me. She was proud of being my secretary, and I was never able to persuade her to give up any part of her share in that unlovely work.

In the talk last night I said I found everything going so

smoothly that if she were willing I would go back to Bermuda in February and get blessedly out of the clash and turmoil again for another month. She was urgent that I should do it, and said that if I would put off the trip until March she would take Katy and go with me. We struck hands upon that, and said it was settled. I had a mind to write to Bermuda by tomorrow's ship and secure a furnished house and servants. I meant to write the letter this morning. But it will never be written, now.

For she lies yonder, and before her is another journey than that.

Night is closing now; the rim of the sun barely shows above the sky-line of the hills.

I have been looking at that face again that was growing dearer and dearer to me every day. I was getting acquainted with Jean in these last nine months. She had been long an exile from home when she came to us three-quarters of a year ago. She had been shut up in sanitariums, many miles from us. How eloquently glad and grateful she was to cross her father's threshold again!

Would I bring her back to life if I could do it? I would not. If a word would do it, I would beg for strength to withhold the word. And I would have the strength; I am sure of it. In her loss I am almost bankrupt, and my life is a bitterness, but I am content: for she has been enriched with the most precious of all gifts—that gift which makes all other gifts mean and poor—death. I have never wanted any released friend of mine restored to life since I reached manhood. I felt in this way when Susy passed away; and later my wife, and later Mr. Rogers. When Clara met me at the station in New York and told me Mr. Rogers had died suddenly that morning, my thought was, Oh, favorite of fortune—fortunate all his long and lovely life—fortunate to his latest moment! The reporters said there were tears of sorrow in my eyes. True—but they were for *me*, not for him. He had suffered no loss. All the fortunes he had ever made before were poverty compared with this one.

Why did I build this house, two years ago? To shelter this vast emptiness? How foolish I was! But I shall stay in it. The spirits of the dead hallow a house, for me. It was not so with other members of my family. Susy died in the house we built in Hartford. Mrs. Clemens would never enter it again. But it made the house dearer to me. I have entered it once since, when it was tenantless and silent and forlorn, but to me it was a holy place and beautiful. It seemed to me that the spirits of the dead were all about me, and would speak to me and welcome me if they could: Livy, and Susy, and George, and Henry Robinson, and Charles Dudley Warner. How good and kind they were, and how lovable their lives! In fancy I could see them all again, I could call the children back and hear them romp again with George—that peerless black ex-slave and children's idol who came one day—a flitting stranger—to wash windows, and stayed eighteen years. Until he died. Clara and Jean would never enter again the New York hotel which their mother had frequented in earlier days. They could not bear it. But I shall stay in this house. It is dearer to me to-night than ever it was before. Jean's spirit will make it beautiful for me always. Her lonely and tragic death—but I will not think of that now.

Jean's mother always devoted two or three weeks to Christmas shopping, and was always physically exhausted when Christmas Eve came. Jean was her very own child—she wore herself out present-hunting in New York these latter days. Paine has just found on her desk a long list of names—fifty, he thinks—people to whom she sent presents last night. Apparently she forgot no one. And Katy found there a roll of bank-notes, for the servants.

Her dog has been wandering about the grounds to-day, comradeless and forlorn. I have seen him from the windows. She got him from Germany. He has tall ears and looks exactly like a wolf. He was educated in Germany, and knows no language but the German. Jean gave him no orders save in that tongue. And so, when the burglar-alarm made a fierce clamor at midnight a fortnight ago, the butler, who is French and knows no German, tried in vain to interest the dog in the supposed burglar. Jean wrote me, to Bermuda, about the incident. It was the last letter I was ever to receive from her bright head and her competent hand. The dog will not be neglected.

There was never a kinder heart than Jean's. From her childhood up she always spent the most of her allowance on charities of one kind and another. After she became secretary and had her income doubled she spent her money upon these things with a free hand. Mine too, I am glad and grateful to say.

She was a loyal friend to all animals, and she loved them all, birds, beasts, and everything—even snakes—an inheritance from me. She knew all the birds: she was high up in that lore. She became a member of various humane societies when she was still a little girl—both here and abroad—and she remained an active member to the last. She founded two or three societies for the protection of animals, here and in Europe.

She was an embarrassing secretary, for she fished my correspondence out of the waste-basket and answered the letters. She thought all letters deserved the courtesy of an answer. Her mother brought her up in that kindly error.

She could write a good letter, and was swift with her pen. She had but an indifferent ear for music, but her tongue took to languages with an easy facility. She never allowed her Italian, French and German to get rusty through neglect.

The telegrams of sympathy are flowing in, from far and wide, now, just as they did in Italy five years and a half ago, when this child's mother laid down her blameless life. They cannot heal the hurt, but they take away some of the pain. When Jean and I kissed hands and parted at my door last, how little did we imagine that in twenty-two hours the telegraph would be bringing words like these:

"From the bottom of our hearts we send our sympathy, dearest of friends."

For many and many a day to come, wherever I go in this house, remembrances of Jean will mutely speak to me of her. Who can count the number of them?

She was in exile two years with the hope of healing her malady—epilepsy. There are no words to express how grateful I am that she did not meet her fate in the hands of strangers, but in the loving shelter of her own home.

*"Miss Jean is dead!"*

It is true. Jean is dead.

A month ago I was writing bubbling and hilarious articles for magazines yet to appear, and now I am writing—this.

*Christmas Day. Noon.*—Last night I went to Jean's room at intervals, and turned back the sheet and looked at the peaceful face and kissed the cold brow, and remembered that heart-breaking night in Florence so long ago, in that cavernous and silent vast villa, when I crept downstairs so many times, and turned back a sheet and looked at a face just like this one—Jean's mother's face—and kissed a brow that was just like this one. And last night I saw again what I had seen then—that strange and lovely miracle—the sweet soft contours of early maidenhood restored by the gracious hand of death! When Jean's mother lay dead, all trace of care, and trouble, and suffering, and the corroding years had vanished out of the face, and I was looking again upon it as I had known and worshipped it in its young bloom and beauty a whole generation before.

About three in the morning, while wandering about the house in the deep silences, as one does in times like these, when there is a dumb sense that something has been lost that will never be found again, yet must be sought, if only for the employment the useless seeking gives, I came upon Jean's dog in the hall down-stairs, and noted that he did not spring to greet me, according to his hospitable habit, but came slow and sorrowfully; also I remembered that he had not visited Jean's apartment since the tragedy. Poor fellow, did he know? I think so. Always when Jean was abroad in the open he was with her; always when she was in the house he was with her, in the night as well as in the day. Her parlor was his bedroom. Whenever I happened upon him on the ground floor he always followed me about, and when I went up-stairs he went too—in a tumultuous gallop. But now it was different: after patting him a little I went to the library—he remained behind; when I went up-stairs he did not follow me, save with his wistful eyes. He has wonderful eyes—big, and kind, and eloquent. He can talk with them. He is a beautiful creature, and is of the breed of the New York police-dogs. I do not like dogs, because they bark when there is no occasion for it; but I have liked this one from the beginning, because he belonged to Jean, and because he never barks except when there is occasion—which is not oftener than twice a week.

In my wanderings I visited Jean's parlor. On a shelf I found a pile of my books, and I knew what it meant. She was waiting for me to come home from Bermuda and autograph them, then she would send them away. If I only knew whom she intended them for! But I shall never know. I will keep them. Her hand has touched them—it is an accolade—they are noble, now.

And in a closet she had hidden a surprise for me—a thing I have often wished I owned: a noble big globe. I couldn't see it for the tears. She will never know the pride I take in it, and the pleasure. To-day the mails are full of loving remembrances for her: full of those old, old kind words she loved so well, "Merry Christmas to Jean!" If she could only have lived one day longer!

At last she ran out of money, and would not use mine. So she sent to one of those New York homes for poor girls all the clothes she could spare—and more, most likely.

*Christmas Night.*—This afternoon they took her away from her room. As soon as I might I went down to the library, and there she lay, in her coffin, dressed in exactly the same clothes she wore when she stood at the other end of the same room on the 6th of October last, as Clara's chief bridesmaid. Her face was radiant with happy excitement then; it was the same face now, with the dignity of death and the peace of God upon it.

They told me the first mourner to come was the dog. He came uninvited, and stood up on his hind legs and rested his fore paws upon the trestle, and took a last long look at the face that was so dear to him, then went his way as silently as he had come. *He knows.*

At mid-afternoon it began to snow. The pity of it—that Jean could not see it! She so loved the snow.

The snow continued to fall. At six o'clock the hearse drew up to the door to bear away its pathetic burden. As they lifted the casket, Paine began playing on the orchestrelle Schubert's *Impromptu*, which was Jean's favorite. Then he played the Intermezzo; that was for Susy; then he played the Largo; that was for their mother. He did this at my request. Elsewhere in this Autobiography I have told how the Intermezzo and the Largo came to be associated in my heart with Susy and Livy in their last hours in this life.

From the windows I saw the hearse and the carriages wind along the road and gradually grow vague and spectral in the falling snow, and presently disappear. Jean was gone out of my life, and would not come back any more. Jervis, the cousin she had played with when they were babies together—he and her beloved old Katy—were conducting her to her distant childhood home, where she will lie by her mother's side once more, in the company of Susy and Langdon.

*December 26th.*—The dog came to see me at eight o'clock this morning. He was very affectionate, poor orphan! My room will be his quarters hereafter.

The storm raged all night. It has raged all the morning. The snow drives across the landscape in vast clouds, superb, sublime—and Jean not here to see.

*2.30 P.M.*—It is the time appointed. The funeral has begun. Four hundred miles away, but I can see it all, just as if I were there. The scene is the library, in the Langdon homestead. Jean's coffin stands where her mother and I stood, forty years ago, and were married; and where Susy's coffin stood thirteen years ago—where her mother's stood, five years and a half ago; and where mine will stand, after a little time.

*Five o'clock.*—It is all over.

When Clara went away two weeks ago to live in Europe, it was hard, but I could bear it, for I had Jean left. I said *we* would be a family. We said we would be close comrades and happy—just we two. That fair dream was in my mind when Jean met me at the steamer last Monday; it was in my mind when she received me at the door last Tuesday evening. We were together; *we were a family!* the dream had come true—oh, preciously true, contentedly true, satisfyingly true! and remained true two whole days.

And now? Now Jean is in her grave!

In the grave—if I can believe it. God rest her sweet spirit!

# KHAKI CONFIDENCES AT CHÂTEAU-THIERRY

*By* DOROTHY CANFIELD FISHER

*Dorothy Canfield Fisher's* Home Fires in France *was one of the really descriptive books brought forth by the Great War. Born in 1879, she is now best known as the author of a series of novels of American life. This article was first published in* Harper's *in the month of the Armistice, November, 1918.*

THEY WERE DETRAINING IN dense brown crowds at what had been the station before German guns had knocked it into a shapeless heap of tumbled bricks; they were pouring in on foot along the road from the west; and when I made my way along the main street to the river I found other khaki-clad lines leaving the little town, marching heavily, unrhythmically, and strongly out across the narrow, temporary wooden bridge, laid hastily across the massive stone pillars which were all that remained of the old bridge.

An old, white-capped woman, who had been one of my neighbors in the days before the little town had known German guns or American soldiers, called out to me:

"Oh, madame! See them! Isn't it wonderful? Just look at them! All day like that, all night like that. Are there any people left in America? And are all your people so big, so fine?"

"Where are they going?" I asked her, taking refuge for a moment in her doorway.

"To the front directly, the poor boys. They'll be fighting in two hours. . . . Do you hear the big guns off there banging away? And they so good, like nice big boys! Their poor mothers!"

I addressed myself in English to a soldier loitering near,

watching the troops pass, "So they are going to the front, these boys?"

After a stare of intense surprise, a broad smile broke over his face. He came closer. "No, ma'am," he said, looking at me hard. "No, these are the Alabama boys just coming back from the front. They've been fighting steadily for five days." He added: "My! it seems good to talk to an American woman. I haven't seen one for four months!"

"Where are you from?" I asked him.

"Just from the Champagne front, with the Third Division. Two of our regiments out there were . . ." He began pouring out exact, detailed military information which I would not have dreamed of asking him. The simple-hearted open confidence of the American soldier was startling and alarming to one who had for long breathed the thick air of universal suspicion. I stopped his fluent statement of which was his regiment, where they had been, what their losses were, where they were going.

"No, no. I mean where are you from in the States?"

I raised my voice to make myself heard above the sudden thunder of a convoy of munition-camions passing by and filling the narrow street from side to side.

"Oh! From Kansas City, Missouri. It's just eight months and seven days since I last saw the old town."

"And how do you like France?"

"Oh, it's all right, I guess! The climate's not so bad. And the towns wouldn't be much off if they'd clean up their manure-piles better."

"And the people, how do you get on with them?"

The camions had passed, and the street was again filled with American infantry, trudging forward with an air of resolute endurance.

"Well enough. They don't cheat you. I forgot and left a fifty-franc bill lying on the table of a house where I'd bought some eggs, and the next morning the woman sent her little girl over to camp to give it back. Real poor-appearing folks they were, too. But I've had enough. I want to get home. Uncle Sam's good enough for me. I want to hurry up and win the war and beat it back to God's country."

He fell away before the sudden assault upon me of an old, old man and his old wife, with the dirt, the hunted look, the crumpled clothes, the desperate eyes of refugees.

"Madame, madame, help us! We cannot make them understand, the Americans! We want to go back to Villers-le-Petit. We want to see what is left of our house and garden. We want to start in to repair the house . . . and our potatoes must be dug."

I had passed that morning through what was left of their village. For a moment I saw their old, tired, anxious faces dimly, as though across the long stretch of shattered heaps of masonry. I answered evasively:

"But you know they are not allowing the civilian population to go back as yet. All this region is still being shelled. It's far too dangerous."

They gave together an exclamation of impatience as though at the futilities of children's talk. "But madame, if *we* do not care about the danger? We never cared! We should not have left, ever, if the soldiers had not taken us away in camions . . . our garden and vineyard just at the time when they needed attention every hour. Well, we will not wait for permission. We will go back, anyhow. The American soldiers are not bad, are they, madame? They would surely not fire on an old man and his wife going back to their home? If madame would only write on a piece of paper that we only want to go back to our home to take care of it . . ."

Their quavering old voices came to me indistinctly through the steady thudding advance of all those feet, come from so far, on so great, so high, so perilous a mission;

come so far, many of them, to meet death more than half-way . . . the poor, old, cramped people before me, blind and deaf to the immensity of the earthquake, seeing nothing but that the comfort of their own lives was in danger. I had a nervous revulsion of feeling and broke the news to them more abruptly than I should have thought possible a moment before:

"There is nothing left of Villers-le-Petit. There is nothing left to go back to."

Well, they were not so cramped, so blind, so small, my poor old people. They took the news standing, and after the first clutch at each other's wrinkled hands, after the first paling of their already ashy faces, they did not flinch.

"But the crops, madame. The vineyards. Are they all gone, too?"

"No, very little damage done there. Everything was kept, of course, intact for camouflage, and the retreat was so rapid there was not enough time for destruction."

"Then we will still go back, madame. We have brought the things for spraying the vineyards as far as here; surely we can get them to Villers-le-Petit, it is so near now. We can sleep on the ground, anywhere. In another week, you see, madame, it will be too late to spray. We have enough for ours, and our neighbors', too. We can save them if we go *now*. If madame would only write on a piece of paper in their language that . . ."

So I did it. I tore a fly-leaf out of a book lying in a heap of rubbish before the ruins of a bombarded house (it was a treatise on Bach's chorales by the French organist, Widor!) and wrote: "These are two brave old people, inhabitants of Villers-le-Petit, who wish to go back there to work under shell-fire to save what they can of their own and their neighbors' crops. Theirs is the spirit that is keeping France alive."

"It probably won't do you a bit of good," I said, "but here it is for what it is worth."

"Oh, once the American soldiers know what we want, they will let us pass, we know." They went off trustfully, holding my foolish "pass" in their hands.

I turned from them to find another young American soldier standing near me. "How do you do?" I said, smiling at him.

He gave a great start of amazement at the sound of my American accent.

"Well, how do you like being in France?" I asked him.

"Gee! Are you really an American woman?" he said, incredulously, his young face lighting up as though he saw a member of his own family. "I haven't talked to one in so *long!* Why, yes, I like France fine. It's the loveliest country to look at, isn't it? I didn't know any country could be kept up so, like a garden. How do they *do* it without any men left? They must be awfully fine people. I wish I could talk to them some."

"Who are these soldiers going through to-day?" I asked. "Are they going out to the front-line trenches, or coming back? I've been told both things."

He answered with perfect certainty and precision: "Neither. They are Second Division troops, from Ohio, mostly, just out of their French training-camp, going up to hold the reserve line. They never have been in action yet."

Our attention was distracted to the inside of a fruit-shop across the street: a group of American soldiers struggling with the sign-language, a flushed, tired, distracted woman shopkeeper volubly unable to conceive that men with all their senses could not understand her native tongue. I went across to interpret. One of the soldiers in a strong Southern accent said:

"Oh, golly, yes! If you *would* do the talkin' fo' us. We

cyan't make out whetheh we've paid heh or not, and we wondeh if she'd 'low us to sit heah and eat ouh fruit."

From the Frenchwoman: "Oh, madame, please, what *is* it they want now? I have shown them everything in sight. How strange that they can't understand the simplest language!"

The little misunderstanding was soon cleared away. I lingered by the counter. "How do you like our American troops, madame?" I asked.

"Very much indeed, if only they could talk. They don't do any harm. They are good to the children. They are certainly as brave as men can be. But there is one thing about them I don't understand. They overpay you, often, more than you ask . . . won't take change . . . and yet if you leave things open, as we always do, in front of the shop, they just put their hands in and help themselves as they go by. I have lost a great deal in that way. If they have so much money, why do they steal?"

I contemplated making a short disquisition on the peculiarities of the American orchard-robbing tradition, with its ramifications, but gave it up as too difficult, and instead sat down at the table with the Americans, who gave me the greeting always repeated: "Great Scott! It's good to talk to an American woman!"

A fresh-faced, splendidly built lad looked up from the first bite of his melon, crying: "Yes, suh, a cantaloup, a' honest-to-the-Lawd cantaloup! I neveh thought they'd *heahd* of such a thing in France."

They explained to me, all talking at once, pouring out unasked military information till my hair rose up scandalized, that this was their first experience with semi-normal civilian life in France, because they belonged to the troops from Georgia—volunteers; that they had been in the front-line trenches at exactly such a place for precisely so many weeks, where such and such things happened, and before that at such another place, where they were so many strong, etc., etc. "So we neveh saw real sto's to buy things till we struck this town. And when I saw a cantaloup I mighty nigh dropped daid! I don't reckon I'm likely to run into a watermelon, am I? I suahly would have to be ca'ied back to camp on a stretcheh if I did!" He laughed out, a boy's cloudless laughter. "But, say, what do you-all think? I paid fo'ty-five cents for this slice—yes, ma'am, fo'ty-five cents for a *slice,* and back home in Geo'gia you pay a nickel for the biggest one in the stor'!" He buried his face in the yellow fruit.

The house began to shake to the ponderous passage of artillery. The boys in khaki turned their staglike heads toward the street, glanced at the long motley-colored, mule-drawn guns, and pronounced, expertly: "The Forty-third heavy artillery going out to Nolepieds; the fellows from Illinois. They've just been up in the Verdun sector and are coming down to reinforce the One-hundred-and-second."

For the first time the idea crossed my head that possibly their mania for pouring out military information to the first comer might not be as fatal to necessary secrecy as it seemed. I rather pitied the spy who might attempt to make coherent profit out of their candor.

"How do you like being in France?" I asked the boy who was devouring the melon.

He looked up, his eyes kindling. "Well, I was plumb crazy to get heah, and now I'm heah, I like it mo' even than I 'lowed I would."

I looked at his fresh, unlined boy's cheeks, his clear, bright boy's eyes, and felt a great wave of pity. "You haven't been in active service yet?" I surmised.

Unconsciously, gaily, he flung my pity back in my face: "You bet yo' life I have. We've just come from the Champagne front, and the sehvice we saw theah was suah active. How about it, boys?"

They all burst out again in rapid, high-keyed, excited voices, longing above everything else for a listener, leaning forward over the table toward me, their healthy faces flushed with their ardor, talking hurriedly because there was so much to say, their tense young voices a staccato clatter of words which brought to me, in jerks, horribly familiar war-pictures, barrage-fires meeting, advancing over dead comrades, hideous hand-to-hand combats . . . all chanted in those eager young voices. . . .

In a pause, I asked, perhaps rather faintly: "And you like it? You are not ever home-sick?"

The boy with the melon spoke for them all. He stretched out his long arms, his hands clenched to knotty masses of muscles; he set his jaw, his blue eyes were like steel, his beautiful young face was all aflame. "Oh, you just get to *love* it!" he cried, shaking with the intensity of his feeling. "You just *love* it! Why, I *neveh* want to go home! I want to stay over heah and go right on killin' *boches* all my life!"

At this I felt stricken with the collective remorse over the war which belongs to the older generation. I said good-by to them and left them to their childlike ecstasy over their peaches and melons.

The artillery had passed. The street was again solidly filled with dusty, heavily laden young men in khaki, tramping silently and resolutely forward, their brown steel casques, shaped like antique Greek shepherd hats, giving to their rounded young faces a curious air of classic rusticity.

An older man, with a stern, rough, plain face stood near me.

"How do you do?" I asked. "Can you tell me which troops these are and where they are going?" I wondered what confident and uninformed answer I should receive this time.

Showing no surprise at my speech, he answered: "I don't know who they be. You don't never know anything about any but your own regiment. The kids always think they do.

They'll tell you this and they'll tell you that, but the truth is we don't know no more than Ann . . . not even where we are ourselves, nor where we're going, most of the time."

His accent made me say: "I wonder if you are not from my part of the country. I live in Vermont, when I'm at home."

"I'm from Maine," he said, soberly, "a farmer, over draft age, of course. But it looked to me like a kind o' mean trick to make the boys do it all for us, so I come along, too." He added, as if in partial explanation, "One of my uncles was with John Brown at Harper's Ferry."

"How do you like it, now you're here?" I asked.

He looked at me heavily. "Like it? It's hell!" he said.

"Have you been in active service?" I used my usual cowardly evasive phrase.

"Yes, ma'am. I've killed some of 'em," he answered me, with brutal, courageous directness. He looked down at his hands as he spoke—big, calloused farmer's hands, crooked by holding the plow-handles. As plainly as he saw it there, I saw the blood on them, too. His stern, dark, middle-aged face glowered down solemnly on those strong farmer's hands. "It's dirty work, but it's got to be done," he said, gravely, "and I ain't a-going to dodge my share of it."

A very dark-eyed, gracefully-built young soldier came loitering by, and stopped near us, ostensibly to look at the passing troops, but evidently in order to share in the phenomenon of a talk in English with an American woman. I took him into the conversation with the usual query:

"How do you do, and how do you like being in France?"

He answered with a strong Italian accent, and I dived into a dusty mental corner to bring out my half-forgotten Italian. In a moment we were talking like old friends. He had been born in Italy, yes, but brought up in Waterbury, Connecticut. His grandfather had been one of Garibaldi's

Thousand, so of course he had joined the American army and come to France among the first.

"Well, there are more than a thousand of you, this time," I said, looking at the endless procession defiling before us.

"*Si, signora,* but it is a part of the same war. We are here to go on with what the Thousand began."

Yes, that was true; John Brown's soul, and Garibaldi's, and those of how many other fierce old fighting lovers of freedom, were marching on there before my eyes, carried like invisible banners by all those strong young arms.

An elderly woman in well-brushed, dowdy black came down the street toward us, an expression of care on her face. When she saw me she said: "Well, I've found you. They said you were in town to-day. Won't you come back to the house with me? Something important. I'm terribly troubled with some American officers. . . . Oh, the war!"

I went, apprehensive of trouble, and found her house, save for a total absence of window-glass, in its customary speckless and shining order. She took me up-stairs to what had been a bedroom and was now an office in the Quartermaster's Department. It was filled with packing-cases, improvised desks, and with serious-faced, youngish American officers who, in their astonishment at seeing me, forgot to take their long black cigars out of their mouths.

"There!" said the woman-with-a-grievance, pointing to the floor, "just look at that! Just *look!* I tell them and I *tell* them, not to put their horrid boxes on the floor, but to keep them on the linoleum, but they are so stupid, they can't understand language that any child could take in! And they drag those boxes, just full of nails, all over the floor. I'm *sick* of them and their scratches!"

A big gun boomed solemnly off on the horizon as accompaniment to this speech.

I explained in a neutral tone to the officers, looking expectantly at me, what was at issue. I made no comments.

None were needed, evidently, for they said, with a gravity which I found lovable, that they would endeavor to be more careful about the floor, that indeed they had not understood what their landlady had been trying to tell them. I gave her their assurance and she went away satisfied.

As the door closed on her they broke into broad grins and pungent exclamations: "Well, how about that! Wouldn't that *get* you? With the town bombarded every night, to think the old lady was working herself up to a froth about her floor-varnish!"

One of them said: "I never thought of it before, but I bet you my Aunt Selina would do just that! I just bet if her town was bombarded she'd go right on shooing the flies out of her kitchen and mopping up her pantry floor with skim-milk! Why, the French are just like *any*body, aren't they? Just like our own folks!"

"They are," I assured him, "so exactly like our own folks, like everybody's folks, that it's impossible to tell the difference."

When I went away the owner of the house was sweeping the garden path clear of broken glass. "This bombardment is such a nuisance!" she said, disapprovingly. "I'd like to know what the place would be like if I didn't stay to look after it."

I looked at her enviously, securely shut away as she was by the rigid littleness of her outlook from any blighting comprehension of what was going on about her. But then, I reflected, there are instances when the comprehension of what is going on is not blighting. No, on the whole, I did not envy her.

Outside the gate I fell in at once with a group of American soldiers. It was impossible to take a step in any direction in the town without doing this. After the invariable expressions of surprise and pleasure over seeing an American woman, came the invariable burst of eager narration of where they had been and what had been happening to them. They seemed to me touchingly like children who have had an absorbing, exciting adventure and must tumble it all out to the first person who will listen. Their haste, their speaking all at once, gave me only an incoherent idea of what they wished to say. I caught odd phrases, disconnected sentences, glimpses through pin-holes. . . .

"One of the fellows, a conscript, that came to fill a vacant place in our lines, he was only over in France two weeks, and it was his first time in a trench. He landed there at six o'clock in the evening, and, just like I'm telling you, at a quarter past six a shell up and exploded and buried him right where he stood. Yes, ma'am, you do certainly see some very peculiar things in this war."

From another, "We took the whole lot of 'em prisoners, and passed 'em back to the rear, but out of the fifteen we took, eight died of sudden heart-failure before they got back to the prisoners' camp."

I tried not to believe this, but the fact that it was told with a laugh and received with a laugh reminded me gruesomely that we are the nation that tolerates the lynching of helpless men by the mob.

From another: "Some of the fellows say they think about the *Lusitania* when they go after the *boches*. I don't have to come down as far as that. Belgium's plenty good enough a whetstone for *my* bayonet."

This reminded me with a thrill that we are the nation that has always ultimately risen in defense of the defenseless.

From another: "Oh, I can't stand the French! They make me tired! And their jabber! I seen some of 'em talk it so fast they couldn't even understand each other! Honest, I did."

From another: "There's something that sort of *takes* me about the life over here. I'm not going to be in any hurry to go back to the States and hustle my head off after the war's over."

From another: "Not for mine. Me for Chicago the day after the *boches* are licked."

I listened to their home voices, running up and down the scale of all the American accents, and reflected on the universality of human nature. Just such entirely varying and contradictory sentiments, just such a mixture of idealism, materialism, narrowness, generosity, inevitably came clattering out from any group of French soldiers speaking their minds freely. There was a good deal of nonsense about this talk of racial differences, I thought to myself.

They were swept away by a counter-current somewhere in the khaki ebb and flow about us, and I found myself with a start next to a poilu, yes, a real poilu, with a faded, horizon-blue uniform and a domed, battered blue French casque.

"*Well!*" I said to him, "things have changed here since the One-hundred-and-forty-second used to come back from the trenches. The town's khaki, and not blue."

He looked at me out of bright brown eyes, smiled, and entered into conversation; and at once I was acutely aware of a strong, unmistakable racial difference. As we talked, I tried desperately with the back of my brain to analyze what it was that made him so different from all the American soldiers I had been seeing. He was a very ordinary little poilu, indeed, such as you see by thousands—a rather short, strongly built, well-knit man, with a rather ugly face, not at all distinguished in line, not at all remarkably clean as to bluish, unshaven chin, nor even as to dingy neck . . . but there was about his every accent, gesture, expression, an amenity, a finish, an ease that not one of the Americans had had, in spite of their perfect self-possession and fluency. Fresh from talking to so many of them, I had a vivid impression of difference.

What was the difference? I racked my brains wildly to

put my finger on it, knowing that in a moment my perception of the phenomenon would pass, my familiarity with the type would reassert itself, and my interlocutor would slip back into the great mass of all other dingy, shabby, polite little poilus with whom I have chatted.

We talked, of course, of the American soldiers, one of whom came up and stood at my elbow, listening with amused astonishment to what seemed to him the insane volubility of our talk.

"Gee!" he said, when I stopped to talk to him, "I wish I could rip it off like that! I have got *combien* and *oui* down fine, but I don't get on any beyond that. Say, what does the Frenchman say about us? Now since that little affair at the Bois de Belleau they think we know a thing or two about the war ourselves, what? They're all right, of course mighty fine soldiers, but, Lord! you'd know by the way any one of them does business, as if he had all the day for it, that they couldn't run a war *fast*, like the way it ought to be run, like the way we're going to run it, now we're here."

I did not think it necessary to translate all of this to the bright-eyed little Frenchman on my other side, who began to talk as the American stopped.

"You asked my opinion of the American troops, madame. I will give it to you frankly. The first who came over made a very bad impression indeed. All who have come since have made the best of impressions. They are remarkably courageous, they really fight like lions, and there could be no better comrades in the world, but, oh, madame! as far as really knowing how to make modern war, they are children, just children. They make all the mistakes we made four years ago. They have so much to learn of the technique of war and they will lose so many men in learning it!"

I did not think it necessary to translate all this to the American, who now shook hands with both of us and turned away. The Frenchman, too, after a quick look at the clock in the church-tower, made his compliments, saluted and disappeared.

I watched his back retreating fixedly, feeling that in an instant more I should have my hand on that slippery ineffable, racial difference. There! It swam up, full and round under my fingers. I closed on it, held it triumphantly to look at it hard . . . and, lo! it was not a racial difference at all, but an infinite difference of age, of maturity. Not that the poilu was materially so much older than our boys, but between them lay the unfathomable abyss of four years of war experience. I realized that he alone, of all the soldiers to whom I had talked, had been able to look outside of himself and see another person there, that he alone had been in a normal frame of mind, had been conscious of what he was saying, had really looked at the person to whom he was talking. This conscious recognition of social contact had given his manner that appearance of social ease which all the familiarity of the Americans had failed to have. They were not conversing, in spite of the fact that they were talking incessantly; they were simply so full of the exciting, rending, upheaving experiences of their lives that they must needs express their excitement, somehow, anyhow, to any one, or choke. The poilu, alas! had lived so long in the rending, exciting upheaving experience that it was second nature to him, that he moved with ease among portents and could turn a phrase and make a gesture among horrors.

Pondering the meaning of this, I walked forward, and, coming to the church door, stepped inside.

It was as though I had stepped into another world. I had found the only place in town where there were no soldiers. The great, gray, dim vaulted interior was empty. After the beat of the marching feet outside, after the shuffling to and fro of the innumerable men quartered in town, after the noisy shops crowded with khaki uniforms, after the incessant thunderous passage of the artillery and munitions-camions, the long, hushed quiet of the empty church rang loud in my ears. I wondered for just an instant if there could be any military regulation forbidding our soldiers to enter the church; and even as I wondered the door opened and a boy in khaki stepped in . . . one out of all those hordes. He crossed himself, took a rosary out of his pocket, knelt, and began his prayers.

Thirty thousand soldiers were in that town that day.

Whatever else we are, I reflected, we are not a people of mystics. But then I remembered the American soldier who had said that Belgium was a good-enough whetstone for his bayonet. I remembered the rough, gloomy farmer who did not want to shirk his share of the world's dirty work. Perhaps there are various kinds of mystics.

Once outside the church, I turned to look up Madame Larçonneur, the valiant market-gardener who had been one of my neighbors, a tired young war-widow with two little children, whom I had watched toiling early and late, day and night, to keep intact the little property left her by her dead soldier husband. I had watched her drawing from the soil of her big garden, wet quite literally by her sweat, the livelihood for her fatherless little girls. I wondered what the bombardment of the town had done to her and her small, priceless home. I found the street, I found the other houses there, but where her little, painfully well-kept house had stood was a heap of stone and rubble, and in the place of her long, carefully tended rows of beans and cabbages and potatoes were shell-holes where the chalky barren subsoil streaked the surface and where the fertile black earth, fruit of years of labor, was irrevocably buried out of sight. Before all this, in her poor, neat black, stood the war-widow with her children.

I sprang forward, horrified, the tears on my cheeks. "Oh, Madame Larçonneur, how awful! How awful!" I cried, putting out both hands to her.

She turned a white, quiet face on me, and smiled, a smile that made me feel infinitely humble. "My little girls are not hurt," she said, drawing them to her, "and as for all this . . . why, if it is a part of getting other people's homes restored to them . . ." Her gesture said that the price was not too high.

The look in her sunken eyes took me for an instant up into a very high place of courage and steadfastness. For the first time that day the knot in my throat stopped aching, I was proud to have her put her work-deformed hands in mine and to feel on my cheek her sister's kiss.

It steadied me somewhat during that difficult next hour, when in the falling twilight I walked up and down between the long rows of raw earth, with the innumerable crosses, each with its new, bright American flag fluttering in the sweet country air. I needed to recall that selfless courage, for my heart was breaking with sorrow, with guilt-consciousness, with protest, as I stood there, thinking of my own little son, of the mothers of the boys who lay there. A squad of soldiers were preparing graves for the next day. As they dug in the old, old soil of the cemetery to make a place for the new flesh come from so far to lie there forever, I looked away toward the little town lying below us, in its lovely green setting, still shaking rhythmically to the ponderous passage of the guns, of the troops, of the camions.

At one side were a few recent German graves, marked with black crosses, and others, marked with stones, dating from the war of 1870, that other nightmare when all this smiling countryside was blood-soaked. Above me, dominating the cemetery, stood a great monument of white marble, holding up to all those graves the ironic inscription, "Love ye one another."

The twilight fell more and more deeply, and became darkness. The dull, steady surge of the advancing troops grew louder. Night had come, night no longer used for rest after labor in the sunlight, night which must be used to hurry troops and more troops forward over roads shelled by day.

They passed by hundreds, by thousands, an endless, endless procession—horses, mules, camions, artillery, infantry, cavalry; obscure, shadowy forms no longer in uniform, no longer from Illinois or Georgia or Vermont, no longer even American; only human young men crowned with the splendor of their strength, going out gloriously through the darkness to victory through sacrifice.

# BEADS[1]

## WAR-TIME REFLECTIONS IN PARIS

*By* Margaret Deland

*Margaret Deland, born in 1857, is author of the* Old Chester Tales, *one of the most distinguished series of short stories written in America. This war-time reflection upon intense experience was published in* Harper's *for July, 1918, and at the time aroused much controversy and criticism, its philosophy being deemed dangerous in time of war.*

OVER HERE IN PARIS, I THREAD my perplexities like many colored beads upon a string. Perhaps, sometime, the pattern of a clear opinion may work itself out. At present my colors are only other people's opinions; and as I put a crimson bead on the string, or a black one, and then some crystal beads—many, many of these—and every now and then a gold bead—many of these, too—I say to myself over and over: "*I* don't know; *I* don't understand. I wonder. . . ."

And so I thread my perplexities.

One thing that puzzles me is the sense of unreality which many of us Americans feel. "Nothing seems real," we say to one another, with bewildered looks. Back of the sense of unrealness is an inarticulate *something* that seems like anger. Yet it is not exactly anger, for anger at least implies the outraged sense of justice, which is deeply righteous. This emotion (whatever it is!) does not wait for any rational process, and cannot by any stretch of self-approval be called "righteous." It rises, with a sudden murderous flare of rage, in quiet, reasonable minds; then sinks down, apparently gone. It lifts again the next day, perhaps at the sight of a blind man clinging to his wife's hand as he stumbles up the steps of the Madeleine. Of course this fury must be rooted in the sense of justice, but it has blossomed into a rank growth that is so remote from our placid experience that it has the quality of a dream. When I see it, or feel it, I slip a crimson bead on my string.

Beside it, in the still unseen design, I put the sinister consciousness in everybody about me of *waiting*. For what? No one knows. Some say for an Allied victory. Some say the same words, but add a question, "*Then* what?" Others —only a very few—say they wait for an Allied defeat; these whisper their confidence that out of defeat will come the real victory—the birth of the Spirit! The Allies (so these people say) need rebirth as much as Germany. On all sides is this inchoate expectancy. . . . And as I think about it I slip a black bead on my string.

Yet perhaps this is a mistake; perhaps the sense of waiting for something undefined ought, as those whisperers say, to be symbolized by the color of Hope? It may be that some minds really are hearing, as they say they hear, very far off, very faintly, from across blood-stained years ahead of us, a Voice:

"*Wait,* I say, on the Lord."

Those who hear that Voice in the unspoken expectancy are waiting with good courage; they are willing to tread even the hard road of Defeat, because they are confident that they will meet Him at its end!

But for most of us the sense of waiting takes the color of Fear, and black beads grow into the pattern. . . . As I look at these, shining among the rest, I wonder whether—there are so many of them!—any far-off interest of tears can possibly repay the nations—all the nations!—for their present pain? Some say it will. "*Vivre pour tout cela,*" said a man whose son has died for France, "*mourir pour tout cela. . . . ça en vaut la peine.*" So men have always said—for themselves; but tears are not too much to pay for the precious knowledge that a man may say it, with passion, of something infinitely dearer than himself—an only son—*mort au champ d'honneur!* Yet marching with the triumph of the Spirit is the grief of the world! A grief which questions and questions. . . . Surely never before have so many broken hearts stormed together the gate of Death, saying: "Where? Where?"

Now, here is a curious thing. In this new, unreal rage that has fallen upon us some of us say we do not know ourselves but through Grief, many French people say, we are beginning to know God! They believe—these people who have wept—that Grief will destroy a materialism which has cried its impudent self-sufficiency into the face of God. If this be true, we shall all share the high knowledge, for it seems as if there were more crystal beads than all the rest put together.

No, it is the golden ones that outnumber the others! Perhaps, after all, there will be no pattern—nothing but a golden string that will hold heaven and earth together. . . .

These are my perplexities, which are jumbled in my mind like beads in a child's box: Why are we angry with this curious kind of anger? Why do we fear something that has no name? Does grief imply a final joy? Is courage to be trusted to make the race gentler? . . . Sometimes I ask Gaston what pattern he thinks my beads will make. Gaston's height indicates that he is eleven, but his little white, pinched, wicked-eyed face suggests that he is at least fifteen. When he happens to think of it, he comes in from the street to answer the bell of the *ascenseur* and carry me up to my floor in this dingy old hotel.

"*Troisième,* Gaston."

"*Oui.* Did Madame observe the newspaper this morning?"

"What about it, Gaston?"

He takes his hand from the wheel of the antiquated mechanism by which the elevator jiggles up and down, and we stop abruptly between floors. Then he fumbles in some tiny pocket of his little blue jacket, brass-buttoned to his sharp white chin, and produces a crumpled newspaper—a single flimsy sheet whose smudged head-lines shout the Caillaux indictment——

"*Traître!*" cries Gaston, shrilly.

"What will be done with him?" I asked, adding mildly, that I should be glad to ascend.

Gaston, grinning, draws his forefinger back and forth across his throat; then he spins his wheel about and we leap with upsetting rapidity to my floor.

Gaston is obligingly ready to cut anybody's throat at any time. He makes his vicious little gesture when various people are named, especially the German Emperor. And everybody who sees him do it nods approval. Here it is—that uprush of rage! We are, all of us non-combatants, accepting killing as a commonplace—just as in our dreams we are matter-of-fact over the most preposterous happenings of joy or horror, and the ages of evolution which have named them "right" or "wrong" are as though they had never been. Possibly the commonplaceness of it is because murder is loose now in the world. Or is it that the "natural man" in us has been masquerading as the "spiritual man" by hiding himself under splendid words—courage, patriotism, justice—and now he rises up and glares at us with blood-red eyes? At any rate, fury is *here,* and most of us are shaken by the surge of it—except the blind man groping and stumbling up the steps of the Madeleine. He, apparently, feels no rage. One soldier said, thoughtfully, "The longer I fight the Germans the better I like them."

But eyes that are not blind sometimes see red. I first realized this in one of the air raids, and I said to myself, like the old woman in Mother Goose: "If this be I, as I suppose it be . . ."

It was nearly midnight when the sirens screamed suddenly from all quarters of the sky at once. It was a screech that ripped the air as if the scroll of the heavens was being rent; and instantly all the lights went out and we were in pitchy darkness, except as the surprised moon peered in between our curtains. There was a gasp of astonishment; then people who were in bed jumped out, fumbled about for more or less clothing, and rushed to windows or out into the street. From my third floor I could see Gaston on the pavement below, dancing up and down like a midge and shrieking with joy at the rattling crash of the air-guns, or the terrible detonations of exploding bombs. A group of American girls leaned appallingly far out of their window and craned their young necks to stare up at the stars of man's ingenuity moving about among the stars of God's serenity and law. They were darting—these stars—zigzagging, soaring up to grapple with one another against the face of the moon; and some of them were dropping death down on our heads. As "efficiency" duplicated the French signal lights of German machines, we did not know which were the stars of murder and which were the stars of defense—only God's stars were candid. And all the while the pretty young Americans (why *do* their fathers and mothers let them come over here?) watched the battle with exactly the same happy excitement that I have seen on their faces at a football game; they were all ready to turn down their pink thumbs for a German aviator, only—"Which *are* the Germans?" one said, distractedly.

A moving star suddenly seemed to stagger . . . then swooped, then fell, straight—straight—straight down, with horribly increasing velocity. We knew that in that flaming star were men keyed to furious living, panting, screaming orders to each other, sweating, tearing at levers, knowing they were plunging from abysmal heights to smash like eggs on some slate roof. As that agonizing star fell, the eager young faces were smiling fiercely, and I could hear panting ejaculations:

"Oh! Oh! *Oh!* Look! See him? *See* him! Oh! I *hope* he's a German!"

And so before their eyes two men dropped to death.

Of course this sort of excitement is as old as human nature. But the difference between the football and arena joy which are without danger (I mean as an animus) and this rejoicing is that these women—and Gaston dancing on the pavement—were themselves in danger of instant death. Only a block or so away two persons were blown to pieces. Yet there was not a quiver of alarm!

After it was all over some one said, with a sort of gasp, a curious thing: "I don't, somehow, believe it." She paused, and caught her breath with a scared look. *"I don't know who I am,"* she said, in a whisper.

Of course the monstrous thing was not real to her; the whole business of war cannot, for a moment, be real to any of us Americans because frightfulness is outside of our experience and our minds do not know how to believe it. As for this especial unreality of the raid, never before has the sky betrayed us; so how could those falling bombs be anything else but of the substance of a dream?

I suppose the indifference to danger was because anger as well as love casts out fear; and down below the unreality there was in all of us a very real and righteous anger that the Germans should make the heavens their accomplice! But as for this other kind of anger, which made the woman who had said, in a whisper, "I don't know who I am," add, smiling fiercely, over clenched teeth, "I *hope* he was a German!"—that scares me. It is a slipping down into the primitive. When I climb out of it I am smirched by the slime of hate. Gaston, and the pretty girls, and certain dull, elderly folk, all were seething with the fury of combat, and grinning with lust for death that made us strangers to ourselves. I heard a calm, fat, gentle, and rather unusually reasonable person say: "I'd like to squeeze his [a German's] throat, in my hands, and feel the blood spurt between my fingers, and see his eyes pop out onto his cheeks!" This is not an expression of justice; it is a desire to commit murder.

I have found this smiling ferocity in many people. Sometimes it is respectable and practical—"No trade ever again with the Boche!" In other words, death by economic strangulation! But oftener it is the open and unashamed vindictiveness which would like to feel the blood spurt. As non-combatants have no chance to sink their fingers into howling throats, they find it a satisfaction to make Gaston's gesture in their minds.

Which makes me wonder, while I thread my beads in so many shades of crimson—Gaston's scarlet, the girls' blush-rose and pink, my own dull red—whether our fury is perhaps *not* ours, but just a ripple creeping into the pools and inlets of our minds from the tide of rage which at certain moments rises—*must* rise!—in the minds of the men in the trenches (the Boche and the Allies) who, without the assistance of personal animosity, must do this wet, dirty, bad-smelling business of killing? They could not do it unless they were carried along on the surge of an emotion which does not wait upon reason. Once they have done what they have to do, this motor rage ebbs. But it does not ebb from the little pools on the shore which it has filled—Gaston's mind, and mine, and many, many other minds, which have no outlet of action; *they* lie harsh and brackish, long after the tide has swept back into the deep. It is the menace to the future of this inactive fury of non-combatants which frightens me, because it is corrosive; it may poison the springs of the idealism which we had hoped would make democracy safe for the world. . . .

Of course it may be more than a ripple of the necessary fury of the trenches; it may be, for all we know, the spume and froth from the lift and heave of a reasoning World-anger which is reproaching humanity for continuing to endure "the foolish business of kings and queens"—a business which has brought the world to its present pass! Some people think Gaston is going to illustrate this World-anger and teach us to be done with our folly. These are the people who say they are "waiting" for victory; but they add the uneasy question, "*Then* what?"

I asked Gaston about this sense of expectancy, in which he himself, although he does not know it, has a place. But he evaded an explanation. I pulled him in from the street, where he had been buying a *petit Suisse* for private consumption in a little niche under the stairs where, when not on the pavement, he curls up like a brass-buttoned rat and sleeps.

"Gaston, I have waited five minutes for the elevator!"

"The *ascenseur* is out of order."

"Gaston, I admire and envy your powers of imagination."

Gaston moved the car up a foot, dropped it six inches, then let it shoot up another foot; here we paused while he experimented with the wheel.

"Madame, the dirty Boches return to-night."

"Who says so?"

"*Toute le monde.*"

"And what will you do, Gaston—go down to the cellar?"

"*Moi?*" shrieked Gaston. "*La cave? Non! Madame a peur?*"

I said I hoped not, I really thought not; but wasn't anybody afraid?

"No *French* people," Gaston said, politely. (The hotel was full of Americans.) After that he became absorbed in the Noah's Ark elevator and confined his remarks to, "*Oh, la-la!*" He did, however, while we hung between the second and third floors, throw me a kind word:

"Did Madame observe the decoration of the new *concierge?*"

"Indeed I did, Gaston!"

"*La Croix de Guerre et la Médaille Militaire!*"

"And when will you receive the *Médaille Militaire?*"

"Madame, my age is such that *je ne la porte pas à présent.* When my age is *en règle* peace will be here."

"When will that be?"

*"Oh, la-la!* Very soon."

"Who says so, Gaston?"

*"Tout le monde."*

"Oh Gaston, you have taken me to the fifth floor!"

Gaston looked patient and lifted his little shoulders to his ears. "Madame was conversing."

So Gaston "waits" for peace. And it is to come soon! It is not only Gaston's world which says so; other worlds declare it, too! But their certainty is not quite so certain as Gaston's *"La-la."*

I asked a *concierge's* wife about it—a woman, heavy-eyed, dressed in black, sitting alone in a chilly little den at the entrance of a hotel. It was dark and rainy, and all Paris was cold, and the mud in the streets that used to be so clean, but are now so filthy, made one think of the mud in the trenches. I spoke of the war and the hope of an early peace, and she agreed listlessly. Oh yes, peace must come, of course.

"Soon?"

She hoped it would be soon. She was very listless.

"Madame," I said, "I rejoice that the American soldiers are here at last."

Then she lifted her somber eyes and looked at me, yet it seemed as if she looked through me, beyond me, at something I could not see.

"Madame," she said, with patient but quite terrible dignity —"Madame, the American soldiers come too late."

The significance of this left me dumb. For what kind of a peace is *she* "waiting"?

I quoted the *concierge's* wife to a man who knows more of the real state of things over here than this poor woman (or Gaston) could possibly know, and, of course, far more than any bewildered American whose especial fear is of generalizing from insufficient data and who only knows that everybody seems to be waiting . . . waiting . . . waiting. He laughed and shrugged with amused disgust.

"Oh, you Americans have not come 'too late.' You may still help us—if you ever really get in. But have no fear, Madame, have no fear! Whether you get in or not, *we* shall never give up while there are any of us left." Then, even while I was slipping a golden bead on my thread, he added, his voice dropping almost to a whisper, *"But there are very few of us left!"*

So he, too, is "waiting" for a peace which he does not define. But some people skirt the edge of a definition. A laconic word or two in the compartment of a train that was dragging itself, hours late, into Paris, was fairly definite. Two elderly French officers in faded blue uniforms were talking together. Their faces were worn and lined, and one man had white hair. Apparently they did not notice the American sitting opposite them, trying to forget French indifference to ventilation by reading a novel. At any rate, they made no effort not to be overhead.

*"Eh bien,"* said one of them, heavily, *"nous sommes finis. Même avec les plus grandes victoires, nous sommes finis."*

The "peace" hinted at in these words is one which civilization is not willing to face. Yet some people think France is facing it. They say that the falling birth-rate has for several years been an anxiety, but that the talk about it now, apropos of a million and a half dead young men, is confession. "While there are any of us left"—we shall not be "finished." But, "There are very few of us left."

In the United States we have known, with horrible disgust, that Germany, facing some such possibility for herself, has —with her customary efficiency—begun to educate her people as to the probable necessity of polygamy. France has not been credited with any such foresight. But it would seem that she has it, and in its train may come extraordinary ethical changes (and for these, too, *tout le monde* "waits"). If Germany officially aproves the Torgas pamphlet on the plurality of wives—"secondary marriages"—France unofficially—but without public or legal disapproval—may read *Mère sans Etre Epouse*—a study of existing conditions, written with dignity and solemnity. It is addressed to the "*jeunes filles et jeunes veuves de France,*" and advocates—what the title indicates. According to this book, France "*ne peut éviter l'abîme qu'en choissisant entre la maternité des célibataires et le polygamie*"—to which last the author is sure the Frenchwoman will never agree. So, while the nation waits for "victory," some people face the fact that victory may bring France to the edge of an "abyss."

The essence of war is the substitution of one set of ideals for another; it offers certain spiritual gains—courage, self-sacrifice, loyalty; against those gains thoughtful persons must set the spiritual losses—one dares not enumerate them! But is one of these losses to be the throwing over, with a *coup de main,* of sex ethics which, imperfect as they are, have taken us so long, so very long, to build up? If this is a possibility hidden in the unspoken *expectancy,* surely the color of Fear has its place in the vaguely growing pattern. At any rate, it seems as if many of these brave people, these people of supreme courage, are *afraid.* They are afraid, not because they are cowardly, but because they are intelligent. Their wisdom shows them two things to be afraid of—first, the kind of peace which may come; and next, the thing which may come after the peace—be the peace what it may!

What will come afterward?

As to the present moment, the French look facts in the face, as we Americans have not yet done. To begin with, many of them feel, so people say, that the war now is as much a state of mind as it is a military situation. That is why they are afraid. Their state of mind has resulted from recognizing perfectly obvious things—first, that they are tired; next, that the English are tired—and hungry; then, that America (not the soldiers, but the nation) which has come into the war, "so late," is neither tired nor hungry; it is something much worse—it is not serious. America is stepping out into the cataclysm with a sunshade and a smiling face. The French do not resent the smiling—they smiled themselves with complete self-confidence when they started in. They do not resent the sunshade—they, too, know the parasitic plague of politicians who bind the hands of War Departments with miles of red tape; they do not even resent the mentality that makes it possible for an American soldier to say, "These here French 'ain't taught *me* nothin'!" It is not these things they fear in us. It is, I think, our fundamental lack of seriousness. Nobody in America is venturing to say that the bright lexicon of Youth *does* contain such a word as failure. The French people are not so—young. When they see us here—with our government's sunshades and smiles—they are kind to us, extraordinarily kind to us! And they are really glad to see us, because they think we may be helpful if we "ever get into the war." But their lexicon is, I think, more complete than ours, so they smile to themselves, now and then, as one smiles at well-meaning and conceited children.

Some of them say, a little impatiently, that the Americans do not know how big it all is, or how far-reaching in its outcome. But the French know! They know that the present situation is as far beyond the declaration of war in 1914 as the declaration of war was beyond that pistol-shot in the street in Sarajevo. They know it is beyond the question of struggle between the Central Powers and the Allies; some of them believe that it has become a cosmic question—that Civilization and Chaos are at grips. The Americans, on the other hand, seem to be under the impression that it is the local issue of throttling Fritz—a thing which they mean to do P.D.Q.! "Oh, the simplicity of us!" said an American long resident in France. "We are provincial in the death struggle!" For the World—not just the Allies, and poor, mad Germany, who happens to be the child who took the candle into the powder-magazine—the whole World is shaking! The French people know it, if we don't, and what their knowledge may do in creating a "state of mind" needs no comment. The two worn and haggard officers in the train put it into words: *"Même avec les plus grandes victoires. . . ."*

You will not wonder that I mark the expectancy in the air by a black bead?

The wife of the *concierge* calls that bead the fear of defeat; the brilliant Frenchman would name it, if he were willing to name it, the fear of conquest; the two officers know it is fear of national extinction.

But there are others, who call it Hope, and not Fear at all. This handful of dreamers have opened their windows toward the east! Their "state of mind" bids them look beyond the gathering darkness toward a Dawn. But they do not deny the terrors of the dark. During the hours before daybreak may come—God knows what! But whatever comes, it will be part of a process which will bring about an adjustment of the social order. It is probable, they say, that Gaston, with his hideous little gesture, will have a hand in it. This is their hope—a new Heaven and a new Earth; Chaos dragged from the throat of Civilization; our code of morals saved from the assault of an efficiency which would reinforce itself by polygamy; the Idealism of Jesus preserved for our children's children! All this through Gaston's surgery. He accomplished, they say, a good deal in 1789. "But that which is coming," said a Frenchman, smiling, "will be for thoroughness, to 1789, as a Sunday picnic, as you call it." Another of the Intellectuals put it in a way which would, I think, have appealed to Gaston:

"It will come," said he, "the new world! But first will come the world revolution. It has already begun in Russia. After the Peace, Germany will explode, then England, then France, and then you people!—with your imitation Democracy. And during the process," he ended, joyously, "it will be *casser des gueules!*"

It is fair, in this connection, and also cheerful, to quote the comment of an American on that reference to the breaking of snouts—and his slang is just as forcible as that of the French editor:

"If anybody said that sort of thing to *me*," said this youngster, grinning, "I should reply, gently but firmly: 'To hell wid yez! There ain't going to be no revolution in *ours!* Why, what have we got to revolute about? *We're* a free people. No, sir! We'll lick these damn Germans out of their boots, and then, so far as the Allies go, everything will be lovely, and the goose hang high!" I fancy many of us at home share this opinion.

The possibility the American denied was put in still another way by a French gentleman, whose serene face, furrowed with suffering, shines with a confidence that is willing to suffer still more—for with him experience has worked Hope.

"Madame," said he, "I had in my country place two horses of an unfriendliness. They *mordaient;* they nipped, as you would say; they *hennissaient!* And two dogs that loved me. They were both my friends, but to each other they were of a ferocity terrible. I had also a gaz'l. . . ."

"Gaz'l?" I queried.

"Madame! Gaz'l. You are acquainted with the gaz'l in your wonderful country of Southern America?"

Some one behind me murmured, "Gazelle," and I said, hastily: "Oh yes, certainly. Pray proceed, Monsieur."

"*Eh bien, mes chevaux* snorted and *mordaient;* my dogs

fought and tore each other; but all, all, united in attacking my gaz'l."

I sympathized.

"My gaz'l was, you understand, of a smell. It was a wild beast, and so was of a smell, *ma pauvre gaz'l!*"

I again pitied the wild beast.

"Madame, it was winter. *Je faisais des réparations* to my stable wherein these animals lived. It became upon a cold day—*froid extrême*—necessary to lift the roof of my *écurie.* I said to my *garde, 'Les animaux* go to perish!' He said, '*Non,* Monsieur, they are very warm.' I said: *'C'est impossible!* What have you done with them?' He replied, 'They are all in one stall.' I said: 'My God! They will destroy one another. The horses will kick each other to death, the dogs will tear each other to pieces—and *ma pauvre gaz'l!*' 'Monsieur,' my *garde* said, *'venez avec moi voir les animaux?'* I accompanied him to the stall. Madame! The cold extreme, the frost of a degree was such, my horses, my dogs, my gaz'l were all togezzer in the stall! ver' close, ver' close; *serrés*—huddled, you would say in your language, so expressive. Yes, close togezzer, because they had been uncomfortable apart! Cold apart! They, to be comfortable, to be warm, was *togezzer. Madame, Democracy was born!*"

"Must we be uncomfortable to learn the meaning of the word?" I said.

"Comfort has not taught you its meaning, in America," he said, smiling a little cynically. "You think you are a democracy? Dear Madame! it is in America an empty word. Many of you are comfortable. Many, many of you are uncomfortable. Not so is the true democracy."

"So, we must all suffer together?" I pondered. . . .

Before this belief that the Kingdom of Heaven may be brought about by pressure from the outside, how was one to say that when the roof was put back on the barn *les animaux* would not again squeal and nip and tear, and the smell of the gaz'l be as pronounced as ever?

It is hardly necessary to say that the immense majority of people do not believe in this possibility of a revolution. They are waiting for victory—complete, complacent, vindictive victory! With no Gaston anywhere in it—except, indeed, as he has been privileged to help in bringing it about, by dying for his country. This comfortable certainty is held by people who have never felt the cold of the lifted roof, and to whom, consequently, huddling is quite unthinkable. They belong in the class with a gentle and very kindly woman in America who said to me some two or three years ago:

"I am tired to death of all this talk about working-people. They *never* wash, and there's a great deal too much done for them, anyhow. All these tiresome girls' clubs! *I* say, let working-girls stay home with their mothers in the evenings, instead of running around to girls' clubs!"

This is almost as far removed from the hope of "huddling" as a scene I remember in my childhood—a big, rocking, family carriage; two fat, strong horses, pulling over a terribly muddy Maryland road. I sat inside with a very majestic and rigid old lady with gray side curls, who never leaned back upon the ancient cushions. We were going, I think, to Hagerstown, to call on some other majestic old lady. As the coach pulled and tugged and I tumbled about like a very small pea in a peck measure, we passed a group of school children, who drew aside to escape the splashing mud from the fetlocks of the fat horses. They didn't escape very much of it, and I can see now their look of dismay at spotted aprons, but the old lady did not notice the aprons. She frowned—and said:

"Fy! fy! What are we coming to? *Not one of them bowed to us!* When *I* was young children in their station respected their betters. Where, *where* shall we end?" she demanded, darkly. She, too, had never huddled.

I remember pondering, as we sank into the muddy ruts, and tugged out to balance on precarious wheels before plunging down again: "Why should the children bow to her? She didn't bow to them."

There is one more hope that a very, very few people feel; it is even more like Fear than the hope of the owner of the gaz'l. I heard it expressed by a little group of Americans, who thought, so some of them said, that the only certain way of ushering in the Kingdom of God was to refrain from ever putting the roof on the stable. "Let 'em all grow their own hair if they want to be warm!" said one of these vaguely speculating folk.

In other words, let us return to the beginnings of things. This will be easy, because, the speaker said, we are seeing the end of a civilization which created the box-stall and is therefore responsible for the differentiation of comfort. "But it must be the whole hog," she went on; "there is no half-way house on the road to regeneration. Gaston won't accomplish it."

This girl, her eyebrows gathering into a frown, seemed to be trying to talk out her perplexities. Some one had said that Nationalism was responsible for the idea that population should be valued by quantity, not quality; naturally, such a standard can contemplate polygamy! "Nationalism is the seed of war," this person said. "*Dulce et decorum* is death for an ideal, but not for a geographical boundary! Christ died for People, not for Nations. We must learn to think of ourselves, not as French or American or German, but as we are born—just poor, little, naked *humans!* When we do that the foolishness of war will end." But the Girl went further than that: "An Allied victory will just strengthen Nationalism," she said, "and, of course, there is going to be an Allied victory! *Must* be, you know. I don't doubt it for a moment! We've simply got to win—only—sometimes I—I wonder . . ."

"I wonder most all of the time," I confessed.

"Isn't it possible," she said, slowly, "that if we just prop up Nationalism we shall prop up for a little while longer this rotten thing that you call civilization? Is it worth while to do that? Civilization is rotten; you can't deny it."

"I'm not denying it."

"It is the expression of a debauched commercialism that has been squeezing the life out of—well, your friend Gaston's body and soul. Look at his nasty, wicked little body! Apparently he has no soul. Your civilization, which is pure materialism, has done it!"

"I do wish you wouldn't call it mine!" one of her hearers said.

"It *is* yours! You batten on it. You grind Gaston's bones to make your bread—"

"Oh, come now!"

"I mean you draw your dividends," she said to the company at large; and some one protested, meekly:

"Not very many now, or very large ones."

"That's not from any excess of virtue on your part," she said, sweetly. "I bet you, none of you ever objected to a melon yet. Well," she went on, frowning, "I know I am all balled up and going off on side-tracks, but what I'm trying to say is, that an Allied victory will only keep the civilization of materialism going a little while longer. I think M. Blank is right, and we shall 'huddle.' But I feel pretty sure that there will come a moment when the gaz'l will suddenly take the whole boxstall; and I sha'n't blame him! Civilization has created him, and it is he who has suffered the most from a war which he did not desire, and did not make, but only fought. When he gets the stall he will die in it, because it isn't Nature— Or turn into a horse, and then we'd have the whole business to do over again!"

Some one said here, that her ideas on evolution would

interest Darwin, but she did not notice the flippant interruption.

"Isn't it possible," she said, "that, to get straightened out, to *live*, in fact, we've got, *all* of us, to get out into the open? Haven't we got to grow our own hair to keep warm? Yes, we must go farther than Gaston's revolution which every one is whispering about; *that* will only be a piece of court-plaster on an ulcer. We will go the whole hog."

This was too preposterous.

"You mean, a return to the primeval slime? Thank you! I prefer the box stall even if the gaz'l is of a smell."

"I don't think your preferences will be consulted. But it does seem"—her face fell into painful lines of sincerity—"it really does seem that the sooner the smash of the whole darned thing comes the better. It isn't any easier to pull a tooth by degrees."

(I may say that this thoughtful woman is a doctor, so her illustrations are natural enough.)

"So that's why," she ended, quietly, "that sometimes, I—I *think* I believe, that it will be better for Germany to win the war!"

There was an outcry at this, "Germany is the apotheosis of materialism!"

"I know. It would be casting out devils by Beelzebub, the Prince of Devils. But a German victory would ice the toboggan and get us down to the bottom more quickly."

A ribald voice suggested that "ice" wouldn't last long in the place to which she seemed bent on sending us. But the girl was in too painful earnest to retort.

"You bet," she said, "we'll drag Germany over the precipice with us, and, once at the bottom, we shall all begin to climb up again. But we must touch bed-rock first."

Everybody laughed, and, of course, nobody took her seriously. Yet this, stripped of slang, is a thing for which, here and there, a very few people are "waiting." They are saying, carefully, with weighed words, something that confesses what this extravagant statement means.

"Not even Gaston's surgery can better conditions that ought not to exist," they say. "We are at the end of our epoch. We must begin all over again."

Of course, very few go as far as this. Gaston is the boundary set by most of the dreamers. Those who do go farther believe, as this girl put it, that an Allied victory will be only a temporary uplifting; that Gaston would be but a palliative, and that it is better, not only for France, but for Western civilization, to get to the bottom as quickly as possible.

"Don't prolong the agony by defeating Germany," one of them said. But whether victory comes, or defeat, Gaston, they say, will do his part. Under his star there will be, perforce, some huddling; and dogs and horses and gaz'l will be quite sure that they are going to live happily for evermore. . . . But after that, the dark. And after *that*, the dawn!

It is a Hope! Eons off, perhaps, but a Hope. The hope of the upward curve of the spiral after it has dipped into the primeval. Back again, these people say, to the beginnings of things, must go our miserable little civilization. Back to some bath of realities, to wash us clean of an unreality which has mistaken geographical boundaries for spiritual values, and mechanics for God. Then, up—up—up—toward the singing heights!

"We will find God," the crystal beads declare! Not in our time, perhaps; perhaps not even in the time of our children; but sometime. "The processes of God are years and centuries."

And as I write, the guns are trained on Paris. . . .

# SPECULATIONS[1]

*By* John Galsworthy

*John Galsworthy, born in 1867, is better known as a dramatist, novelist, and author of* The Forsyte Saga *than as essayist. He is essentially, however, a critic of life, and his ideas find congenial expression in the essay form. This essay was first published in* Harper's *for April, 1918.*

WHEN—IN WORDS OF THE OLD song—"we survey the world around, the wondrous things that there abound," and especially the developments of these last years, there must come to some of us a doubt whether civilization is going to have a future. Mr. Lowes Dickenson, in a very able book called *The Choice Before Us*, has outlined the alternate paths which the world may tread after this war—the path of "National Militarism" or the path of "International Pacifism." He has pointed out with great force the terrible dangers on the first of these two paths, the ruinous strain and ultimate destruction which a journey down it will inflict on every nation. But holding, like myself, a brief for the second path, he was not, in that book, at all events, concerned to point out the dangers which beset it. Man is instinctively averse to committing himself definitely to any particular direction, and no doubt the world will go wabbling on between these two paths much as it did in the past, but with a decided and immediate leaning toward the latter; not so much from deliberate choice as from natural reaction after a ruinous dash down the former. The world is never doctrinaire, human nature never uniform—it will never as one man join the Salvation Army. Sheer exhaustion, and disgust with suffering, sacrifice, and sudden death, will almost surely force us all into some sort of international quietude and order, and for the first time in the history of man organized justice, such as for many centuries has ruled the relations between individuals, may begin to rule the relations between states, and free us from war for a period which with good fortune may be almost indefinitely prolonged. The perpetuation of a great change like that in the life of mankind is, like the perpetuating of smaller changes, very much a question of getting an adequate machinery of law into running order; something which men can see is there and pin their faith to; something to which they can get used and feel that they would miss if it were dissolved; something which works and has proved its utility. If an international court of justice, backed by international force, makes good in the settlement of two or three national disputes, allays two or three crises, it will with each success be the firmer and more difficult to uproot; it may very well become as much a matter of course in the eyes of the nations as our national courts of justice are in the eyes of individual citizens.

Making, then, the large but by no means hopeless assumption that such a change may come, how is the life of civilized man going to "pan out"?

In *Erewhon*, Samuel Butler's amusing satire on civilization, there is a country, "Nowhere," whose inhabitants had broken up all machinery, abandoned the use of money, and lived in a strange Elysium of health and beauty.

I confess that I often wonder how, without something of the sort, modern man is to be prevented from being exploited to death by the physical and economic machinery he has devised for his benefit. The problem for modern man becomes more and more the problem of becoming master, not slave, of his own civilization; for the history of the last hundred and fifty years is surely one long story of ceaseless banquet and acute indigestion. Certain Roman emperors are popularly supposed to have taken emetics during their feasts, that they might regain their appetites; it would appear that modern man has not that cynical wisdom, or perhaps his appetite is so insatiable that he does not mind feeling sick all the time.

Few will deny, certainly not this writer, that to be clean, warm, well fed, healthy, decently leisured, and free to move quickly about the world are pure benefits. These are presumably the prime objects of man's toil and ingenuity, the ideals supposed to be served by the discovery of steam, electricity, modern industrial machinery, telephony, flying—all those amazing conquests of the present age which have crowded one on the other so fast that we have never had time to assimilate and digest them. Each as it came we have hailed as an incalculable benefit to mankind, and so it was, or would have been if modern man had not the appetite of a cormorant and the assimilative powers of an elderly gentleman. Our civilization is in a state of chronic dyspepsia, which, in spite of all our science—maybe because of our science—is rapidly increasing. We discover, and hurl our discoveries broadcast at a society utterly uninstructed in the proper use of them. Take an instance from Britain—the discovery of the spinning-jenny, whence came the whole system of Lancashire cotton-factories which drained the countryside of peasants and caused that deterioriation of physique from which as yet there has been no recovery. Here was an invention which was to effect a tremendous saving of labor and be a great benefit to mankind. Exploited by greedy persons without knowledge, scruple, or humanity, it also caused untold miseries and grievous national harm. That and similar inventions have been the forces which dotted beautiful counties of England with the blackest and most ill-looking towns in the world, changed the proportion of country to town dwellers from about three as against two in 1761, to two as against seven in 1911. And parallels can no doubt be found in the history of America. The standard of wealth has gone up, of course. A few years ago in America I heard a colored man on a ferry-boat complaining of his weekly wage: "Fohteen dollars! What kin yeh do with fohteen dollars?" Fifty-six shillings a week. There were still plenty of English agricultural laborers then getting fourteen shillings a week. I once had a long talk with one of our very old shepherds on the South Downs, whose youth and early married life were lived on eight shillings (two dollars) a week; and he was no exception. The standard of wealth may have gone up, though money purchases much less than it used to; but has the standard of health? Has the standard of beauty, or the standard of happiness? They certainly might have, with proper use and understanding, but, as a matter of fact, have they? I think not, in Britain, among the great bulk of the population; I doubt if they have in any European country.

Or take the discovery of flying. To what use has it been put, so far? To practically none save the destruction of life. About five years before the war some of us in England tried to initiate an international movement to ban the use of flying for military purposes. The effort was entirely abortive. The fact is that man has never gone in front of events, has always insisted on buying experience through hard facts. And I am inclined to think that we shall continue to advance backward unless we operate on our inventors and render their genius sterile, until such time as we have mastered, digested, and learned to use for our real benefit the inventions of the last century or so; until, in sum, we know how to run our machines of every sort in a sane way instead of letting them run us. But since such an operation is a policy of perfection which will never be undertaken by any nation with a sense of humor, our only chance will be the international banning of certain deadly dangers, under pain of instant and universal boycott; and the establishment in every country of some wise, controlling agency which shall make sure that no inventions are exploited under conditions obviously harmful to men, either within or without the country of use. Suppose, for instance, that the spinning-jenny had come before such a board of wisdom, one imagines they might have said, "If you want to use this thing, you must satisfy us that your employees are going to work under conditions favorable to health." Or take the introduction of rubber. They might have said: "You are bringing in this new and evidently very useful article. We shall send out and see the conditions under which you obtain it." And, having seen, they would have added, "You will alter those conditions, and use the natives humanely, or we will ban your use of this article."

The history of modern civilization shows, I think, that while we can only trust individualism to produce discovery, we absolutely cannot trust it to apply discovery without some sort of State check in the interests of health and happiness. Certain results of inventions and discoveries cannot, of course, be foreseen, but national boards of control which comprise the first brains of the generation could foresee a good many and save mankind from the most rampant evils which arise from raw and unconsidered exploitation. The child who discovers that there is such a thing as candy, if left to itself, can only be relied on to make itself and its companions sick.

Let us stray for a moment into the realms of art; for I understand that the word Art is claimed for what we call the "film"! This new discovery went as you please for a few years in the hands of inventors and commercial agents. In these few years a rampant public taste for cowboy, crime, and Chaplin films has been developed, so that a commission which has just been sitting on the matter in England finds as a conclusion that the public will not put up with more than a ten-per-cent. proportion of educational film in the course of an evening's entertainment. Now the film as a means of transcribing actual life of all sorts is admittedly of absorbing interest and great educational value; but, owing to a false start, we cannot get it swallowed in more than extremely small doses as a food and stimulant, while it is gulped down as a drug or irritant. As to the film's value as art, I am skeptically trying to keep an open mind. All that one can say at present is that the case is non-proven. A film is a very restless thing, and I cannot think of any work of art, as hitherto we have understood the word, to which that description could be applied, unless perchance it be a Wagner opera, which to me has ever seemed a bastard. When we think that art has existed for very many thousand years, if we remember that the Cro-Magnon men of Europe decorated the walls of their caves quite beautifully, we see that art is indeed long; and that it must always require the verdict of at least a generation to tell us what is art and what is not, among the new experiments which are continually being made. When I was watching the great American film "Intolerance" I kept on wondering whether I was getting anything from it emotionally that I could not have got much more intensely from ordinary drama. I came to the conclusion that I was not. But I was certainly getting from it a more rapid and extensive brushing-up of knowledge than I should have got in two or three hours from a stage play. In other words, its value to me was educational, not esthetic—always supposing that the knowledge I gained was correct. Almost the next evening I saw Captain Beazley's film of his marvelous South American wanderings. That I found to be pure educational gain from beginning to end. Judging from those two films, I felt that the proper function of the cinema was the broadening of the mind through the presentation of life as it is. The film, of course, is in its first youth, but, honestly, I see no signs as yet that it will ever overcome, in the art sense, the handicap of its physical conditions so as to equal or surpass in depth the emotionalizing power of ordinary drama. But since it takes the line of least resistance and makes a rapid, lazy, superficial appeal to the mind, through the eye, instead of through the spoken word, it may very well oust the drama. And to my thinking, of course, that will be all to the bad.

During the filming of my own play, "Justice," I attended rehearsal to see Mr. Gerald du Maurier play the cell scene. In that scene there is not a word spoken in the play, so that there is no difference in kind between the appeal of play and film. But I was at least twice as much affected by the live rehearsal for the film as when I saw the dead result of that rehearsal on the film itself. The film sweeps up into itself a far wider surface of life in a far shorter space of time; but the medium is flat, and has no blood in it, and in my experience no amount of surface and quantity in art ever makes up for lack of depth and quality.

One dwells on the film because it is a pretty good illustration of the whole tendency of modern civilized life under the too rapid development of machines. Roughly speaking, our life seems to be turning up yearly more and more ground to less and less depth.

There is an American expression "highbrow," which, complimentary in origin, has become in some sort a term of contempt, as we use the word academic. Doubts and speculations on the trend of modern life are liable to be labeled "highbrow" at once, and to drop like water off a duck's back. There is an idea, I think, that any one who doubts our triumphant progress must be tabooed for a pedant. That does not alter the fact, however, that we are getting feverish, rushed, and complicated. We have multiplied conveniences to such an extent that we do nothing but produce them and leave ourselves no time to "live" and enjoy. We mistake "life" for living. We were rattling into a new species of barbarity when the war came, and may perhaps continue to rattle after it is over. It is herd-life in every country which is working the change; herd-life based on machines, money, and the dread of being dull. Every one knows how fearfully strong that dread is. But to be capable of being dull is in itself a disease. All modern life seems, in a way, to be a process of creating disease, then finding a remedy for that disease, which in its turn creates another disease, demanding fresh remedy, and so on. We pride ourselves, for example, on modern sanitation; but what is modern sanitation if not one huge palliative and preventive of evils which have arisen from herd-life; and does it not enable herd-life to be intensified? That old shepherd on our South Downs had probably never even come into contact with modern sanitation, yet he was very old, very hardy, very healthy, and very contented. He had a sort of inner life and satisfaction that we moderns have nearly all of us lost, and how we are ever to get it back again I do not know. The true elixirs—for there be two, I think—are open-air life and a proud pleasure in one's work; and the trouble is that we have evolved a mode of existence in which it is comparatively rare to find those two conjoined. In old countries such as Britain the evil is at present vastly more accentuated than it is in a new country such as America. On the other hand, the itch which most men have to go to hell is such that the farther off they are from that Elysium the faster they seem to run toward it; and, I take it, machines are now driving America on even more rapidly than they are driving Europe. America has tremendous space to cover; it must take her perhaps two or three generations yet to get into Britain's state of congestion, but that she will reach it I doubt not, unless modern civilization begins to take itself very severely in hand. We are, I suppose, awakening to the dangers of "Gadarening"—rushing down the high cliff into the sea, possessed by the devils of machinery; but if any man would see how slender is the hold of our alarm, let him ask himself how much of the present mode of existence he is prepared to alter—not in the lives of other people, but in his own. Altering the habits of other people seems to be a most delightful occupation; one would have the greatest hopes of the future if we had nothing before us but that. We have capital vision for the motes in other eyes. Indeed, if we were to pile the intolerant one on the other, they would reach to that moon they wish for. Ah! and if only, having reached it, they could be forced to take up abode there! And this writer would be of the company, for he is hopelessly intolerant of intolerance! We are all ready to burn houses down if we can make sure of our opponents being at home in them—like the long-ago Irishman in Froude, a Geraldine or Desmond, who, when indicted for burning down the cathedral at Armagh, defended himself thus: "As for the cathedral, 'tis true I burned it, but sure an' I wouldn't have, only they told me the archbishop was inside."

Seriously, how to get ourselves reformed without reforming other people or being reformed by them—two processes of which one knows not which is the more objectionable—is one of the puzzles of the future. Moreover, even the legitimate province of reformers is strictly limited to the negative activities of securing evidence for the public eye, and working for the prohibition by law of acts manifestly cruel, dishonest, or otherwise anti-social; and, granted that the word anti-social embraces everything obviously baneful, still, it hardly includes the prevailing mood of men's minds or the prevailing trend of their civilization. We can certainly not force men to live in the open, or to take a proud pleasure in their work, or to enjoy beauty, or not to concentrate themselves on making money. No amount of legislation will make us "lilies of the field" or "birds of the air," or prevent us from worshiping false gods, or neglecting to reform ourselves. The only hope lies in what we call education. Unfortunately, in order to educate, one must oneself be educated. "Democracy, at present, offers the spectacle of a man running down a road followed at a more and more respectful distance by his own soul." For democracy I should have used the broader words "modern civilization." For modern civilization has so far lent itself flaccidly to the habit of redress after the event, blindly grouped itself into holes which were avoidable, and has to pull itself painfully out, only to blunder into others. It foresees nothing. It is at present purely empirical, if one may be forgiven for using a "highbrow" word.

Politics are popularly supposed to govern the direction, and politicians to be the guardian angels, of civilization. This is an error; they have little or no power over its growth. They are of it and move with it. Their concern is rather with the body than with the mind—or shall we say soul?—of a national organism. We have at present no fixed point a little higher than medium from which leverage can be applied or direction given to general tastes. Politically speaking, America has the best Constitution yet discovered; not, perhaps, a better type of politician, but certainly a Constitution superior to ours. America has in the person of her elected President a real central force which can operate with swiftness and decision, and bring in practically all the advantages of autocracy without in any way departing from the principle of government of the people by the people for the people. The British Prime Minister's position is not nearly so detached, nor is his power so great or so swift.

Believing, as I do, that education, not politics, is the only agent capable of controlling or altering the direction of civilization, I think it a thousand pities that neither America nor Britain nor, so far as I know, any other nation, has as yet evolved machinery through which there might be elected a supreme director, or say a little board of three directors, of the nation's spirit, an educational president, as it were, with position and power analogous to that of America's elected political President. With us the Minister of Education is, as a rule, just an ordinary man of affairs, and member of the Government for the time being—though we happen at the moment to have an expert, an admirably different type of man. Why cannot education be regarded, like religion in the past, as something apart and very sacred; not merely a department of ordinary political administration? Ought not the heart and brains of a nation to be perpetually on the lookout to secure the election of the highest mind and finest spirit of the day? The appointment of such a man, or triumvirate of men, would certainly need a special sifting process of election, analogous to, but closer and more careful than, the American Presidential election by delegates. One might use for the purpose the actual body of teachers in the country, to elect delegates to finally select the flower of the national flock. It would be worth any amount of trouble to insure that we always had the best man or men. And when we had got them we should give them a mandate as real and substantial as America gives now to her political President. We should intend them not for mere lay administrators and continuers of custom, but for true fountain-heads and initiators of higher ideals of conduct, learning, manners, and health. Hitherto the supposed direction of ideals—in practice almost none—has been left to religion. Religion as a motive force is at once too personal, too lacking in unanimity, and too specialized to control the educational needs of a modern state; moreover, religion, as I understand it, is essentially emotional and individual, and, when it becomes practical and worldly, strays outside its true province and loses all force. Education, as I want to see it, would take over the control of social ethics, learning, and health, but make no attempt to usurp the emotional functions of religion. It would merely prevent religion from amateurish entrance into fields with which it has no direct concern.

America, in her political system, has established the very agency essential to the pressing out from democracy of the best that there is in it. She has, in working order, a sort of endless band of force—throwing up what is presumably the best American politician of the day till he forms a head or apex whence political virtue runs down again with accelerated swiftness into the toes of the people who elected him. She uses the principle of Nature herself, the symbol of which is neither the circle nor the spire, but circle and spire mysteriously conjoined.

But, if it be not politics so much as education which checks and changes our attitude to life, what we must do in every modern state, if we want to master our own civilization, is to establish in education that principle of Nature which America already follows in politics, and get an endless band of force and virtue into running order.

Talk and theorize as we will, we all know from every-day life and business that the real, the only real problem is to get the best men, the right men, to run the show. When we get them the show runs well; when we don't all is dust and ashes. The capital defect of modern civilization based on democracy is the difficulty of getting best men quickly enough. Democracy, to be sound, must secure and utilize not an autocracy, but an aristocracy of mind. The first, the really vital concern of the elected head of education would be the discovery and employment of the best men, best heads of schools and colleges, whose chief concern, in turn, would be the discovery and employment of best subordinates. The better the teacher the better the ideals. Indeed, the only hope of raising ideals is to raise the standard of teachers and teaching.

To readers in a land not one's own one has ever the fear of seeming as strange and comic as was that native interpreter in Egypt who, when the authorities complained that he had overstayed his leave of absence, wrote back: "My absence is impossible. Some one has removed my wife. My God! I am annoyed!" Still, even the habitually cautious must take the risk of making a fool of himself sometimes; and I ramble on about such remote things as civilization, education, and the future, to American readers, for this reason: America, after the war, is going to be more emphatically than ever in material things the most important and powerful nation of the earth, and all, especially we British, have a legitimate and breathless interest in the use she will make of her power, the turn she will give to her civilization, the lead she will set. All these depend, not on her material wealth, not on her armed power, not even primarily on her world policy; they depend really on what the attitude toward life, and the ideals of her citizens, are going to be. Americans have one quality for which I look in vain in the Old World—eagerness and openness of mind; they have also, for all their absorption in success, the aspiring eye. They *do* want the good thing. These qualities, in combination with material strength, give America the chance to lead a world which, after the war, may—one hopes—be on the single plane of democratic development; but they impose on her a corresponding and rather awful responsibility. If she does not set her face firmly against "Gadarening," then we are all bound for downhill. If she goes in for spread-eagleism, if her aspirations are not at once both high and humble, toward quality, not quantity, we are all in danger of being commonized. If she should get that purse-and-power-proud fever which comes from national success and overfeeding, we are all bound for another world flare-up. The burden of proving that a democratic "live and let live" world-civilization can stand will be on her shoulders more than on those of any other nation. It will all depend on what Americans make of their inner life, on their individual habits of thought, on what they reverence and what they despise. If they despise meanness and cruelty, injustice and oppression, shoddiness and blatancy; if they reverence chivalry, freedom, toleration, good order, and pride of work —America's star will shine before all the peoples not so blessed by fortune. She will be loved, not feared; she will lead in spirit and in truth, not in mere money and guns. She stands at the door of her real greatness, and she is malleable as yet, and will be for a long time to come. Is she to become a great statue, or a mere amorphous abortion? That is for America the long decision, a decision to be worked out not so much in her Senate and her Congress as in her homes and schools. On Americans, and America's conduct after the war, I verily believe the destiny of civilization for the next century will hang. She cannot take herself too seriously nor too humbly. If she mislays—indeed, if she does not improve—the power of self-criticism, that special dry American humor which the great Lincoln had, she will soon develop the intolerant provincialism which has so often been the bane of the earth and the undoing of great nations. If she gets a swelled head, the world will get cold feet. Above all, if she does not solve the problems of town life, of distribution of wealth, of national health, and of the mastery of our inventions, she is in for a cycle of mere anarchy, disruption, and dictatorships into which we shall all follow. The motto, "Noblesse oblige," applies as much to democracy as ever it did to the old-time aristocrat. It applies with terrific vividness to America. Great are the gifts bestowed on her by ancestry and nature. Behind her stand conscience, enterprise, independence, and adventure. Such were the companions of the first Americans, and are the comrades of the American citizens to this day. America has abounding energy, an unequaled spirit of discovery, a vast and wonderful country not half discovered. I remember sitting on a bench overlooking the Grand Cañon of Arizona, into which the sun was shining and snowstorms whirling all at once. All that most marvelous natural work of art was flooded to the brim with tawny gold, and white, and wine-dark shadows, so that the colossal carvings, as of huge rock-gods and beasts, along its sides were made living by the very mystery of the light and darkness. I remember sitting there, and an old gentleman passing close behind, leaning a little toward me, and saying in a sly, gentle voice, "How are you going to tell it to the folks at home?" America has so much that one despairs of telling to the folks at home; so much wide and noble beauty to be to her an inspiration and uplift toward great and free thought and vision; so much music, so many pictures, such great poems wrought in the large. She has Nature on her side to make of her and keep her a noble people. In Great Britain—all told, not half the size of Texas—there is a quiet beauty of a sort that America perhaps has not. I walked not long ago from Worthing on the Sussex coast to the little village of Steyning, just north of the South Downs. It was such a day as one rarely gets in England. When the sun was dipping and there came on the cool, chalky hills the smile of late afternoon, and across a smooth valley on the rim of the Down one saw a tiny group of trees, one little building, and a stack against the clear pale-blue sky, it was like a glimpse of heaven, so utterly pure in line and color, so removed and touching. There is much loveliness in Britain, but not in the grand manner. America has the grand manner in her scenery, the grand manner in her blood, for Americans are all the children of adventure. She has had already past-masters in greatness and dignity, but she has still before her as a nation the grand manner in achievement. America knows her dangers and her failings, her own qualities and powers; what, perhaps, she cannot realize so well as one who comes from the Old World is the intense concern and interest and the real sympathy, deep down behind a stolid and often provoking surface, with which we of the old country watch her, knowing that what she does reacts on us above all nations, and will ever react more and more. Beyond surface differences and irritations, the English-speaking peoples are fast bound together. May it not be in misery and iron! If America grows to full height and dignity and walks upright, so will Britain; if she goes bowed under the weight of money and materialism, we too shall creep our ways. We run a long race, we nations; a generation is but a day. But in a day a man may leave the track and never again recover it.

We moderns have an inclination to ride new things to death. Take a petty illustration—rag-time music! Seeing how it has extended to Britain, and beyond, one would think it a splendid discovery; yet it suggests little or nothing but the love-making of two darkies. We are riding it to death; but, unfortunately, its jigging, jogging, jumpy jingle refuses to die, and America's children and ours grow up in the tradition of its soul-forsaken sounds. Take another tiny illustration—the new dancing, developed from cake-walk to fox-trot, by way of tango, and invading Britain and beyond as invincibly as rag-time. Has it not precisely the same spiritual origin? I would ask, are these things worthy? They have not exactly the grand manner. Take the "snappy" side of journalism. To its flash-light emphasis no words can do justice. In one great city a few years ago the press snapped a certain writer and his wife in their bedroom, and next day there appeared a photograph of two intensely wretched-looking beings, under the head-line, "Blank and wife enjoy gaiety and freedom in the air." A friend told me that as he set his foot on a car leaving another great city a young lady grasped him by the coat-tail and cried, "Now, Mr. Asterisk, what are your views on a future life?" All this is but the excrescence of vitality and interest. Perhaps! But fine men are not the better-looking for being covered with spots. And are these excrescences not symptoms of a sort of fever which lies within our modern civilization, of a restlessness which is going to make achievement of great aims and great work more difficult? We Britons, as a people, are admittedly lethargic; we err as much on the side of stolidity as Americans on the side of restlessness; yet we are both subject to these excrescences. I know not what is the experience in America, but in Britain we are finding out that there is something terribly catching about vulgarity; taste is on the down-grade, following the tendencies of herd-life. It is not a process to be proud of.

Fortunately, vulgarity does not seem able to attack the real inner man. If there is a lamentable increase of vulgarity in our epoch, there is also an inspiring development of certain qualities. Those who were watching human nature before the war were pretty well aware of how, under the surface, unselfishness, a certain ironic stoicism, and a warm humanity were increasing. These are the great town virtues, the fine products of herd-life. A big price is being paid for them, but they are almost priceless. The war has revealed them in full bloom. *Revealed them, not produced them!* Who, in the future, with this amazing show before him, will dare to talk about the need of war to preserve courage and unselfishness? All these wonders of endurance and bravery and sacrifice have been displayed by the simple untrained citizens of countries fifty years deep in peace! Never, I suppose, in the world's history was there a more peaceful century than the last hundred years. Never in the world's history has there been so marvelous a display in war of the bed-rock virtues. The soundness at core of the modern man has had one long triumphant demonstration. Take that wonderful little story of a certain British superintendent of the pumping-station at some oil-wells in Mesopotamia. A valve in the oil-pipe had split, and a fountain of oil was being thrown up on all sides; while, thirty yards off and nothing between, the furnaces were in full blast. To prevent a terrible conflagration and great loss of life, and save the oil-wells, it was necessary to turn off the furnaces. To do that meant dashing through the oil spray and arriving saturated at the furnaces. The superintendent, without a moment's hesitation, sprang through the oil spray, turned off the furnaces, and died. Modern man has been doing things like that all through this war.

We Britons are an insular people, ignorant, for the most part, of anything outside our own empire; and it has struck me as a rather wonderful tribute to America that one could go the length of Britain and find hardly a creature who was not confident that Americans will display the same endurance, bravery, and unselfishness that we have seen displayed by our own men all these years. Instinctively, we know and feel it. There is something proud in Americans as in ourselves, something undefeated and undefeatable. It comes of our common cult of freedom and of the individual conscience, and in both our countries is a growing, not a withering, quality.

When you come to think of it, this modern man is a very new and marvelous creature. Without realizing it we have evolved a fresh species of stoic, even more stoical and broader (because less self-conscious) than were the ancient stoics. He has cut loose from leading-strings and stands on his own feet. The modern man's religion is to take what comes without flinching or complaint, as part of the day's work which an unknowable God, Providence, Creative Principle, or whatever it be called, has appointed. Far from inclining to believe in the new, personal, elder-brotherly God of Mr. Wells, my observation tells me that modern man at large has turned his face quite the other way, toward the confronting of life and death without aid from fetiches, be they cloaked never so adroitly in turned garments. By courage and kindness modern man exists, warmed by the glow of the great human fellowship, content to know that the mystery of his being is unknowable, and that if he does not help himself, and help his fellows, he cannot find the peace within which satisfies. To do his bit, and to be kind! It is by that creed rather than by any mysticism that the modern man finds the salvation of his soul. His religion is to be a common, or garden, hero, without thinking anything of it. Instead of giving our men the Victoria Cross, or Distinguished Service Order, we should make them bishops. For, of a truth, this is the age of conduct, and these have proved themselves past-masters in the bed-rock virtues. Does not the only real spiritual warmth, not tinged by Pharisaism, egotism, or cowardice, come from the feeling of doing your work well and helping others? Is not the rest all embroidery, luxury, pastime, pleasant sound, and incense? The modern man, take him in the large, does not believe in salvation to beat of drum, or that by leaning up against another person, however idolized and mystical, he can gain support. He is a realist with too deep a sense perhaps of the romantic mystery which surrounds existence to pry into it. The modern man, like modern civilization, is the creature of west and north, of atmospheres, climates, manners of life, which foster neither inertia, reverence, nor mystic meditation. He is essentially the man of action, and in ideal action finds his only true comfort. No attempts to discover for him new gods and symbols will divert him from the path made for him by Nature and the whole trend of his existence. I am sure that padres at the front in France and Flanders see that the men whose souls they are supposed to tend are living the highest form of religion; that, in their courage, their unselfish humanity, their endurance without whimper of things worse than death, they have gone beyond all pulpit and death-bed teachings. And who are these men? Just all the early manhood of the race, just modern man as he was before the war began and will be when the war is over.

The modern world, of which Americans are perhaps the

truest types, stands revealed, from beneath all its froth, frippery, and vulgar excrescences, sound at heart—a world whose implicit motto is, "The good of all humanity." Herd-life, which is its characteristic, brings many evils, has many dangers. To preserve a sane mind in a healthy body is the problem. We English-speaking races are by chance, as it were, the advance-guard of modern man. It will be for us to find the answer to this problem. Because of our common language, our ties of blood and tradition, and our geographical positions, the action and reaction between us is such that we shall only find it if we work together, in no selfish or exclusive spirit. We want the betterment not only of Britain and America, but of the whole world, and with that the betterment of each man's lot.

When from all our hearts this great weight is lifted; when no longer in those fields Death sweeps his scythe, and our ears at last are free from the rustling thereof—then will come the test of magnanimity in all countries. Will modern man rise to the ordering of a sane, a free, a generous life? This earth is made too subtly, of too multiple warp and woof, for prophecy. When he surveys the world around, the wondrous things that there abound, the prophet closes foolish lips—besides, have not writers, as the historian says, "that undeterminateness of spirit which commonly makes literary men of no use in the world?" But we do know that we English-speaking peoples will go to the adventure of peace with something of the same purpose and spirit in our hearts, with something of the same outlook.

Our world is fair and meant to be enjoyed. Who dare affront this world of beauty with mean views? There is no darkness but what the ape in us still makes; and, for all his monkey tricks, modern man is at heart farther from the ape than man has ever been.

To do our jobs really well, and to be brotherly! If in Britain and America, in all the English-speaking nations, we can put that simple faith of modern man into practice, what may not this world of ours become? Shall the highest product of creation be content to pass his little day in a house like unto bedlam? When the present great task in which we have joined hands is ended, when once more from the shuttered house the figure of Peace steps forth and stands in the sun, and we may go our ways again in the beauty and wonder of a new morning, let it be with the vow in our hearts, "No more of madness—neither in war nor peace!" The world is wide, and Nature bountiful enough for all, if we keep sane minds in healthy bodies.

The past of America has been like a fairy-tale; her present is an epic, her future may well become a legend of inspiration and guidance to us of the Old World.

Each of us loves his own country best, be it a little land or the greatest on earth; but jealousy is the dark thing, the creeping poison. Where there is true greatness, let us acclaim it; where there is true worth, let us prize it as if it were our own.

# WITHIN THE RIM[1]

*By* HENRY JAMES

WITH AN INTRODUCTION BY ELIZABETH ASQUITH

---

*This reaction of a great cosmopolitan to the cataclysm which led him to change his citizenship and brought on his death belongs in a volume which covers the war years for the intrinsic interest of its subject as well as for its excellence. Novelist, critic, and refiner of the language, Henry James was born in 1843, and died in 1916. This essay was published in* Harper's *for December, 1917, and has not before been reprinted.*

IT HAS BEEN SUGGESTED TO ME that I should explain how "Within the Rim" came to be written. Those who knew Henry James, not as a name, but as a man, will approach this sketch less with the detached interest of critics than with the warm sympathy of friends, and to them these few details of its origin may be of interest. "Within the Rim" was one of the last things Henry James ever wrote, and one of the few things he wrote about the war.

In November, 1914, I organized a matineé which laid the financial foundations of the Arts Fund—a scheme started by Miss Constance Collier for the relief of artists in distress owing to the war.

We had naturally relied on dramatic and musical entertainments as our chief sources of income, but as all the four arts had benefited equally by our fund, we wished to give to painting and literature an opportunity of making their contributions through the medium of an album. I was lunching with Henry James in February, 1915, and he promised to write something for us. "It must be about the war," he said. "I can think of nothing else." Three

[1] Copyright 1917 by Harper & Brothers.

weeks later he asked me to lunch with him again in order that he might read me what he had written.

I can see him now, sitting in front of the fire, his tongue caressing the words—conducting his verbal orchestration with his foot, as if by beating time he could force his complicated passages into a shape intelligible to the listener.

After it was over he brushed aside my thanks and began talking about the war and then the younger generation till gradually, under the spell of his conversation, lunch faded into tea and it was time for me to go. I asked for the precious manuscript, but he told me he would send it round by messenger, as I was certain to leave it in the taxi. I assured him that I would look after it and cherish it as if it were a child. So he confided it to my care.

Ultimately the Committee of the Arts Fund abandoned the idea of an album.

I told Henry James and asked him if he would like me to return him his manuscript, but he said, "It is yours, my dear child, to do what you will with."

The last time I saw him was in November, 1915, at a view of my sister's wedding-presents. I again asked him whether he really wanted me to keep "Within the Rim," and he assured me that he did. He then inquired what I would wear as a bridesmaid. "Orange," I told him. "I shall see you tomorrow as a flame," he said. Thirty-six hours later he had his stroke and I never saw him again.

Now that he is dead, I am publishing "Within the Rim" for the purpose for which he originally intended it.

It is his legacy to the literature of the war and to the English nation, for it shows him not only as a great artist, but as a great soldier fighting our battles.

ELIZABETH ASQUITH.

THE FIRST SENSE OF IT ALL to me after the first shock and horror was that of a sudden leap back into life of the violence with which the American Civil War broke upon us, at the North, fifty-four years ago, when I had a consciousness of youth which perhaps equalled in vivacity my present consciousness of age. The illusion was complete, in its immediate rush; everything quite exactly matched in the two cases; the tension of the hours after the flag of the Union had been fired upon in South Carolina living again, with a tragic strangeness of recurrence, in the interval during which the fate of Belgium hung in the scales and the possibilities of that of France looked this country harder in the face, one recognised, than any possibility, even that of the England of the Armada, even that of the long Napoleonic menace, could be imagined to have looked her. The analogy quickened and deepened with every elapsing hour; the drop of the balance under the invasion of Belgium reproduced with intensity the agitation of the New England air by Mr. Lincoln's call to arms, and I went about for a short space as with the queer secret locked in my breast of at least already knowing how such occasions helped and what a big war was going to mean. That this was literally a light in the darkness, or that it materially helped the prospect to be considered, is perhaps more than I can say; but it at least added the strangest of savours, an inexpressible romantic thrill, to the harsh taste of the crisis: I found myself literally knowing "by experience" what immensities, what monstrosities, what revelations of what immeasurabilities, our affair would carry in its bosom—a knowledge that flattered me by its hint of immunity from illusion. The sudden new tang in the atmosphere, the flagrant difference, as one noted, in the look of everything, especially in that of people's faces, the expressions, the hushes, the clustered groups, the detached wonders, and slow-paced public meditators, were so many impressions long before received and in which the stretch of more than half a century had still left a sharpness. So I took the case in and drew a vague comfort, I can scarce say why, from recognition; so, while recognition lasted, I found it come home to me that we, we of the ancient day, had known, had tremendously learnt, what the awful business is when it is "long," when it remains for months and months bitter and arid, void even of any great honour. In consequence of which, under the rapid rise of presumptions of difficulty, to whatever effect of dismay or of excitement, my possession of something like a standard of difficulty, and, as I might perhaps feel too, of success, became in its way a private luxury.

My point is, however, that upon this luxury I was allowed after all but ever so scantly to feed. I am unable to say when exactly it was that the rich analogy, the fine and sharp identity between the faded and the vivid case broke down, with the support obscurely derived from them; the moment anyhow came soon enough at which experience felt the ground give way and that one swung off into space, into history, into darkness, with every lamp extinguished and every abyss gaping. It ceased quite to matter for reassurance that the victory of the North had been so delayed and yet so complete, that our struggle had worn upon the world of the time, and quite to exasperation, as could well be remembered, by its length; if the present complication should but begin to be as long as it was broad no term of comparison borrowed from the past would so much as begin to fit it. I might have found it humiliating, in fact however I found it of the most commanding interest, whether at certain hours of dire apprehension or at certain others of the finer probability, that the biggest like convulsion our generations had known was still but too clearly to be left far behind for exaltations and terrors, for effort and result, as a general exhibition of the perversity of nations and of the energy of man. Such at least was the turn the comparison took at a given moment in a remembering mind that had been steeped, so far as its restricted contact went but in the Northern story; I did, I confess, cling awhile to the fancy that what loomed perhaps for England, what already did so much more than loom for crucified Belgium, what was let loose in a torrent upon indestructible France, might correspond more or less with the pressure of the old terrible time as the fighting South had had to know it, and with the grim conditions under which she had at last given way. For the rest of the matter, as I say, the difference of aspect produced by the difference of intensity cut short very soon my vision of similitude. The intensity swallowed up everything; the rate and the scale and the speed, the unprecedented engines, the vast incalculable connections, the immediate presence, as it were, of France and Belgium, whom one could hear pant, through the summer air, in their effort and their alarm, these things, with the prodigious might of the enemy added, made me say, dropping into humility in a manner that resembled not a little a drop into still greater depths, "Oh no, that surely can't have been 'a patch' on this!" Which conclusion made accordingly for a new experience altogether, such as I gratefully embrace here an occasion not to leave unrecorded.

It was in the first place, after the strangest fashion, a sense of the extraordinary way in which the most benign conditions of light and air, of sky and sea, the most beautiful English summer conceivable, mixed themselves with all the violence of action and passion, the other so hideous and piteous, so heroic and tragic facts, and flouted them as with the example of something far superior. Never were desperate doings so blandly lighted up as by the two unforgettable months that I was to spend so much of in looking over from the old rampart of a little high-perched Sussex town at the bright blue streak of the Channel, within a mile or two of us at its nearest point, the point to which it had receded after washing our rock-base in its earlier ages; and staring at the bright mystery beyond the rim of the furthest opaline reach. Just on the other side of that finest of horizon-lines history was raging at a pitch new under the sun; thinly masked by that shameless smile the Belgian horror grew; the curve of the globe toward these things was of the scantest, and yet the hither spaces of the purest, the interval representing only charm and calm and ease. One grew to feel that the nearer elements, those of land and water and sky at their loveliest, were making thus, day after day, a particular prodigious point, insisting in their manner on a sense and a wondrous story which it would be the restless watcher's fault if he didn't take in. Not that these were hints or arts against which he was in the least degree proof; they penetrated with every hour deeper into the soul, and, the contemplations I speak of aiding, irresistibly worked out an endless volume of references. It was all somehow the history of the hour addressing itself to the individual mind—or to that in any case of the person, at once so appalled and so beguiled, of whose response to the whole appeal I attempt this brief account. Roundabout him stretched the scene of his fondest frequentation as time had determined the habit; but it was as if every reason and every sentiment conducing to the connection had, under the shock of events, entered into solution with every other, so that the only thinkable approach to rest, that is to the recovery of an inward order, would be in restoring them each, or to as many as would serve the purpose, some individual dignity and some form.

It came indeed largely of itself, my main help to the reparatory, the reidentifying process; came by this very chance that in the splendor of the season there was no mistaking the case or the plea. "This, as you can see better than ever before," the elements kept conspiring to say, "is the rare, the sole, the exquisite England whose weight now hangs in the balance and your appreciation of whose value, much as in the easy years you may have taken it for granted, seems exposed to some fresh and strange and strong determinant, something that breaks in like a character of high color in a play." Nothing could have thrilled me more, I recognise, than the threat of this irruption or than the dramatic pitch; yet a degree of pain attached to the ploughed-up state it implied—so that, with an elderly dread of a waste of emotion, I fear I almost pusillanimously asked myself why a sentiment from so far back recorded as lively should need to become any livelier, and in fact should hesitate to beg off from the higher diapason. I felt as the quiet dweller in a tenement so often feels when the question of "structural improvements" is thrust upon him; my house of the spirit, amid everything about me, had become more and more the inhabited, adjusted, familiar home, quite big enough and sound enough for the spirit's uses and with any intrinsic inconvenience corrected long since by that principle's having cultivated and formed, at whatever personal cost (since my spirit was essentially a person) the right habits, and so settled into the right attitude, for practical, for contented occupation. If, however, such was my vulgar apprehension, as I put it, the case was taken out of my hands by the fate that so often deals with these accidents, and I found myself before long building on additions and upper storeys, throwing out extensions and protrusions, indulging even, all recklessly, in gables and pinnacles and battlements—things that had presently transformed the unpretending place into I scarce know what to call it, a fortress of the faith, a palace of the soul, an extravagant, bristling, flag-flying structure which had quite as much to do with the air as with the earth. And all this, when one came to return upon it in a considering or curious way, because to and fro one kept going on the old rampart, the town "look-out," to spend one's aching wonder again and again on the bright sky-line that at once held and mocked it. Just over that line were unutterable things, massacre and ravage and anguish, all but irresistible assault and cruelty, bewilderment and heroism all but overwhelmed; from the sense of which one had but to turn one's head to take in something unspeakably different and that yet produced, as by some extraordinary paradox, a pang almost as sharp.

It was of course by the imagination that this latter was quickened to an intensity thus akin to pain—but the imagination had doubtless at every turn, without exception, more to say to one's state of mind, and dealt more with the whole unfolding scene, than any other contributive force. Never in all my life, probably, had I been so glad to have opened betimes an account with this faculty and to be able to feel for the most part something to my credit there; so vivid I mean had to be one's prevision of the rate at which drafts on that source would require cashing. All of which is a manner of saying that in face of what during those horrible days seemed exactly over the way the old inviolate England, as to whom the fact that she *was* inviolate, in every valid sense of the term, had become, with long acquaintance, so common and dull, suddenly shone in a light never caught before and which was for the next weeks, all the magnificence of August and September, to reduce a thousand things to a sort of merciless distinctness. It was not so much that they leaped forth, these things, under the particular recognition, as that they multiplied without end and abounded, always in some association at least that caught the eye, all together overscoring the image as a whole or causing the old accepted synthesis to bristle with accents. The image as a whole, thus richly made up of them—or of the numberless testifying touches to the effect that we were not there on our sea defense as the other, the harried, countries were behind such bulwarks as they could throw up—was the central fact of consciousness and the one to which every impression and every apprehension more or less promptly related themselves; it made of itself the company in which for the time the mind most naturally and yet most importunately lived. One walked of course in the shade of the ambiguous contrast—ambiguous because of the dark question of whether it was the liabilities of Belgium and France, to say nothing of their awful actualities, that made England's state so rare, or England's state that showed her tragic sisters for doubly outraged: the action of the matter was at least that of one's feeling in one's hand and weighing it there with the last tenderness, for fullest value, the golden key that unlocked every compartment of the English character.

Clearly this general mystery or mixture was to be laid open under stress of fortune as never yet—the unprecedentedness was above all what came over us again and again, armaments unknown to human experience looming all the while larger and larger; but whatever face or succession of faces the genius of the race should most turn up the main mark of them all would be in the difference that, taken together, couldn't fail to keep them more unlike the peoples off there beyond than any pair even of the most approved of these peoples are unlike each other. "Insularity!"—one had spent no small part of one's past time in mocking or in otherwise fingering the sense out of that word; yet here it was in the air wherever one looked and as stuffed with meaning as if nothing had ever worn away from it, as if its full force on the contrary amounted to inward congestion. What the term essentially signified was in the oddest way a question at once enormous and irrelevant; what it might *show* as signifying, what it was in the circumstances actively and most probably going to, seemed rather the true consideration, indicated with all the weight of the evidence scattered about. Just the fixed *look* of England under the August sky, what was this but the most vivid exhibition of character conceivable and the face turned up, to repeat my expression, with a frankness that really left no further inquiry to be made? That appearance was of the exempt state, the record of the long safe centuries, in its happiest form, and even if any shade of happiness at such an hour might well seem a sign of profanity or perversity. To *that* there were all sorts of things to say, I could at once reflect, however; wouldn't it be the thing supremely in character that England should look most complacently herself, irradiating all her reasons for it, at the very crisis of the question of the true toughness, in other words the further duration, of her identity? I might observe, as for that matter I repeatedly and unspeakably did while the two months lasted, that she was pouring forth this identity, as atmosphere and aspect and picture, in the very measure and to the very top of her consciousness of how it hung in the balance. Thus one arrived, through the succession of shining days, at the finest sense of the case—the interesting truth that her consciously not being as her tragic sisters were in the great particular was virtually just her genius, and that the very straightest thing she could do would naturally be not to flinch at the dark hour from any profession of her genius. Looking myself more askance at the dark hour (politically speaking I mean) than I after my fashion figured her as doing in her mass, I found it of an extreme of quite an endless fascination to trace as many as possible of her felt idiosyncrasies back to her settled sea-confidence, and to see this now in turn account for so many other things, the smallest as well as the biggest, that, to give the fewest hints of illustration, the mere spread of the great trees, the mere gathers in the little bluey-white curtains of the cottage windows, the mere curl of the tinted smoke from the old chimneys matching that note, became a sort of exquisite evidence.

Exquisite evidence of a like general class, it was true, didn't on the other side of the Channel prevent the awful liability to the reach of attack—its having borne fruit and been corrected or averted again was in fact what half the foreign picture meant; but the foreign genius was other, other at almost every point; it had always in the past and on the spot, one remembered, expressed things, confessed things, with a difference, and part of that difference was of course the difference of history, the fact of exemption, as I have called it, the fact that a blest inviolacy was almost exactly what had least flourished. France and Belgium, to refer only to them, became dear accordingly, in the light I speak of, because, having suffered and suffered, they were suffering yet again, while precisely the opposite process worked for the scene directly beneath my eyes. England was interesting, to put it mildly—which is but a shy evasion of putting it passionately—because she hadn't suffered, because there were passages of that sort she had publicly declined and defied; at the same time that one wouldn't have the case so simple as to set it down wholly to her luck. France and Belgium, for the past, confessed, to repeat my term; while England, so consistently harmonised, with all her long unbrokenness thick and rich upon her, seemed never to do that, nor to need it, in order to practice on a certain fine critical, not to mention a certain fine prejudiced, sensibility. It was the season of sensibility now, at any rate for just those days and just that poor place of yearning, of merely yearning, vigil; and I may add with all emphasis that never had I had occasion so to learn how far sensibility may go when once well wound up. It was saying little to say I did justice easiest at once and promptness to the most advertised proposal of the enemy, his rank intention of clapping down the spiked helmet, than which no form of headgear, by the way, had ever struck one as of a more graceless, a more telltale platitude, upon the priceless genius of France; far from new, after all, was that measure of the final death in him of the saving sense of proportion which only gross dementia can abolish. Those of my generation who could remember the detached and frustrated purpose of a renewed Germanic pounce upon the country which, all but bled to death in 1871, had become capable within five years of the most penetrating irony of revival ever recorded, were well aware of how in that at once sinister and grotesque connection they had felt notified in time. It was the extension of the programme and its still more prodigious publication during the quarter of a century of interval, it was the announced application of the extinguisher to the quite other, the really so contrasted genius of the expression of which surrounded me in the manner I have glanced at, it was the extraordinary fact of a declared non-sufferance any longer, on Germany's part, of either of the obnoxious national forms disfiguring her westward horizon, and even though by her own allowance they had nothing intellectually or socially in common save that they were objectionable and, as an incident, crushable—it was this, I say, that gave one furiously to think, or rather, while one thanked one's stars for the luxury, furiously and all but unutterably to feel.

The beauty and the interest, the now more than ever copious and welcome expression, of the aspects nearest me found their value in their being so resistingly, just to that very degree of eccentricity, with that very density of home-grownness, what they were; in the same way as the character of the sister-land lately joined in sisterhood showed for exquisite because so ingrained and incorrigible, so beautifully all her own and inimitable on other ground. If it would have been hard really to give the measure of one's dismay at the awful proposition of a world squeezed together in the huge Prussian fist and with the varity and spontaneity of its parts oozing in a steady trickle, like the sacred blood of sacrifice, between those hideous knuckly fingers, so, none the less, every reason with which our preference for a better condition and a nobler fate could possibly bristle kept battering at my heart, kept in fact pushing into it, after the fashion of a crowd of the alarmed faithful at the door of a church. The effect was literally, yes, as of the occasion of some great religious service, with prostrations and exaltations, the light of a thousand candles and the sound of soaring choirs—all of which figured one's individual inward state as determined by the menace. One could still note at the same time, however, that this high pitch of private emotion was by itself far from meeting the case as the enemy presented it; what I wanted of course to do was to meet it with the last lucidity, the fullest support of particular defensive pleas or claims—and this even if what most underlay all such without exception came back to my actual vision, that and no more, of the general sense of the land. The vision was fed and fed to such a tune that in the quest for reasons, that is for the particulars of one's affection, the more detailed the better, the blades of grass, the outlines of leaves, the drift of clouds, the streaks of mortar between old bricks, not to speak of the call of child-voices muffled in the comforting air, became, as I have noted, with a hundred other like touches, casually felt, extraordinary admonitions and symbols, close links of a tangible chain. When once the question fairly hung there of the possibility, more showily set forth than it had up to then presumed to be, of a world without use for the tradition so embodied, an order substituting for this, by an unmannerly thrust, quite another and really, it would seem, quite a ridiculous, a crudely and clumsily improvised story, we might all have resembled together a group of children at their nurse's knee disconcerted by some tale that it isn't their habit to hear. We loved the old tale, or at least I did, exactly because I knew it; which leaves me keen to make the point, none the less, that my appreciation of the case for world-variety found the deeply and blessedly familiar perfectly consistent with it. This came of what I "read into" the familiar; and of what I did so read, of what I kept reading through that uplifted time, these remarks were to have attempted a record that has reached its limit sooner than I had hoped.

I was not then to the manner born, but my apprehension of what it was on the part of others to be so had been confirmed and enriched by the long years, and I gave myself up to the general, the native image I thus circled around as to the dearest and most precious of all native images. That verily became at the crisis an occupation sublime; which was not after all so much an earnest study of fond arrangement of the mixed aspects as a positive, a fairly sensual bask in their light, too kindled and too rich not to pour out by its own force. The strength and the copious play of the appearances acting in this collective fashion carried everything before them; no dark discrimination, no stiff little reserve that one might ever have made, stood up in the diffused day for a moment. It was in the opposite way, the most opposite possible, that one's intelligence worked, all along the line; so that with the warmth of the mere sensation that "they" were about as good, above all when it came to the stress, as could well be expected of people, there was the acute interest of the successive points at which one recognised why. This last, the satisfaction of the deepened intelligence, turned, I may frankly say, to a prolonged revel—"they" being the people about me and every comfort I had ever had of them smiling its individual smile straight at me and conducing to an effect of candor that is beyond any close notation. They didn't know how good they were, and their candor had a peculiar loveability of unconsciousness; one had more imagination at their service in this cause than they had in almost any cause of their own; it was wonderful, it was beautiful, it was inscrutable, that they could make one feel this and yet not feel with it that it at all practically diminished them. Of course if a shade should come on occasion to fall across the picture that shade would perhaps be the question whether the most restless of the faculties mightn't on the whole too much fail them. It beautified life, I duly remembered, it promoted art, it inspired faith, it crowned conversation, but hadn't it—always again under stress—still finer applications than these, and mightn't it in a word, taking the right direction, peculiarly conduce to virtue? Wouldn't it indeed be indispensable to virtue of the highest strain? Never mind, at any rate—so my emotion replied; with it or without it we seemed to *be* taking the right direction; moreover the next-best thing to the imagination people may have, if they can, is the quantity of it they may set going in others, and which, imperfectly aware, they are just exposed to from such others and must make the best of: their advantage becoming simply that it works, for the connection, all in their favour. That of the associated outsider the order of whose feelings, for the occasion, I have doubtless not given a wholly lucid sketch of, cultivated its opportunity week after week at such a rate that, technical alien as he was, the privilege of the great partaking, of shared instincts and ideals, of a communion of race and tongue, temper and tradition, put on before all the blest appearances a splendor to which I hoped that so long as I might yet live my eyes would never grow dim. And the great intensity, the melting together of the spiritual sources so loosed in a really intoxicating draught, was when I shifted my watch from near east to far west and caught the enemy, who seemed ubiquitous, in the long-observed effort that most fastened on him the insolence of his dream and the depth of his delusion. There in the west were those of my own fond fellowship, the other, the ready and rallying partakers, and it was on the treasure of our whole unquenchable association that in the riot of his ignorance, this at least apparently armor-proof, he had laid his unholy hands.

# THE COUNTRY NEWSPAPER[1]

*By* William Allen White

*William Allen White, editor of* The Emporia Gazette, *whose editorial, "What is the Matter with Kansas?" made him and Kansas famous, is a novelist, critic, and statesman, as well as one of the leading journalists of the United States. This essay was first published in* Harper's *in May, 1916. He was born in 1868.*

THE COUNTRY TOWN IS ONE of those things we have worked out for ourselves here in America. Our cities are not unlike other cities in the world; the trolley and the omnibus and the subway, the tender hot-house millionaire and the hardy, perennial crook are found in all cities. Class lines extend from city to city well around the globe. And American aversion to caste disappears when the American finds himself cooped in a city with a million of his fellows. But in the country town—the political unit larger than the village and smaller than the city, the town with a population between three and one hundred thousand—we have built up something distinctively American. Physically, it is of its own kind; the people for the most part live in detached wooden houses on lots with fifty feet of street frontage, and from one hundred to one hundred and fifty feet in depth. Grass is the common heritage of all the children—grass and flowers. A kitchen-garden smiles in the back yard, and the service of public utilities is so cheap that in most country towns in America electricity for lighting and household power, water for the kitchen sink and the bathroom, gas for cooking, and the telephone with unlimited use may be found in every house. In the town where these lines are written there are more telephones than there are houses, and as many water intakes as there are families, and more electric lights than there are men, women, and children. Civilization brings its labor-saving devices to all the people of an American country town. The uncivilized area is negligible, if one measures civilization by the use of the conveniences and luxuries that civilization has brought.

In the home, the difference between the rich and the poor, in these towns, is denoted largely by the multiplication of rooms; there is no very great difference in the kinds of rooms in the houses of those who have much and those who have little. And, indeed, the economic differences are of no consequence. The average American thinks he is saving for his children, and for nothing else. But if the child of the rich man and the child of the poor man meet in a common school, graduate from a common high-school, and meet in the country college or in the state university—and they do associate thus in the days of their youth—there is no reason why parents should strain themselves for the children; and they do not strain themselves. They relax in their automobiles, go to the movies, inhabit the summer boarding-house in the mountains or by the sea, and hoot at the vulgarity and stupidity of those strangers who appear to be rich and to be grunting and sweating and saving and intriguing for more money, but who really are only well-to-do middle-class people.

In the American country town the race for great wealth has slackened down. The traveler who sees our half-dozen great cities, who goes into our industrial centers, loafs about our pleasure resorts, sees much that is significantly American. But he misses much also if he fails to realize that there are in America tens of thousands of miles of asphalted streets arched by elms, bordered by green lawns, fringed with flowers marking the procession of the seasons, and that back from these streets stand millions of houses owned by their tenants—houses of from five to ten rooms, that cost from twenty-five hundred to twenty-five thousand dollars, and that in these houses live a people neither rural nor urban, a people who have rural traditions and urban aspirations, and who are getting a rather large return from civilization for the dollars they spend. Besides the civilization that comes to these people in pipes and on wires, they are buying civilization in the phonograph, the moving picture, the automobile, and the fifty-cent reprint of last year's fiction success. The Woman's City Federation of Clubs is bringing what civic beauty it can lug home from Europe and the Eastern cities; the opportune death of the prominent citizen is opening playgrounds and hospitals and parks; and the country college, which has multiplied as the sands of the sea, supplements the state schools of higher learning in the work of bringing to youth opportunities for more than the common-school education.

Now into this peculiar civilization comes that curious institution, the country newspaper. The country newspaper is the incarnation of the town spirit. The newspaper is more than the voice of the country-town spirit; the newspaper is in a measure the will of the town, and the town's character is displayed with sad realism in the town's newspapers. A newspaper is as honest as its town, is as intelligent as its town, as kind as its town, as brave as its town. And those curious phases of abnormal psychology often found in men and women, wherein a dual or multiple personality speaks, are found often in communities where many newspapers babble in many voices arising from the disorganized spirits of the place. For ten years and more the tendency in the American country town has been toward fewer newspapers. That tendency seems to show that the spirit of these communities is unifying. The disassociated personalities of the community—the wrangling bankers, the competing public utilities, the wets and the drys, the Guelfs and the Ghibellines in a score of guises that make for discord in towns—are slowly knitting into the spirit of the place. So one newspaper in the smaller communities—in communities under fifteen thousand, let us say—is becoming the town genus! And in most of the larger towns—so long as they are towns and not cities—one newspaper is rising dominant and authoritative because it interprets and directs the community. The others are merely expressions of vagrant moods; they are unhushed voices that are still uncorrelated, still unbridled in the community's heart.

It is therefore the country newspaper, the one that speaks for the town, that guides and cherishes the town, that embodies the distinctive spirit of the town, wherein one town differeth from another in glory—it is that country newspaper, which takes its color from a town and gives color back, that shall engage our attention at present. That newspaper shall be our vision.

Of old in this country the newspaper was a sort of poor relation in the commerce of a place. The newspaper required support, and the support was given, somewhat in charity, more or less in return for polite blackmail, and the rest for business reasons. The editor was a tolerated person. He had to be put on the chairmanship of some important committee in every community enterprise to secure his help. In times of social or political emergency, he sold stock in his newspaper company to statesmen. That was in those primeval days before corporations were controlled; so the editor's trusty job-press never let the supply of stock fall behind the demand. Those good old days were the days when the editor with the "trenchant pen" stalked to glory through libel-suits and shooting scrapes, and when most American towns were beset by a newspaper row as by a fiendish mania.

But those fine old homicidal days of the newspaper business are past, or are relegated to the less civilized parts of the land. The Colonel and the Major have gone gallantly to dreams of glory, perhaps carrying more buckshot with them to glory than was needed for ballast on their journey; but still they are gone, and their race has died with them. The newspaper man of to-day is of another breed. How the Colonel or the Major would snort in derision at the youth who pervades the country newspaper office to-day. For this young man is first of all a manufacturer! The shirt-tail full of type and the cheese press, which in times past were held as emblems of the loathed contemporary's plant, have now grown even in country villages, to little factories. The smallest offices now have their typesetting-machines. The lean, sad-visaged country printer, who had tried and burned his wings in the editorial flight, is no more. Instead we have a keen-eyed, dressy young man who makes eyes at the girls in the front office, and can talk shows with the drummer at the best hotel, or books with the high-school teacher in the boarding-house. This young gentleman operates the typesetting-machine. Generally he is exotic; frequently he is a traveler from far countries, but he rides in the Pullman and the clay of no highway ever stains his dainty feet. In the country town, in the factory that makes even the humblest of our country dailies, the little six and eight page affairs, all unknown, unhonored, and unsung, three or four and sometimes half a dozen of the smart, well-fed, nattily dressed machine operators are hired, and the foreman—the dear old pipe-smoking, unshaven foreman who prided himself in a long line of apprentice printers, the foreman who edited copy, who wrote the telegraph heads and ruled the reporters in the front office with an iron rod of terror, the foreman who had the power of life and death over every one around the building but the advertising man, the foreman who spent his princely salary of fifteen dollars a week buying meals for old friends drifting through with the lazy tide of traffic between the great cities, the foreman who could boast that he once held cases on the *Sun* and knew old Dana—that foreman is gone; in his place we know the superintendent. And, alas! the superintendent is not interested in preserving the romance of a day that is past. He is not bothered by the touch of a vanished hand. When the vanished hand tries to touch the superintendent of the country newspaper office to-day, a ticket to the Associated Charities' wood-yard is his dull response. The superintendent is interested largely in efficiency. The day of romance is past in the back room of the country newspaper.

But in the front room, in the editorial offices, in the business office even, there abides the spirit of high adventure that is incarnate in these marvelous modern times. Never before were there such grand doings in the world as we are seeing to-day. Screen the great war from us, and still we have a world full of romance, full of poetry, full of an unfolding progress that is like the gorgeous story of some enchanter's spell. Where in all the tales of those *Arabian Nights' Entertainments* is anything so wonderful as wireless telegraphy, so weird and uncanny as talking over the seas without wires? What is Cinderella and her romance compared with the Cinderella story to-day—the story that tells us how the world is turning into her prince, shortening her hours of work, guaranteeing her a living wage, keeping her little brothers and sisters away from the factory and in school, and pensioning her widowed mother that she may care for her little flock! How tame is the old Cinderella story beside this! And Sindbad is losing his load, too—slowly, as the years form into decades, Sindbad is sloughing off the old man of the sea; the twelve-hour day is almost gone, and the eight-hour day is coming quickly; the diseases and accidents of labor are falling from his shoulders, being assumed by his employer; his bank savings are guaranteed by his government; his food is no longer poisoned; his tenement is ceasing to be a pit of infection; his shop is no longer a place of torture. And every day the newspaper brings some fresh and inspiring chapter of these great stories to their readers. Stories of progress are the magnificent tales of sorcery and wizarding that come gleaming in celestial light across the pages of our newspapers every day. And in our country papers we rejoice in them, because we know the heroes. We know Cinderella; she works in our button-factory. We knew her father, who lived on Upper Mud Creek and was a soldier in the big war of the 'sixties. We know Sindbad; he is our neighbor and friend. He is not a mere number and a wheel-tender to us. We played with him as boys; we went to school with him in the lower grades before he had to leave, when his father died, to support the family. We see Cinderella and Sindbad every day, and when we read of their good fortunes we feel kindly toward the paper that tells us of these fine things. We open the country paper and say, "How blessed on the mountains are the feet of them that bring glad tidings," and so we read it, every line. It is the daily chronicle of the doings of our friends.

Of course our country papers are provincial. We know that as well as any one. But then, so far as that goes, we know that all papers are provincial. How we laugh at the provincialisms of the New York and Boston and Chicago papers when we visit the cities! For the high gods of civilization, being jealous of the press, have put upon all newspapers this spell: that every one must be limited in interest to its own town and territory. There can be no national daily newspaper, for before it reaches the nation its news is old and dull and as clammy as a cold pancake. News does not keep. Twelve hours from the press it is stale, flat, and highly unprofitable. However the trains may speed, however the organization of the subscription department and the press-room may perfect itself, the news spoils before the ink dries, and there never may be in our land a cosmopolitan press. So the cities' papers find that they must fill up those spaces, which in a nation-wide paper should be filled with the news from the far corners of our land, with city news. Thus in every country paper we have the local gossip of its little world. And our country papers are duplicated on a rather grander scale in the cities. What we do in six or eight or ten or twelve pages in the country, the city papers do in twenty or forty pages. What they do with certain prominent citizens in the social and criminal and financial world, we do also with our prominent citizens in their little worlds.

And in the matter of mere circulation, our American country newspapers are a feeble folk, yet they do as a matter of fact build their homes upon the rock. The circulation of daily newspapers in our cities—towns of over four hundred thousand—aggregates something over eleven millions. The other daily newspapers in the country circulate more than twelve millions, and the weeklies circulate twenty millions more, and most of these weeklies are printed in our small country towns. We have, therefore, a newspaper circulation of nearly thirty-four millions outside of our great cities, and only eleven millions in the great cities. At least so says our latest census bulletin. And the money we country editors have invested is proportionately larger than that our city brethren have invested.

But the beauty and the joy of our papers and their little worlds is that we who live in the country towns know our own heroes. Who knows Murphy in New York? Only a few. Yet in Emporia we all know Tom O'Connor—and love him. Who knows Morgan in New York? One man in a hundred thousand. Yet in Emporia who does not know George Newman, our banker and merchant prince? Boston people pick up their morning papers and read with shuddering horror of the crimes of their daily villain, yet read without that fine thrill that we have when we hear that Al Ludorph is in jail again in Emporia. For we all know Al; we've ridden in his hack a score of times. And we take up our paper with the story of his frailties as readers who begin the narrative of an old friend's adventures.

The society columns of our city papers set down the goings and comings, the marriages and the deaths of people who are known only by name; there are gowns realized only in dreams; there are social functions that seem staged upon distant stars. Yet you city people read of these things with avidity. But our social activities, chronicled in our country papers, tell of real people, whose hired girls are sisters to our hired girls, and so we know the secrets of their hearts. We know a gown when it appears three seasons in our society columns, disguised by its trimming and its covering, and it becomes a familiar friend. To read of it recalls other and happier days. And when we read of a funeral in our country newspapers, we do not visualize it as a mere church fight to see the grand persons in their solemn array on dress parade. A funeral notice to us country readers means something human and sad. Between the formal lines that tell of the mournful affair we read many a tragedy; we know the heartache; we realize the destitution that must come when the flowers are taken to the hospital; we know what insurance the dead man carried, and how it must be stretched to meet the needs. We can see the quiet lines on each side of the walk leading from the house of sorrow after the services—the men on one side, the women on the other—waiting to see the mourning families, and to be seen by them; we may smile through our tears at the uncongenial pall-bearers and wonder what common ground of mirth they will find to till on the way back from the cemetery. In lists of wedding-guests in our papers we know just what poor kin was remembered, and what was snubbed. We know when we read of a bankruptcy just which member of the firm or family brought it on, by extravagance or sloth. We read that the wife of the hardware merchant is in Kansas City, and we know the feelings of the dry-goods merchant who reads it and sees his own silks ignored. So when we see a new kind of lawn-mower on the dry-goods merchant's lawn, we don't blame him much for sending to the city for it.

Our papers, our little country papers, seem drab and miserably provincial to strangers; yet we who read them read in their lines the sweet, intimate story of life. And all these touches of nature make us wondrous kind. It is the country newspaper, bringing together daily the threads of the town's life, weaving them into something rich and strange, and setting the pattern as it weaves, directing the loom, and giving the cloth its color by mixing the lives of all the people in its color-pot—it is this country newspaper that reveals us to ourselves, that keeps our country hearts quick and our country minds open and our country faith strong.

When the girl at the glove-counter marries the boy in the wholesale house, the news of their wedding is good for a forty-line wedding-notice, and the forty lines in the country paper give them self-respect. When in due course we know that their baby is a twelve-pounder, named Grover or Theodore or Woodrow, we have that neighborly feeling that breeds the real democracy. When we read of death in that home we can mourn with them that mourn. When we see them moving upward in the world, into a firm, and out toward the country club neighborhood, we rejoice with them that rejoice. Therefore, men and brethren, when you are riding through this vale of tears upon the California Limited, and by chance pick up the little country newspaper with its meager telegraph service of three or four thousand words—or, at best, fifteen or twenty thousand; when you see its array of countryside items; its interminable local stories; its tiresome editorials on the waterworks, the schools, the street railroad, the crops, and the city printing, don't throw down the contemptible little rag with the verdict that there is nothing in it. But know this, and know it well: if you could take the clay from your eyes and read the little paper as it is written, you would find all of God's beautiful sorrowing, struggling, aspiring world in it, and what you saw would make you touch the little paper with reverent hands.

# "THE GENTLEMAN'S REVIEW"[1]

*By* F. M. Colby

---

*F. M. Colby, born in 1865 and died in 1925, for many years editor of the* International Year Book, *was one of the most incisive writers of ironic essay in English of his time. He wrote much upon literature, but more upon life direct. This essay was first published in "The Lion's Mouth" of* Harper's *for January, 1920.*

I WISH I COULD DO JUSTICE TO a certain sort of British literary journalism which I shall have to typify under the imaginary title of *The Gentleman's Review,* because to pick out a single one of the several competitors would be invidious. The essential point of *The Gentleman's Review* is that it is written by persons of the better sort for persons of the better sort. And not only must the writer be a better sort of person; he must constantly say that he is a better sort of person, and for pages at a time he must say nothing else. I have read long articles which when boiled down told the reader nothing else. I have read articles on socialism, patriotism, labor programs, poetry, the vulgarity of America and of the Antipodes, and on divers other subjects which did literally tell nothing else to the socialist, laborer, poet, or American or Antipodean outcast who read them. The gentility of the writers is never merely suggested; it is announced, and usually in terms of severity. A coal-heaver reading *The Gentleman's Review* would be informed in words of unsparing cruelty that he is low. Indeed, it seems the main purpose—at times the only purpose—for which *The Review* exists—to tell coal-heavers and other outside creatures that they are low. And by outside creatures I mean almost everybody. I mean not only all Americans, all Canadians, and other inhabitants of a hemisphere which, to say the least, is in the worst possible taste as a hemisphere, besides being notoriously external to the British Isles. I mean almost everybody in the right kind of hemisphere. I mean almost everybody in the British Isles, or even on the better streets of London. Only a handful of people can read the typical article of *The Gentleman's Review* without feeling that they are at the bottom of a social precipice.

The ideal of the true-born Gentleman's Reviewer is not only social exclusiveness, but mental exclusiveness. He does not argue against an idea of which his disapproves; he shows that idea to the door. In a long paper on socialism he will say at the start that he must really refuse to speak of socialism. The right sort of people do not speak of socialism. They have dismissed it from their minds. And he devotes his paper to developing the single point that the only way to deal with socialists is to expunge them from your list of acquaintances the moment you find out that they are socialists, and thereafter not to say a single word to them beyond conveying the bare information that they have been expunged. I recall just such a paper as this, and I recall the impression it made on seven extremely dignified persons whose successive letters to the editor, all dated from respectable London clubs, declared that in the opinion of the writers the danger of socialism could not be averted in any other way: Gentlemen must dismiss socialists from their company just as they had dismissed socialism from their minds. That done, socialism would perish.

A writer on a Labor-party program in *The Gentleman's Review* would no more think of meeting the arguments for the Labor-party program than he would think of meeting the laboring-man himself. Why bother to prove a Labor-party program unsound in face of the towering absurdity that there should be such a thing as a Labor party and that it should have such a thing as a program? There are social certitudes that gentlemen do not discuss. When Labor raises a question, the Gentleman's Reviewer, if he is true to type, will simply raise an eyebrow. When woman's progress was blackening the sky, I read dozens of articles in *The Gentleman's Review* on woman's suffrage from which I am sure no reader could make out anything whatever except that a shudder was running through some gentlemanly frames. At the threat of a revolt of the working-class some time ago, *The Gentleman's Review* became speechless almost immediately as to the nature of the revolt. It could only say that some labor leader had been impolite to a duke, and that it feared the lower classes might, if they kept on in their present courses, become impolite to dukes. The thought of other perils more horrible than that shocked it to silence. But perhaps it could not think of other things more horrible than that. There are things in this world that minds of this gentlemanly quality really must decline to meet. They are most of the things in this world.

It is at its best in rebuking other people's manners while unconsciously displaying its own. Take American manners, for instance. Forty years ago it was saying we were rude because we were young. It is still saying so. "Centuries of polite international tradition"—we are to understand that it took at least that much to make a Gentleman's Reviewer—are not behind us Americans. "Instinctive delicacy and sympathy with the feelings of others"—such as are displayed in the pages of *The Review*—"are not commonly possessed by the very young"—meaning, of course, possessed by Americans. Why, then, aspire to the courtesy and tact of ripe old world-wise Europe?

As a rude young thing I should not think of aspiring to it, if I did not read on the very next page, perhaps, that the whole share of the United States in the war, from the very beginning of it to the very end of it, was merely a "military parade." Then the "delicacy" and the "sympathy" and the "polite international tradition" of this fine old world-wise representative are suddenly brought not only within my reach, but within easy reach of almost any one. The cook and the bootblack and the garbage-man and I, and every sort of low American, including colored people, may now burst out spontaneously and joyously and unashamed with all the crudities inherent in our natures, knowing that we can go no farther in bad manners than the writers quoted have already gone—for the simple reason that there is no farther to go. If that is the degree of "traditional international politeness" required by the rich and mellow culture of an older world, why need a Ute or a Yahoo despair of it? Raw man from Oklahoma though I am, utterly unfinished, confined almost exclusively to the companionship of cows, backgroundless, uncouth, in social experience a tadpole, even I can be as delicately urbane as these exponents of an Old World culture.

Now I confess I have idealized the situation in representing this element of snobbery as the sole constituent of any single periodical. It may constitute only a part of a magazine or newspaper, and it may appear only sporadically. Several magazines which it pervaded largely at one time have since died of it, and others seem about to die. But it is still to be found in reassuring quantities, though scattered, and one could at any time, by judicious selection, make up a *Gentleman's Review*. I believe it is not only harmless, but desirable. It is not representative of the English people or of any English class. It is the unconscious burlesque—often a very good one—of insularity and pretension, and the world is the better for a good burlesque. It is no more like the courteous and witty Englishman one meets in life or in books or in the newspapers than is James Yellowplush. If Major Pendennis or the elder Osborne or Podsnap or Turveydrop came to life again and turned into literary persons, they would write like *The Gentleman's Review*. And it is pleasant to meet again the Pendennises, Podsnaps, and Turveydrops. Finally it has supplied many objects of entertaining satire to the best English writers of plays and fiction during our own generation. There is only one bad thing about it and that is entirely the fault of my fellow-countrymen. Owing to the unfortunate colonialism of the American literary class, there are quarters in which this sort of thing is taken seriously. I believe when that happens it is a surprise, even to the Gentleman's Reviewer himself. I believe even he is secretly aware that, whatever nature's reason for presenting him to a patient world may be, it cannot be for any such purpose as that.

# DO WE DESPISE THE NOVELIST?[1]

*By* W. L. George

*W. L. George, born in 1882, was well known as a writer of acute essays upon women and upon literature before he became a novelist. Indeed, his best work was unquestionably in the essay form. This article was first published in* Harper's *for March, 1918. He died in 1926.*

THERE ARE TIMES WHEN ONE wearies of literature; when one reads over one's first book, reflects how good it was, and how greatly one was misunderstood; when one considers the perils and misadventures of so accidental a life and likens one's self to those dogs described by Pliny, who run fast as they drink from the Nile for fear they should be seized by the crocodiles; when one tires of following Mr. Ford Madox Hueffer's advice, "to sit down in the back garden with pen, ink, and paper, to put vine leaves in one's hair and to write"; when one remembers that in Flaubert's view the literary man's was a dog's life (metaphors about authors lead you back to the dog), but that none other was worth living. In those moods, one does not agree with Flaubert; rather, one agrees with Butler:

Those that write in rhyme still make
The one verse for the other's sake;
For one for sense and one for rhyme,
I think's sufficient at one time.

One sees life like Mr. Polly, as "a rotten beastly thing." One sighs for adventure, to be a tramp or a trust magnate. One knows that one will never be so popular as Brown's Meat Extract; thence is but a step to picture oneself as less worthy.

We novelists are the showmen of life. We hold up its mirror, and, if it look at us at all, it mostly makes faces at us. Indeed, a writer might have with impunity sliced Medusa's head; she would never have noticed him. The truth is that the novelist is a despised creature. At moments when, say, a learned professor devotes five columns to showing that a particular novelist is one of the pests of society, the writer feels exalted. But as society shows no signs of wanting to be rid of the pest, the novelist begins to doubt his own pestilency. He is wrong. In a way, society knows of our existence, but does not worry; it shows this in a curiously large number of ways, more than can be enumerated here. It sees the novelist as a man apart—as a creature fraught with venom, and, paradoxically, a creature of singularly lamb-like and unpractical temperament.

Consider, indeed, the painful position of a respectable family; its sons make for Wall Street every day; its daughters for Fifth Avenue and fashion, or for the East Side, good works, and social advancement. Imagine that family, which derives a steady income, shall we say in the neighborhood of fifty thousand dollars a year, enough to keep it in modest comfort, confronted with the sudden infatuation of one of its daughters for an unnamed person, met presumably on the East Side where he was collecting copy. You can imagine the conversation after dinner:

Sadie: "What does he do, Papa? Oh, well, he's a novelist."

Papa: "What! A novelist? One of those long-haired, sloppy-collared ragamuffins without any soles to their boots? Do you think that because I've given you an automobile I'm going to treat you to a husband? A saloon loafer!" (We are always intemperate.) . . . "A man whom your mother and sisters . . ." (Our morals are atrocious.) . . . "I should not wonder if the police . . ." (We are all dishonest, and yet we never have any money.) . . . "I was talking to the minister . . ." (We practise no religion, except that occasionally we are Mormons.)

And so on, and so on. Papa won't have it, and if in the end Papa does have it (which he generally does when Sadie has made up her mind), he finds that Sadie's eyes are *not* blacked, but that Sadie's husband's boots *are* blacked; that the wretched fellow keeps a balance at the bank, can ride a horse, push a perambulator, drive a nail; but he does not believe it for a long time. For it is, if not against all experience, at any rate against all theory that a novelist should be eligible. The bank clerk is eligible, the novelist is not. We are not "safe"; we are adventurers, we have theories, and sometimes the audacity to live up to them. We are often poor, which happens to other men, and this is always our own fault, while it is often their misfortune. Of late years we have grown still more respectable than our forefathers, who were painfully so: Dickens lived comfortably in Marylebone; Thackeray reigned in a luxurious house near Kensington Square and in several first-class clubs; Walter Scott reached a terrible extreme of respectability—he went bankrupt, but later on paid his debts in full. Yet we never seem quite respectable, perhaps because respectability is so thin a varnish. Even the unfortunate girls whom we "entice away from good homes" into a squalor of the arts do not think us respectable. For them half the thrill of marrying a novelist consists in the horror of the family which must receive him; it is like marrying a quicksand, and the idea is so bitter that a novelist who wears his hair long might do well to marry a girl who wears hers short. He will not find her in the bourgeoisie.

The novelist is despised because he produces a commodity not recognized as "useful." There is no definition of usefulness, yet everybody is clear that the butcher, the car conductor, the stock-jobber are useful; that they fulfil a function necessary to the maintenance of the state. The pugilist, the dancer, the vaudeville actor, the novelist, provide nothing material, while the butcher does. To live, one wants meat, not novels. We need not pursue this too far and ask the solid classes to imagine a world without arts; presumably they could not. It is enough to point the difference and to suggest that we are deeply enthralled by the Puritan tradition which calls pleasure, if not noxious, at any rate unimportant; the maintenance of life is looked upon as more essential than the enjoyment thereof, so that many people picture an ideal world as a spreading corn-field dotted with cities that pay good rents, connected by railroads which pay good dividends. They resemble the revolutionary who on the steps of the guillotine said to Lavoisier, *"La République n'a pas besoin de savants."* This is obvious when the average man (which includes many women) alludes to the personality of some well-known writer. One he has come to respect—Mr. Hall Caine, because popular report says that his latest novel brought him in about half a million dollars; but such men as Mr. Arnold Bennett and Mr. H. G. Wells leave strange shadows upon his memory. Of Mr. Bennett he says: "Oh yes, he writes about the North Country, doesn't he? Or is it the West Country? Tried one of his books once. I forget its name, and, now I come to think of it, it may have been by somebody else. He must be a dreary sort of chap, anyhow; sort of Methodist."

Mr. H. G. Wells is more clearly pictured: "Wells? The fellow who writes about flying-machines and men in the moon? Jules Verne sort of stuff, isn't it? He's a Socialist."

And so out with Mr. Bennett, one of our best modern stylists, who, in spite of an occasional crowding of the canvas, has somehow fixed for us the singular and ferocious tribe from which he springs; so out with Mr. Wells with his restless, impulsive, combative, infinitely audacious mind. The average man says, "Flying-machines," and the passion of Mr. Wells for a beautiful, if somewhat over-hygienic, world is swept away. Those are leading instances. Others, such as Mr. Conrad, Mrs. Edith Wharton, O. Henry, Mr. Galsworthy, are not mentioned at all; if the name of Henry James is spoken, it leads up to a gibe at long sentences.

The attitude is simple; we are not taken seriously. Novelists have to take mankind seriously because they want to understand it; mankind is exempt from the obligation because it does not conceive the desire. We are not people who take degrees, who can be scheduled and classified. We are not doctors of science, licentiates of music schools. We are just men and women of some slight independence, therefore criminals; men who want to observe and not men who want to do, therefore incredible. And so, because we cannot fall into the classes made for those who can be classified, we are outside of class, below class. We are the mistletoe of the social oak.

It is perhaps in search of dignity and status that the modern novelist has taken to journalism. Journalism raises a novelist's status, for a view expressed by a fictitious character is not taken seriously, while the same view fastened to an event of the day acquires importance, satisfies the specific function of the press, which is more and more that of a champion of—found causes. The newspaper is a better jumping-off ground than the pulpit or the professorial chair; it enjoys a vast circulation, which the novel does not; it conveys an idea to millions of people who would never think of buying a newspaper for the sake of an idea, but who buy it for news, murder cases, or corn-market reports; it is a place where a writer may be serious, *because the newspaper is labeled as serious, while the novel is labeled as frivolous.*

This is vital to the proposition, and explains why so many novelists have sought refuge in the press. It is not exactly a question of money. Journalism rewards a successful novelist better than does the novel, though successful novelists make very good incomes; they often earn as much as the red-nosed comedian with the baggy trousers and the battered derby. Thackeray, Washington Irving, Kingsley, and notably Dickens knew the value of journalism. Dickens was the most peculiar case, for it is fairly clear that *Nicholas Nickleby* helped to suppress the exploiting schools and that *Oliver Twist* was instrumental in reforming workhouse law; both works were immensely successful, but Dickens felt that he wanted a platform where he could be always wholly serious—for this *Daily News* was born in 1846. Likewise, Mr. Wells has written enormously upon war and economics; Mr. Arnold Bennett has printed many political articles; Mr. Galsworthy has become more direct than a novelist can be, and writing largely on Cruelty to Animals, Prison Reform, etc. It is the only way in which we can be taken seriously. We must be solemn, a little dull, patriotic or unpatriotic, socialistic or conservative; there is only one thing we may not be, and that is creative and emotional.

It should be said in passing that even the press does not think much of us. Articles on solid subjects by novelists are printed, well paid for, sought after; it does a paper good to have an article on Demon Finance by Mr. Dreiser, or on Feminism by Mr. Zangwill. The novelist amounts to a poster; he is a blatant advertisement; he is a curiosity, the man who makes the public say, "I wonder what the *Daily* is up to now." But be assured that Mr. Zangwill's views on Feminism do not command the respectful treatment that is accorded a column leader in the *Times;* he is too human; he sparkles too much; he has not the matchless quality of those leaders which compel you to put on an extra stamp if you have to send the paper through the post.

The newspapers court the novelist as the people of a small town court the local rich man, but neither newspaper nor little town likes very much the object of its courtship. Except when they pay him to express them, the newspapers resent our having any views at all; the thought behind is always, "Why can't the fellows mind their own business, and go on writing about love and all that sort of stuff?" During the war, references to novelists who express their views have invariably been sneering; it is assumed that because we are novelists we are unable to comprehend tactics, politics—in fact, any "ics," except perhaps the entirely unimportant esthetics. But the peculiarity of the situation is that not a voice has been raised against professors of philology who write on finance, against bishops dealing with land settlement, against doctors when they remap Europe, against barristers, business men. They may say anything they like; they are plain, hard-headed men, while our heads are soft enough to admit a new idea.

To define the attitude of the press is in modern times to define the attitude of the state. From our point of view this is frigid. In America there are no means of gauging a novelist's position, for your classification rests upon breeding, celebrity, and fortune. Ours rests upon breeding and reliability. You are more adventurous than we. Britannia rides in a chariot, while your national emblem foreshadowed the aeroplane. And so, in America, it may profit a man as well to be a Jack London as an Elihu Root. You have no means of recognizing status, while in England we have honors. We distribute a great many honors, and indeed the time may come, as Mr. Max Beerbohm says, when everybody will be sentenced to a knighthood without the option of a fine. Honors are rather foolish things, monuments that create a need for circumspection; they are often given for merits not easily perceived, but still they are a *rough* test of status. Setting aside money, which is the primary qualification, and justifies Racine in saying that without money honor is but a disease, a title is a fairly clear sign of distinction. Sir Edward Shackleton, Sir Douglas Haig, Sir Frederick Treves, Lord Reading, Sir William Crookes, Lord Lister—all those titles are obvious recognition of prominence in polar exploration, the army, the law, medicine, research, as the case may be; there are scores of medical knights, many law lords, many major-generals, and admirals endowed with the Knight Commandership of the Bath. We do not complain. They deserve their honors, most of them. They deserve them more than the politicians who have received for long service rewards that ability could not give them, than the Lord Mayors who are titled because they sold, for instance, large quantities of kitchen fenders. When we consider the arts, we observe a discrepancy. The arts do not ask for honors; they are too arrogant, and know that born knights cannot be knighted. Only they claim that an attempt should be made to honor them, to grant them Mr. Gladstone's and Mr. Chamberlain's privilege of refusing honors.

Consider, for instance, the Order of Merit, one of the highest honors that the British Crown can confer. At the end of last year it numbered twenty-one members. Among them were some distinguished foreigners—Prince Oyama, Prince Yamagata, and Admiral Togo; historians, pro-consuls, four admirals, and one novelist, Mr. Thomas Hardy. We do not complain that only Mr. Thomas Hardy was chosen, for there is nobody else to set at his side—only we do complain that in this high order four admirals find a place. Are we then so rich in admiralty, so poor in literature? The same is still truer when we come to the inferior orders, which are still fairly high, such as the Commandership of the Bath. That ancient order is almost entirely recruited from among soldiers, sailors, politicians, and civil servants; it does not hold the name of a single novelist. Only one novelist, Sir Gilbert Parker, is a Privy Councilor, though the position is honorific and demands no special knowledge. On the Privy Council you find labor members of Parliament, barristers, coal-owners, sellers of chemicals and other commodities. In all the other orders it is the same thing; for novelists there are neither Commanderships of the Bath, nor of the Victorian Order, nor St. Michael and St. George, no honors great or minor; no man has ever in England been offered a peerage *because* he wrote novels; and yet he has been offered a peerage because he sold beer. George Meredith was not offered a peerage, even though some think that his name will live when those of captains and kings have melted into dust. Our little band of recognized men such as Sir James Barrie, Sir Rider Haggard, Sir Arthur Conan Doyle—small is the toll they have taken of public recognition; perhaps they should not expect it; perhaps they have been recognized only because of certain political activities; but must we really believe that so many lawyers and so few writers are worthy of an accolade? Is the novelist worthless until he is dead? This picture may seem too black, and, indeed, it is mainly that of Great Britain, where contempt for literature has risen to a peculiar degree, but even in your country it applies. Make an imaginative effort; see yourself in the reception-room of some rich man in New York, where a "crush" of celebrities is taking place. A flunky at the head of the stairs announces the guests. He announces: "Mr. Charles Evans Hughes! . . . Mr. W. D. Howells! . . . The Bishop of Oklahoma!" Who caused a swirl in the "glided throng"? The notable cleric? The former candidate for the Presidential chair? Or your premier novelist? Be honest in your reply to yourself, and you will know who, at that hypothetical reception, created a stir. The stir, according to place or period, greeted the politician or the bishop, and only in purely literary circles would Mr. Howells have been preferred. For the worship of crowds goes to power rather than to distinction; to the recognized functionary of the state, to him whose power can give power, to all the evanescent things and seldom to those stockish things, the mile-stones on the road to eternity. The attitude of the crowd is the attitude of the state, for the state is only the crowd, and often just the mob; it is the chamberlain of ochlocracy, the leader who follows. In all times the state has shown its indifference, its contempt, for the arts, and particularly for literature. Now and then a prince, such as Louis of Bavaria, Philip of Spain, Lorenzo the Magnificent, has given to literature more than respect. He has given love, but that only because he was a man before a prince. The prince must prefer the lawyer, the politician, the general, and indeed of late years what prince was found to patron George Meredith or Henry James?

The attitude of the state to the novelist defines itself most clearly when a royal commission is appointed. In England royal commissions are *ad hoc* bodies appointed by the Government from among men of political influence and special knowledge, to investigate a special question.

As a rule they are well composed. For instance, a royal commission on water-supply would probably comprise two or three members of Parliament of some standing, the president of the Institute of Civil Engineers, a professor of sanitation, a canal expert, one or two trade-unionists, one or two manufacturers, and a representative of the Home Office or the Board of Trade. Any man of position who has shown interest in public affairs may be asked to sit on a royal commission—provided he is not a novelist. Only one novelist has attained so giddy a height—Sir Rider Haggard. How it happened is not known; it must have been a mistake. We are not weighty enough, serious enough, to be called upon, even if our novels are so weighty and so serious that hardly anybody can read them. We are a gay tribe of Ariels, too light to discuss even our own trade. For royal commissions concern themselves with our trade, with copyright law, with the restriction of the paper-supply. You might think that, for instance, paper-supply concerned us, for we use cruel quantities, yet no recognized author sat on the commission; a publisher was the nearest approach. Apparently there were two great consumers of paper, authors and grocers, but the grocers alone were consulted. What is the matter with us? Is our crime that we put down in indecent ink what we think and feel, while other people think and feel the same, but prudently keep it down? Possibly our crimes are our imagination and our tendency to carry this imagination into action. Bismarck said that a state conducted on the lines of the Sermon on the Mount would not last twenty-four hours; perhaps it is thought that a state in the conduct of which a novelist had a share would immediately resolve itself into a problem play. Something like that, though in fact it is unlikely that Ariel come to judgment would be much more fanciful in his decrees than the historic Solomon.

All this because we lack solidity—and yet the public calls us commercial, self-advertisers, money-grubbers. It is thought base that we should want three meals a day, though nobody suggests that we can hope to find manna in the street, or drink in our parks from the fountain Hippocrene. We are told that we make our contracts too keenly, that we are grasping, that we are not straight—and yet we are told that we are not business men. What are we to do? Shall we form a trade-union and establish a piece rate? Shall we sell our novels by the yard? May we not be as commercial and respected as the doctor who heals with words and the lawyer who strangles with tape?

Now and then the defenses of society and state are breached and a novelist enters Parliament. Mr. Hilaire Belloc, Mr. A. E. W. Mason followed Disraeli into the House of Commons, but it is very extraordinary. No one knows how these gentlemen managed to convince the electors that with their eye "in fine frenzy rolling" they would not scandalize their party by voting against it. (Those writing chaps, you know, they aren't *safe!*)

It must be said that once in Parliament the novelists did not have a very good time; they were lucky in having been preferred to a landowner, or a pawnbroker, but once in they had not the slightest chance of being preferred to those estimable members of society. It was not a question of straight votes; it never came to that, for Mr. Belloc soon disagreed with both sides and became a party of one, while Mr. A. E. W. Mason as a rush light flickered his little flicker and went out. It is as well; they would never have been taken seriously. It is almost a tradition that they should not be taken seriously, and it is on record in most of the worldly memoirs of the nineteenth century that the two main objections to Disraeli were his waistcoats and his authorship of *Contarini Fleming*. Nero liked to see people burned alive; Disraeli wrote novels. Weaknesses are found in all great men.

There seems in this to lie error as well as scandal. When a new organization is created, say for the control of lamp-oil, obviously a novelist should not be made its chairman, but why should a blotting-paper merchant be preferred? Indeed, one might side with Mr. Zangwill, who demands representation for authors in the Cabinet itself, on the plea that they would introduce the emotion which is necessary if the Cabinet is to manage impulsive mankind. As he finely says, we are professors of human nature; if only some university would give us a title and some initials to follow our name, say P.H.N., people might believe we knew something of it. But the attitude of the state in these matters is steadfast enough. It recognizes us as servants rather than citizens; if in our later years we come upon hard times, we can be given, through the Civil List, pensions which rescue us from the indignities of the poorhouse, but no more. Mostly these pensions benefit our heirs, but the offering is so small that it shocks; it is like tipping an ex-President a dollar. Thus Mr. W. B. Yeats enjoys a pension of $750, Mr. Joseph Conrad, of $500. Why give us pensions at all if they must be alms? One cannot be dignified on $500 a year;

one can be dignified on $25,000 a year, because the world soon forgets that you ride a gift house, if that horse is a fine, fat beast. The evidence is to be found in the retiring pensions of our late lord chancellors, who receive $25,000 a year; of our judges, $5,000 to $18,750; in the allowances made to impoverished politicians, which attain $10,000. Out of a total of $1,600,000 met by our Civil List, literature, painting, science, research, *divide* every year $6,000. Nor do the immediate rewards show greater equality. Lord Roberts was voted $500,000 for his services in South Africa; Mr. Thomas Hardy has not yet been voted anything for *The Dynasts*. I suspect that America is just as dull.

The shame of literature is carried on even into the following generations. The present Lord Nelson, who is not a poor man, for he owns seven thousand acres of land, is still drawing a pension of $25,000 a year, earned by his august ancestor, but the daughter of Leigh Hunt must be content with $250. We are unknown. We are nobody; Rouget de l'Isle, author of "La Marseillaise," gave wings to the revolutionary chariot, but tiny, bilious, tyrannic Robespierre rode in it, and rides in it to-day through the pages of history, while men go to their death singing the words of Rouget de l'Isle and know him not.

Even in our own profession of authorship the novelist is an object of disdain. We are less than the economists, the historians, the political writers; we amuse while they teach; they bore, and as they bore it is assumed that they educate, dullness always having been the sorry companion of education. Evidence is easily found; there exists a useful, short encyclopedia called *Books that Count.* It contains the names of about four thousand authors, out of whom only sixty-three are novelists. Divines whose sermons do not fetch five cents at the second-hand bookseller's, promoters of economic theories long dispatched, partisan historians, mendacious travelers—they crowd out of the *Books That Count* the pale sixty-three novelists, all that is left of the large assembly that gave us *Tom Jones* and *The Way of All Flesh.* This attitude we observe in most reference-books. We observe it, for instance, in the well-known *Who's Who Year Book,* which, amazing as it seems, contains no list of authors. The book contains a list of professors, including dental surgery, a list of past presidents of the Oxford Union, a list of owners of Derby winners, but not a list of authors. The editors of this popular reference book know what the public wants; apparently the public wants to know that Mr. Arthur H. King is general manager of the Comercial Bank of London, Ltd.—but the public does not want to know that Mr. Anatole France is a great man. The only evidence of notice is a list of our pseudonyms. It matters that Mr. Richard Le Gallienne should write under the name of "Logroller," for that is odd. Mr. Le Gallienne, being an author, is a curiosity; it matters to nobody that he is a man.

What is the area of a novelist's reputation? How far do the ripples extend when he casts a novel into the whirlpool of life? It is difficult to say, but few novelists were ever so well known to the people as were in their time such minor figures as Rockefeller or Dingley, nor is there a novelist to-day whose name can vie with that of, say, Mr. Roosevelt. It is strange to think that Dickens himself could not in his own day create as much stir as such obscure personages as Captain Waddell, Peabody or President Johnson. He lacked political flavor; he was merely one of the latter-day prophets who lack the unique advertisement of being stoned. It will be said that such an instance is taken from the masses of the world, most of whom do not read novels, while all are affected by the politician, but in those circles that support literature the same phenomenon appears: the novel may be known; the novelist is not. The novel is not respected and, indeed, one often hears a woman at a big lending library ask for "three of the latest novels." New novels! Why not new potatoes? She takes the books away calmly, without looking at the titles or the names. She is quite satisfied; sometimes she does not care very much whether or not she has read those novels before, for she does not remember them. They go in at one ear and come out at the other, presumably, as a judge said, because there is nothing to stop them.

It is undeniable that the great mass of readers forgets either names or titles; many forget both. Some of the more educated remember the author and ask their library for "something by Henry Sydnor Harrison," because he writes such sweet, pretty books, a definition where slander subtly blends with veracity. But, in most cases, nothing remains of either author or title except in hazy impression; the reader is not quite sure whether the book she liked so much is *Fraternity* or the *Corsican Brothers*. She will know that it had something to do with family, and that the author's name began with "G"—unless it was "S." It cannot be otherwise, so long as novels are read in the way they are read—that is to say, if they are taken as drugs. Generally, novels are read to dull the mind, and many succeed, ruining the chances of those whose intent is not morphean, which fulfil the true function of art—*viz.*, to inflame. The object of a novel is not to send the reader to sleep, not to make him oblivious of time on a railway journey; it is not to be propped up against a cruet and consumed between the chop and the pudding; it is meant to show character, to stimulate observation, to make life vivid, and as life is most vivid when it is most unpleasant, the novel that is worth reading is set aside. For such novels stir the brain too much to let it go to sleep. Those novels are judged in the same way as the baser kind, and that is perhaps why the novel itself stands so low. It does stand low, at least in England, for it is almost impossible to sell it to the public. Inquiries made of publishers show that they expect to sell to the circulating libraries seventy to seventy-five per cent. of the copies printed. To sell to a circulating library is not selling; it is lending at one remove; it means that a single copy bought by a library is lent out to anything between twenty and a hundred people. Sometimes it is read by more, for it is sold off when the subscribers no longer want to hire it. It goes to a town of the size of, say, Tacoma. Discarded after a year or so by this second set of subscribers, it may be sold off for two or three cents, with one thrown into the dozen for luck, and arrive with its cover hanging on in a way that is a testimonial to the binder, with its pages marked with thumbs, stained with tears, or, as the case may be, with soup, at some small stationer's shop in a little market town, to go out on hire at two cents a week, until it no longer holds together, and goes to its eternal rest in the pulping machine. On the way, nobody has bought it except to let it out, as the padrone sends out the pretty Italian boys with an organ and a monkey. The public have not bought the books to read and to love. The twenty-five or thirty per cent. actually sold have been disposed of as birthday or Christmas presents, because one has to give something, and because one makes more effect with a well-bound book for a dollar than with two dollars' worth of chocolates. Literature has been given its royalty on the dollar of economy. Yet, impossible as the novel finds it to tear its dollar from the public, the theater easily wheedles it into paying five dollars or more for two stalls. It seems strange that two people will pay five dollars to see a dramatized novel on the boards, yet would never dream of giving a dollar for the original book. That is because theater seats must be paid for, while books can be borrowed. Plays, and especially players, can be remembered; a book may be returned. It goes so far that novelists are continually asked "where one can get their books," meaning "where they can be borrowed"; often they are asked to lend a copy, while no one begs a ride from a cabman. Things are not as bad as that in America; why the lending library has not asserted itself in your country is difficult to say, for clotted masses of population are the atmosphere in which it lives. It may be due to your novels being published at a cheap rate; it may be that a large proportion of your population is not clotted, but is so scattered that a library could not reach it; it may be that the high quality of the American magazine has created a reading public. Or it may be that you are just barbarians with all the generosity of the savage, and that when your civilization is ancient you will acquire the vices of ours. That is what generally happens in the course of civilization.

In England, the public of the novel is almost exclusively feminine. Few men read novels, and a great many nothing at all except the newspaper. They say that they are too busy, which is absurd when one reflects how busy is the average woman. The truth is that they are slack and ignorant. They have some historic reason to despise the novel, or it is quite true that in the nineteenth century, with a few exceptions, such as Thackeray, Jane Austen, Charlotte Brontë, Nathaniel Hawthorne, Dickens, Scott, George Eliot, the three-volume novel was trash. It dealt generally with some rhetorical Polish hero, a high-born English maiden, cruel parents, and Italian skies. Right up to 1885 that sort of thing used to arrive every morning in a truck at the lending library, but if it still arrives in truckloads, it should not be forgotten that other novels arrive, too. That is what the men do not know. If they read at all you will find them solemnly taking in "The Reminiscences of Mr. Justice X. Y. Z.," or "Shooting Gazelles in Bulbulland," "Political Economics," or "Economic Politics" (it means much the same either way up). All that sort of thing—that frozen, dried-up, elderly waggishness, that shallow pomp, is mentally murderous. Sometimes men do read novels, mostly detective stories, sporting or very sentimental tales. When observed, they apologize and say something about resting the brain. That means that they do not respect the books they read, which is base; it is like keeping low company, where one can yawn and put one's boots on the sofa. Now no company is low unless you think it is. As soon as you realize that and stay, you yourself grow naturalized to it. Likewise, if you read a book without fellowship and respect for its author, you are outraging it. But mankind is stupid, and it would not matter very much that a few men should read novels in that shamefaced and patronizing way if they were not so open about it. If they do not apologize, they boast that they never read a novel; they imply superiority. Their feminine equivalent is the serious-minded girl who improves her mind with a book like *Vicious Viscounts of Venice;* if she reads novels at all, she holds that, like good wine, they improve with keeping, and must be at least fifty years old. By that time the frivolous author may have redeemed his sins.

It is because of all these people, the people who borrow and do not cherish, the people who skim, the people who indulge and cringe, and the people who do not indulge at all, that we have come to a corruption of literary taste, where the idea is abashed before the easy emotion, where religiosity expels religion, and the love passion turns to heroics or to maundering, that the success of the second-rate has come about. It is a killing atmosphere. It is almost incomprehensible, for when the talk is of a political proposal, say of land settlement in the Northwest, or of a new type of oil engine, hardly a man will say, "I am not interested." He would be ashamed to say that. It would brand him as a retrograde person. Sometimes he will say, "I do not like music," but he will avoid that if he can, for music is an evidence of culture; he will very seldom confess that he does not care for pictures; he will confess without any hesitation that he does not care for any kind of book. He will be rather proud to think that he prefers a horse or a balance-sheet. It will seldom occur to him that this literature of which some people talk so much can hold anything for him. It will not even occur to him to try, for literature is judged at Jedburgh. It hardly ever occurs to any one that literature has its technique, that introductions to it are necessary; a man will think it worth while to join a class if he wants to acquire scientific knowledge, but seldom that anything in the novel justifies his taking preliminary steps. It is not that literature repels him by its occasional aridity; it is not that he has stumbled upon classics, which, as Mr. Arnold Bennett delightfully says, "are not light women who turn to all men, but gracious ladies whom one must long woo." Men do not think the lady worth wooing. This brings us back to an early conclusion in this chapter: novelists are not useful; we are pleasant, therefore despicable. Our novels do not instruct; all they can do is to delight or inflame. We can give a man a heart, but we cannot raise his bank interest. So our novels are not worthy of his respect because they do not come clad in the staid and reassuring gray of the text-book; they are not dull enough to gain the respect of men who appreciate only the books that bore them, who shrink away from the women who charm them and turn to those who scrag their hair off their foreheads, and bring their noses, possibly with a cloth, to a disarming state of brilliancy.

Sometimes, when the novelist thinks of all these things, he is overcome by a desperate mood, decides to give up literature and grow respectable. He thinks of becoming a grocer, or an attorney, and sometimes he wants to be the owner of a popular magazine, where he will exercise, not the disreputable function of writing, but the estimable one of purchasing. Then the mood passes, and he is driven back to Flaubert's view that it is a dog's life, but the only one. He decides to live down the extraordinary trash that novelists produce. Incredible as truth may be, fiction is stranger still, and there is no limit to the intoxications of the popular novelist.

The novel is a commodity, and if it seeks a wide public it must make for a low one: the speed of a fleet is that of its slowest ship; the sale of a novel is the capacity of the basest mind. Only it might be remembered that all histories are not accurate, all biographies not truthful, all economic text-books not readable. Likewise, it should be remembered, and we need quote only Mr. W. D. Howells, in evidence, that novels are not defined by the worst of their kind. . . . It is men's business to find out the best books; they search for the best wives; why not for the best novels? There are novels that one can love all one's life, and this cannot be said of every woman.

There are to-day in England about twenty men and women who write novels of a certain quality, and about as many who fail, but whose appeal is to the most intelligent. These people are trying to picture man, to describe their period, to pluck a feather from the wing of fleeting time. They do not write about radium murders, or heroines clad in orchids and tiger-skins. They strive to seize a little of the raw life in which they live. The claim is simple; even though we may produce two thousand novels a year which act upon the brain in the evening as cigarettes do after lunch, we do put forth a small number of novels which are the mirror of the day. Very few are good novels, and perhaps not one will live, but many a novel, concerned with labor problems, money, freedom in love, will have danced its little dance to some purpose, will have created unrest—always better than stagnation, will have aroused controversy, anger; impelled some people, if not to change their life, at least to tolerate that others should do so. *The New Machiavelli, Huckleberry Finn, The White Peacock, The Rise of Silas Lapham, Ethan Frome*—none of those perhaps is a supreme book, but every one of them is a hand-grenade flung at the bourgeoisie; we do not want to kill it, but we do want to wake it up.

It is the bourgeoisie's business to find out the novels that will wake it up; it should take as much pains to do this as to find out the best cigar. The bourgeoisie has congestion of the brain; the works of scholars will stupefy it still more; only in the novelists of the day, who are rough, unpleasant, rebellious, restless, will they find a remedy.

Whether the reading public can discern that undying flame in the choking smoke of books written for money and not for love, is another question. Every year more novels are published, but when one considers the novelists of the past, Thackeray's continual flow of sugary claptrap, the incapacity of Dickens to conceive beauty, the almost unrelieved, stagey solemnity of Walter Scott, the novelist of to-day is inclined to thank God that he is not as other men. Those old writers trod out paths for us, but they walked blindfold; let us recognize their splendid qualities, their feeling for atmosphere, their knowledge of men, but we find more that is honest and hopeful in a single page of *Tono-Bungay* than in all the great Victorians put together. Yes, we are arrogant. Why not? Why should it be natural to us to see our faults and not our talents? We are held in contempt, but such was the fate of every prophet; they make us into mummers and we learn mummery, but Balzac and Turgenev rise from their own dust. We are not safe people, or quiet people; not tame rabbits in a hutch, nor even romantic rogues; most of us are no more romantic than jockeys.

It is, perhaps, because we are not safe (and are we any less safe than mining magnates?) that we are disliked. We are disliked, as Stendhal says, because all differences create hatred; because by showing it its face in the glass we tend to disrupt society, to exhibit to its shocked eyes what is inane in its political constitution, barbarous in its moral code. We are queer people, nasty people, but we are neither nastier nor queerer than our fellows. We are merely more shameless, and exhibit what they hide. We have got outside, and we hate being outside; we should so much like to enlist under the modern standard, the silk hat, and yet we are arrogant. Doctors, judges, bishops, merchants, think little of us; we regret it and we rejoice in it. We are unhappy and exalted adventurers in the frozen fields of human thought. We are the people who make the "footprints on the sands of time." Later on, the bourgeoisie will tread in them.

# FAME[1]

*By* HENRY MILLS ALDEN

*Henry Mills Alden, for many years editor of* Harper's Magazine, *wrought powerfully for criticism and morals in his department, "The Editor's Study." This essay was published anonymously in July, 1907. He was born in 1836, and was editor of the Magazine from 1869 until his death in 1919.*

THE DESIRE FOR FAME, AS A motive to literary expression, seems to us hardly worth considering, thought it is generally assumed to be the strongest incentive, and the noblest, provided it be an aspiration and not an ambition.

"The thoughts of the boy are long, long thoughts," and in this expansion of the youthful mind the prospect is as immense as the retrospect, and the future is thronged with as eminent personages, the creatures of his imagination, as the past is with those history has made him acquainted with. He is a part of this coming eminence, since it has no shape except in his own dreams, but the vista stretching out before him and his relation to it are as vague as his dreams are. What he is to meet is so different from what he feigns, after the fashion of the past, that whatever definite goal he may set before him is likely to vanish and the veil of his cherished vision to be broken the moment he enters upon his course.

No great writer has ever consciously striven for a deathless fame. Such a writer is wholly absorbed in his work. Any vague desire he may have hitherto nourished is displaced by a distinct vision of beauty and truth which eclipses every ulterior objec , demanding only and imperatively its own embodiment. Like Horace, he must be able to say *exegi monumentum* before he exclaims *Non omnis moriar!*

It was in an essay showing the advantages of obscurity

that Cowley said, "I love and commend a true, good fame, because it is the shadow of virtue, not that it doth any good to the body which it accompanies, but it is an efficacious shadow, and, like that of St. Peter, cures the diseases of others." The writer's immortality is not his own concern, but that of his posterity. To the student of literature it is of interest because the conditions which determine it are inseparable from those which determine the evolution of literature itself.

We have reached a stage in this evolution—have reached it indeed at the very point in time where we now stand—in which the conditions affecting an author's prosperity with his present audience, as related to that which he may hope for with any possible audience of the future, challenge our attention. We are witnessing the culmination of a movement which began two centuries ago and which marked a distinct breach with antiquity. It was initiated with the advent of periodical literature in popular miscellanies, a literary transformation through the diversion of genius into new channels, new modes of expression. It had an earlier cradling, since it was really due to an audience which had expanded beyond the limits of that society of the erudite hitherto addressed by select authors—the society for which books like Burton's *Anatomy of Melancholy* was written, and which had fostered pedantry in the best writers, off the stage, ever since there had been any English writing.

The wider audience consisted, on the one hand, of the elegant and refined who, since the Restoration, had welcomed poets like Herrick and Butler—the author of "Hudibras"—and Gay and Prior, and, on the other, of the common people, for whom Bunyan had written, and who had been educated under non-conformist and democratic influences. This audience demanded a more familiar communication, and periodical literature, heralded by the already successful newspaper and bold pamphleteer, assumed that office. But in this undertaking the periodical was very soon surpassed by the novel of English society, which in its earliest examples, from the pen of Henry Fielding, was far less antique than Doctor Johnson's magazine essays, and which, in its familiar appeal and idiomatic speech, inherited from the *Spectator*. The novel was then something quite separate from the periodical; when they coalesced in the next century they together finally accomplished the literary revolution which each had independently initiated.

The full effect of the transformation is apparent only in our own time, but, from the first establishment of ready channels for familiar communication between writers and a large body of readers, it is obvious that both writing and reading began to mean something different from what they had meant before. The real modernity of literature was then ushered in, and it has been developed along with that modernity of our life which has been intensified by the employment of steam and electricity for the annihilation of distance in space and time. The breach with antiquity was a departure, not from what we call the ancient and medieval world—it came too late for definition in those stereotyped terms—but from an old order of life as well as of literature in which the people were supinely participant but had no initiative, no voice but that of assent. This order had maintained itself long after the Renaissance, and for more than two centuries after the discovery of America. It was an aristocratic régime; class distinctions had the fixity of established types, marked by clearly visible external insignia; letters and the fine arts were under noble patronage; the social organization of every realm was consolidated by military discipline and, in every movement, impelled by arbitrary sovereignty, marched with processional regularity, as if keeping step to martial music: altogether a picturesque and impressive spectacle, in which monarchs and prelates and warriors shone with varied and conspicuous distinction.

The harmony of the order itself was sustained, by whatever frequent and devastating conflicts the peace of the world was disturbed. Its stability survived those delimitations of empires which were forever transforming the map of Europe and Asia and America. The entire period of its existence was studded with Great Events, chiefly wars, and literature seemed mainly to be the reflection of these, from Homer's story of the siege of Troy to Addison's celebration of the Battle of Blenheim. The writers whose renown is bound up with the splendors they reflected were for the most part poets, who kept step with that old processional. When the people began to have a voice in public affairs and a popular audience began to determine the course of literature, making its demands felt there, the ancient régime was doomed, and a writer's renown came to depend upon his partnership with his readers—with their thought and feeling—as to both his matter and manner. His predecessors had shared the glory of the great ones of the earth, and their fame was that of a like spectacular eminence. Whatever greatness they had in themselves was recognized only by the few who still could read them, but their names shone forever in the literary heavens, remote and unassailable.

Such popular audiences as there had been in the old régime were not made up of readers, were indeed illiterate, listeners and lookers-on at stage representations, at forensic displays, and at stately political or religious functions. Whatever argument or theme there was in these, something for the ear and the mind beyond the visible spectacle and pomp, was familiar, not in the intimate appeal, but as relating to myths, sentiments, typical ideas, held in common, and dramatically or symbolically illustrated. The popular participation was simply that of response, however ready and enthusiastic, to an outwardly imparted, traditional communication.

Now it was a mentally developed popular audience of

readers, which compelled the participation of writers in its own world—a world which was growing away from mute dependency and becoming something on its own account. In eighteenth-century England it was a divided audience, a considerable part of which was still bound by old social traditions, and all of which, including even the non-conformist and democratic, was frankly conventional. But the very existence of such an audience was significant, connoting the beginning of a new era in literature, in which writers were divested of courtly attire and seen plain, submitting themselves to the estimate and near regard of a contemporary public.

Thus prose came into vogue and was developed at the expense of poetry. One hardly remembers the names of the poets-laureate of that period. The popular periodical reinforced as well as initiated every characteristic feature of this prose development. It promoted the brokenness of literary structure, since brevity and variety were the necessary conditions of its existence and of its successful appeal to an audience demanding the short essay. We can understand why Burke was not a contributor to magazines, preferring to institute that massive year-book, the *Annual Register,* which he wrote himself and kept up from 1759 to 1788, finding through this medium full scope for the amplitude and elaboration of his splendid prose. But he had that intense interest in contemporaneous things which distinguishes the periodical, making it always the mirror of its time. The society novel, which in Fielding's time was far from brief, was wholly engaged in the portrayal of contemporary character and manners. The concentration of public attention upon affairs of the moment was a distinguishing feature of the century. The wit of Horace and the satire of Juvenal, revived in "Imitations," found their butts and victims near at hand.

The Romantic revival in the latter part of the century

showed a strong tendency toward a reversion to older types, but it stopped short of antiquity, was more Gothic than it was, in a general sense, medieval in its inspiration, radically national, and, for the poets, was more Elizabethan than Gothic. The true character of the revival was apparent in the next century, after it had been relieved of its barbaric conceits, and Scott had indulged in his picturesque historical revels. Two more Great Events had in the mean time been added to those which thronged the historical retrospect, but radically different from the most of these—the war of American Independence, and the French Revolution, with its Napoleonic sequel; and it was these more than Romanticism which inspired Byron and Wordsworth and the whole Lake School of poets. In the clearing up after the storm eighteenth-century conventionalism had disappeared.

The *laudator temporis acti,* always with us, forever protests against the passing of the picturesque. The breaking up of the antique seems to him a corruption in our life and literature, as to the purists new locutions indicate corruption in our language. It does not appear strange that an author as well versed in Elizabethan poetry as Charles Lamb was should have exclaimed: "Hang the age! I'll write for antiquity." But Lamb and Leigh Hunt and Hazlitt were making a greater prose literature and for a wider, more eagerly postulant, and better educated audience than Johnson and Chesterfield were making a century earlier. Here too we find the periodical leading the way. It was the golden though brief period of the *London Magazine;* and *Blackwood's Magazine* and the *Edinburgh Review* were in the buoyant youth of their remarkable careers. The next two generations were to witness the full fruition of Victorian literature in its few great poets and its many great novelists, and at the same time a marvellous expansion of industry and commerce, fatal to the old-time leisure, filling the towns with human drudges and with the dust and soot and noise of factories, and awakening the indignant protests of Ruskin and Carlyle.

Then it was, midway in the nineteenth century, that prose rioted in its triumph over poetry—being especially rampant in the two authors just mentioned—monopolizing all its charms, save that of the measured line; and some of the poets—notably Whitman and to some extent Browning—broke up the very mould of their own art, as if envious of the freedom enjoyed by the prose masters. This preeminence of "loosened speech" is more evident in our day than ever before. It is not that the age has become prosaic or mechanical or from any decay of imaginative powers. On the contrary, it is the imagination which has been cultivated, and in lines leading away from its old devices—lines of revolt against artifice of every sort, metrical, rhetorical, dramatic, or even epigrammatic. In breaking altogether with antiquity we at last break with tradition and behold the truth of our human life divested of masks—that is, we behold it in its own investment and not in the old clothes put upon it.

We have come, then, in this extremė emancipation, to that art "which nature makes." The communication between writer and reader is not familiar through a symbolism traditionally imposed, but it has a new familiarity, made possible through the response of the developed sensibility of the reader to the creative faculty of the writer, so that the communication is immediate, as if in the light shared by both, flashed from the living truth itself. Only through that response is the disclosure completed. In this conjugation of minds in the world of the imagination, the participation of the audience is an indispensable factor, determining the prosperity of the writer, whose felicity is confined to such creative communication. The temple of fame is displaced by the house of life. The writer is remembered only so long as he is read. This has been true of authors for at least a hundred years. How different is their case as to perpetuity of fame from that of the great but seldom read authors from Homer to Pope!

In our characterization of the communication between the writer and reader of to-day as familiar, we have had in view the attitude which both have in common toward nature and human life—seeking a real comprehension of the truth in these. The old methods of mastery in literature have suffered no change save that determined by the sincerity of this quest. The world of man and nature is, as it ever must be, participant in every artistic communication and essential to its meaning—the harbor for all anchorages of the spirit. Objective embodiment is as necessary as ever; the accordant background, the atmosphere—every feature of a picture—but all for the psychical significance of the truth disclosed. The distinction of the new art from the old is that the world enters not as a contrived spectacle, and the picture exists for its reality, not for picturesqueness.

The more of the world there is in a story, or in an essay which is a genuine creation of the imagination, the greater the interest, since the truth of life has thus an ampler interpretation, in its natural complement, and the scope of human sympathy is enlarged. Other things being equal, it is upon a writer's knowledge of the world and his mastery of the art of faithfully communicating it that his influence and the extent of his recognition depend.

Science, therefore, within its limitations, which must always be narrower than those of literature, but which have been infinitely enlarged as compared with what they were in the eighteenth century, is a finer inspiration to the imaginative writer of our day than the most stirring of events ever could have been to his predecessors. What it was to Tennyson every reader of that poet knows. No other kind of knowledge has so impressed the minds of men with the conviction of the unity of all life and of a universal kinship which Wordsworth prophetically intimated. Science, with its limitations, not only yields real disclosures of the physical world, and thus confirms the quest of literature for truth in life, but has pursued its discoveries to the line of contact of the physical with the psychical, furnishing the imagination with luminous suggestions leading beyond nature's fixed cycles into the spiritual domain. It is not the materialism of science which could degrade literature, but a conventional materialism of our own unscientific fashioning.

Science is forever on the brink of some new mystery, and none of our old fables or fairy-tales can match its romances. The proverb that truth is stranger than fiction—that is, than contrived fiction—has a fresh meaning not thought of in its making. Imaginative fiction entertains this stranger truth—the truth of evil as well as of good—following it without fear or disdain, whatever veritable shape it may take and whithersoever it leads.

This new order of communication is not a logical presentment of exact or absolute truth. The illusion remains. Nature has its own prismatic refractions of light, through the rain-drops giving us the rainbow, and through the humid clouds the hues of the sunset sky. The illusions of life as presented in really great imaginative writing to-day are produced naturally, not artificially.

The prosperity of writers with readers of their own generation is no security for their hold upon posterity. In present conditions it would almost seem that the near regard is won at the expense of the future. It may be that hereafter each new generation must, because of its new and more exigent demands, have and cherish only its own authors.

# TOLSTOY[1]

### *By* WILLIAM DEAN HOWELLS[1]

*William Dean Howells, one of the most distinguished novelists and critics of the American nineteenth century, was born in 1837 and died in 1920. This essay was first published in* Harper's Bazar, *but belongs to the series of comments upon writers and writing which he wrote through many years for* Harper's. *It was thanks to Howells that Russian fiction was brought to the attention of the American public.*

I COME NOW, THOUGH NOT QUITE in the order of time, to the noblest of all these enthusiasms—namely, my devotion for the writings of Lyof Tolstoy. I should wish to speak of him with his own incomparable truth, yet I do not know how to give a notion of his influence without the effect of exaggeration. As much as one merely human being can help another I believe that he has helped me; he has not influenced me in æsthetics only, but in ethics, too, so that I can never again see life in the way I saw it before I knew him. Tostoy awakens in his reader the will to be a man; not effectively, not spectacularly, but simply, really. He leads you back to the only true ideal, away from the false standard of the gentleman, to the Man who sought not to be distinguished from other men, but identified with them, to that Presence in which the finest gentleman shows his alloy of vanity, and the greatest genius shrinks to the measure of his miserable egotism. I learned from Tolstoy to try character and motive by no other test, and though I am perpetually false to that sublime ideal myself, still the ideal remains with me, to make me ashamed that I am not true to it. Tolstoy gave me heart to hope that the world may yet be made over in the image of Him who died for it, when all Cæsar's things shall be finally rendered unto

Cæsar, and men shall come into their own, into the right to labor and the right to enjoy the fruits of their labor, each one master of himself and servant to every other. He taught me to see life not as a chase of a forever impossible personal happiness, but as a field for endeavor towards the happiness of the whole human family; and I can never lose this vision, however I close my eyes, and strive to see my own interest as the highest good. He gave me new criterions, new principles, which, after all, were those that are taught us in our earliest childhood, before we have come to the evil wisdom of the world. As I read his different ethical books, *What to Do, My Confession,* and *My Religion,* I recognized their truth with a rapture such as I have known in no other reading, and I rendered them my allegiance, heart and soul, with whatever sickness of the one and despair of the other. They have it yet, and I believe they will have it while I live. It is with inexpressible astonishment that I hear them attainted of pessimism, as if the teaching of a man whose ideal was simple goodness must mean the prevalence of evil. The way he showed me seemed indeed impossible to my will, but to my conscience it was and is the only possible way. If there is any point on which he has not convinced my reason it is that of our ability to walk this narrow way alone. Even there he is logical, but as Zola subtly distinguishes in speaking of Tolstoy's essay on "Money," he is not reasonable. Solitude enfeebles and palsies, and it is as comrades and brothers that men must save the world from itself, rather than themselves from the world. It was so the earliest Christians, who had all things common, understood the life of Christ, and I believe that the latest will understand it so.

I have spoken first of the ethical works of Tolstoy, because they are of the first importance to me, but I think that his æsthetical works are as perfect. To my thinking they transcend in truth, which is the highest beauty, all other works of fiction that have been written, and I believe that they do this because they obey the law of the author's own life. His conscience is one ethically and one æsthetically; with his will to be true to himself he cannot be false to his knowledge of others. I thought the last word in literary art had been said to me by the novels of Tourguenief, but it seemed like the first, merely, when I began to acquaint myself with the simpler methed of Tolstoy. I came to it by accident, and without any manner of preoccupation in *The Cossacks*, one of his early books, which had been on my shelves unread for five or six years. I did not know even Tolstoy's name when I opened it, and it was with a kind of amaze that I read it, and felt word by word, and line by line, the truth of a new art in it.

I do not know how it is that the great Russians have the secret of simplicity. Some say it is because they have not a long literary past and are not conventionalized by the usage of many generations of other writers, but this will hardly account for the brotherly directness of their dealing with human nature; the absence of experience elsewhere characterizes the artist with crudeness, and simplicity is the last effect of knowledge. Tolstoy is, of course, the first of them in this supreme grace. He has not only Tourguenief's transparency of style, unclouded by any mist of the personality which we mistakenly value in style, and which ought no more to be there than the artist's personality should be in a portrait; but he has a method which not only seems without artifice, but is so. I can get at the manner of most writers, and tell what it is, but I should be baffled to tell what Tolstoy's manner is; perhaps he has no manner. This appears to me true of his novels, which, with their vast variety of character and incident, are alike in their single endeavor to get the persons living before you, both in their action and in the peculiarly dramatic interpretation of their emotion and cogitation. There are plenty of novelists to tell you that their characters felt and thought so and so, but you have to take it on trust; Tolstoy alone makes you know how and why it was so with them and not otherwise. If there is anything in him which can be copied or burlesqued it is this ability of his to show men inwardly as well as outwardly; it is the only trait of his which I can put my hands on.

After *The Cossacks* I read *Anna Karenina* with a deepening sense of the author's unrivalled greatness. I thought that I saw through his eyes a human affair of that most sorrowful sort as it must appear to the Infinite Compassion; the book is a sort of revelation of human nature in circumstances that have been so perpetually lied about that we have almost lost the faculty of perceiving the truth concerning an illicit love. When you have once read *Anna Karenina* you know how fatally miserable and essentially unhappy such a love must be. But the character of Karenin himself is quite as important as the intrigue of Anna and Vronsky. It is wonderful how such a man, cold, Philistine and even mean in certain ways, towers into a sublimity unknown (to me, at least), in fiction when he forgives, and yet knows that he cannot forgive with dignity. There is something crucial, and something triumphant, not beyond the power, but hitherto beyond the imagination of men in this effect, which is not solicited, not forced, not in the least romantic, but comes naturally, almost inevitably, from the make of man.

The vast prospects, the far-reaching perspectives of *War and Peace* made it as great a surprise for me in the historical novel as *Anna Karenina* had been in the study of contemporary life; and its people and interests did not seem more remote, since they are of a civilization always as strange and of a humanity always as known.

I read some shorter stories of Tolstoy's before I came to this greatest work of his: I read *Scenes of the Siege of*

*Sebastopol*, which is so much of the same quality as *War and Peace;* and I read *Policoushka* and most of his short stories with a sense of my unity with their people such as I had never felt with the people of other fiction.

His didactic stories, like all stories of the sort, dwindle into allegories; perhaps they do their work the better for this, with the simple intelligences they address; but I think that where Tolstoy becomes impatient of his office of artist, and prefers to be directly a teacher, he robs himself of more than half his strength with those he can move only through the realization of themselves in others. The simple pathos, and the apparent indirectness of such a tale as that of *Policoushka*, the peasant conscript, is of vastly more value to the world at large than all his parables; and *The Death of Ivan Ilyitch*, the Philistine worldling, will turn the hearts of many more from the love of the world than such pale fables of the early Christian life as "Work while ye have the Light." A man's gifts are not given him for nothing, and the man who has the great gift of dramatic fiction has no right to cast it away or to let it rust out in disuse.

Terrible as the *Kreutzer Sonata* was, it had a moral effect dramatically which it lost altogether when the author descended to exegesis, and applied to marriage the lesson of one evil marriage. In fine, Tolstoy is certainly not to be held up as infallible. He is very distinctly fallible, but I think his life is not less instructive because in certain things it seems a failure. There was but one life ever lived upon the earth which was without failure, and that was Christ's, whose erring and stumbling follower Tolstoy is. There is no other example, no other ideal, and the chief use of Tolstoy is to enforce this fact in our age, after nineteen centuries of hopeless endeavor to substitute ceremony for character, and the creed for the life. I recognize the truth of this without pretending to have been changed in anything but my point of view of it. What I feel sure is that I can never look at life in the mean and sordid way that I did before I read Tolstoy.

Artistically, he has shown me a greatness that he can never teach me. I am long past the age when I could wish to form myself upon another writer, and I do not think I could now insensibly take on the likeness of another; but his work has been a revelation and a delight to me, such as I am sure I can never know again. I do not believe that in the whole course of my reading, and not even in the early moment of my literary enthusiasms, I have known such utter satisfaction in any writer, and this supreme joy has come to me at a time of life when new friendships, not to say new passions, are rare and reluctant. It is as if the best wine at this high feast where I have sat so long had been kept for the last, and I need not deny a miracle in it in order to attest my skill in judging vintages. In fact, I prefer to believe that my life has been full of miracles, and that the good has always come to me at the right time, so that I could profit most by it. I believe if I had not turned the corner of my fiftieth year, when I first knew Tolstoy, I should not have been able to know him as fully as I did. He has been to me that final consciousness, which he speaks of so wisely in his essay on "Life." I came in it to the knowledge of myself in ways I had not dreamt of before, and began at least to discern my relations to the race, without which we are each nothing. The supreme art in literature had its highest effect in making me set art forever below humanity, and it is with the wish to offer the greatest homage to his heart and mind, which any man can pay another, that I close this record with the name of Lyof Tolstoy.

# AMERICAN APHORISMS[1]

By BRANDER MATTHEWS[1]

*A writer of short stories, a dramaitc critic, for many years an authority on the history of the drama and professor of dramatic literature in Columbia since 1892, Professor Brander Matthews has also been widely known as a writer upon usage in English. This essay was first published in* HARPER'S *in November, 1915. He was born in 1852.*

AT THE BEGINNING OF AN address which John Morley delivered before the Edinburgh Philosophical Institute nearly thirty years ago, he told his hearers that he had often been asked for a list of the hundred best books, and that he had once been requested to supply by return of post the names of the three best books in the world. "Both the hundred and the three are a task far too high for me," he confessed; and then he declared that he would prefer to indicate what is "one of the things best worth hunting for in books"—the wisdom which has compacted itself into the proverb, the maxim, the aphorism, the pregnant sentence inspired by "common sense in an uncommon degree." Morley asserted that the essence of the aphorism is "the compression of a mass of thought and observation into a single saying"; and he added that it ought "to be neither enigmatical nor flat, neither a truism on the one hand, nor a riddle on the other."

The lecturer did not provide a definition of the lofty, searching aphorism which should serve to distinguish it from the humbler proverb; and yet the distinction is perhaps contained in this last quotation, since the democratic proverb tends toward the truism, whereas the more aristocratic aphorism inclines toward the enigma. Lord John Russell once called a proverb "All men's wisdom and one man's

[1] From "The Tocsin of Revolt"; copyright, 1922, by Charles Scribner's Sons. By permission of the publishers (1922).

wit"; and proverbial wisdom appeals at once to the mass of mankind, whereas the less universal truth, packed into the subtler aphorism, is likely to demand a little time for consideration before it can win its welcome. In fact, the more keenly the maker of an aphorism has peered into the inner recesses of human nature, the less likely is his maxim to attain immediate acceptance from the multitude, who are optimistically content to see only the surface of life, and who prefer not to probe too deeply into the fundamental egotism of man. So it is that the swift apprehension of some of the shrewdest of La Rochefoucauld's sayings might almost be made to serve as a test of intelligence and of knowledge of the labyrinthian intricacies of the human soul.

We may easily find ourselves quarreling over the veracity of an aphorism, whereas a proverb is almost indisputable; it proves itself as simply and as instantly as the assertion that two and two make four. This immediate obviousness of a proverb does not prevent it from being irreconcilable with another proverb stating the equally obvious opposite. "Penny wise and pound foolish" may seem to contradict "Take care of the pence and the pounds will take care of themselves." But, after all, the contradiction is only apparent, since it takes both of these sayings to contain the whole truth that we must be careful in little things, no doubt, but we must also be able to discern boldly the moment when little things must be sacrificed for greater things. More than one humorist has seen fit to poke fun at this peculiarity of proverbial wisdom without any impairment of the authority of either of the contradictory assertions.

The maxim we may trace to its source and tag with the name of its maker, but the proverb is not individual, even if it must have been minted by one man's wit. "Penny wise and pound foolish" might have been uttered in any age, and it is only the modern expression for a rule of conduct inherited from the remotest past. An equivalent phrase must have been uttered soon after the development of articulate speech; and we may be assured that it was almost as familiar to the cave-dwellers as it is to us. It did not have to be transmitted by inheritance from the dead languages to the living; it sprang into being by spontaneous generation in every tongue, ancient and modern. By the very fact that it is of universal validity, and therefore of universal utility, it is to be found in every land, in every language, and in every age.

The maxim, on the other hand, is more frankly individual; it is due not to the wisdom of the many, but only to the penetrating wit of one; and therefore it is often racial, revealing the tongue and the era of him who first put the piercing thought into apt words. So it is likely to have local color, a flavor of the soil in which it grew. Some of the aphorisms of Confucius may be universal, no doubt, but others—and not a few of them—are essentially Chinese; and I cannot help feeling that I discover a Roman quality in the saying of Marcus Aurelius, that "The best way to get revenge is to avoid being like the one who has injured you." This is not only Roman; it seems to have also an individual liberality disclosing a truly imperial mind.

Many of the maxims of the caustic La Rochefoucauld are marked with the time and place of their making—the France of the aged Richelieu and of the youthful Louis XIV. When the French observer asserted that "You are never so easily cheated as when you are trying to cheat somebody else," he is declaring a truth which might have been uttered by Aristophanes, by Molière, or by Mark Twain, a truth upon which are established the schemes of the green-goods men and the gold-brick operators in New York in the twentieth century; but when he tells us that "Virtue would not go far if vanity did not keep it company," there we can detect the Frenchman of the seventeenth century. It is true that Sainte-Beuve credits La Rochefoucauld with large imagination—not a frequent possession of the French—finding evidence for this in another of these maxims, "We cannot gaze fixedly at the sun, or at death." But most of these searching and scorching sentences are directly due to the disenchantment which envenoms La Rochefoucauld's scalpel; and this disenchantment was the result of a recoil of that social instinct which is a predominant French characteristic.

Of course, among the mass of French aphorisms there are a host which lack local color. When Madame de Boufflers suggested that "The only perfect people are those we do not know," she was making a remark that might have been uttered by an Italian or by a Spaniard. When the Spanish Gracian declared that "The ear is the area-gate of truth, but the front-door of lies," he was saying something that might have been said by an Englishman or by a Roman. And when Bacon asserted that "Extreme self-lovers will set a house on fire an it were but to roast their eggs," the wording is British, but the thought is one that might readily have occurred to a Frenchman, and which might be easily paralleled in the pages of La Rochefoucauld.

There is little that is significantly Oriental in this specimen of the wisdom of the East: "If you censure your friend for every fault he commits, there will come a time when you will have no friend to censure." A Frenchman could very well have said that, although he might have phrased it more felicitously. On the other hand, many of the sayings of Nietzsche we could not well credit to an inquisitor of any other nationality or of any other century. "There are two things a true man likes—danger and play; and he likes woman because she is the most dangerous of playthings." That is one of them, and there is another: "All women behind their personal vanity cherish an impersonal contempt for Woman." And yet even in Nietzsche we may find now and again a sentence which might have been set down on the tablets of that lonely stoic, Marcus Aurelius: "A slave cannot *be* a friend, and a tyrant cannot *have* a friend."

The perennial commonplaces of observation are reincarnated in every generation, born again, century after century, in every quarter of the globe, since man himself changes only a little, even though mankind has ever the delusion of progress. It was an unknown but a most modern American who was once moved to the biting accusation against certain of his contemporary countrymen that they sought "first, to get on, then to get honor, and finally to get honest." Nevertheless, this bitter gibe was anticipated by the old Greek poet Phokylides, who expressed his wish, "first to acquire a competence, and then to practise virtue." John Fiske once wrote an essay to indicate a few of the many points of resemblance between the Athenians of old and the Americans of to-day; and we need not despair of yet finding a Greek wit who had already dwelt on that disadvantage of "swapping horses while crossing a stream" which Lincoln once pointed out with his customary shrewdness.

It is perhaps because of their superior social instinct that the French are the modern masters of the maxim; and even if we who speak English are more abundant and more adroit in aphorism than those who speak German or those who speak Italian, we must confess our constant inferiority to those who speak French, a language that lends itself to epigram because it has been suppled to the needs of its makers, the race most distinguished among the moderns for their intelligence, as the Athenians were among the ancients. And of the two peoples who have English for their mother-tongue, we Americans, despite our superficial and superabundant loquacity, seem to be able to achieve the sententious at least as often as the British. Lincoln was a master of the compact and pregnant phrase; so was Emerson before him, and so was Franklin a century earlier.

In his autobiography Franklin tells how he utilized "the

little spaces that occurred between the remarkable days" in the almanac (which he issued annually for twenty-five years, and which was the basis of his own comfortable fortune) to contain "proverbial sentences, chiefly such as inculcated industry and frugality as the means of procuring wealth, and thereby securing virtue—it being more difficult for a man in want to act always honestly, as, to use here one of these proverbs, 'it is hard for an empty sack to stand upright.'" Most of these proverbs were borrowed from "the wisdom of many ages and nations," as Franklin himself acknowledges, but not a few of them seem to be due to his own witty wisdom; and that just quoted appears to be one of these. Taken as a whole, the sayings of Poor Richard range rather with the lowly proverb than with the more elevated and more incisive aphorism; and Morley chose to dismiss them with curt contempt as "kitchen maxims about thrift in time and money." Yet the saying about the empty sack rises a little above the level of the kitchen maxim; and so does that other which declares that "If you would have your business done, go; if not, send." One of Franklin's biographers records that when Paul Jones, after his victory in the *Ranger*, went to Brest to await the new ship which had been promised him, he was tormented for months by excuses and delays despite his appeals to Franklin, to the royal family, and to the king himself. Then at last he chanced to pick up *Poor Richard*, and the saying just quoted hit home. He took the hint, "hurried to Versailles, and there got an order for the ship which he renamed in honor of his teacher, *Bon Homme Richard*."

Emerson gives us "golden nuggets of thought," so Mr. Brownell suggests; but he does not mold them into beads and link them into necklaces. His essays lack unity, except that of theme and of tone; and his sentences are, as he himself confessed, "infinitely repellent particles." No one of his essays is artistically composed, and every one of his sentences is sufficient unto itself, with a careful adroitness of composition of which he alone in his time had the secret. He is master of the winged phrase, barbed to flesh itself in the memory. In his sentence there is not only meat, but meat dressed to perfection, cooked to a turn, and not lacking sauce. "No writer ever possessed a more distinguished verbal instinct, or indulged it with more delight," to quote again from Mr. Brownell; Emerson "fairly caresses his words and phrases and shows in his treatment of them a pleasure nearer sensuousness, perhaps, than any other he manifests."

None the less is it difficult to detach from his pages the exact maxim as we find it in Bacon and La Rochefoucauld and Vauvenargues. Emerson's thoughts are elevated and often subtle but they do not often fall precisely into the form of the aphorism. He tells us that "the man in the street does not know a star in the sky"; but that is not quite a maxim, even if it escapes being a truism. He asserts that "It is as impossible for a man to be cheated by any one but himself as for a thing to be and not to be at the same time"; but that can hardly be called an aphorism, wise as it is and incisive. Perhaps the explanation lies in the fact that Emerson is wholly devoid of malice—the malice that edges La Rochefoucauld's shafts which sting into our consciousness. Emerson has few delusions about the ultimate infirmities of mankind, but he is never malevolently pessimistic. He is clear-eyed, beyond all question, and yet he remains optimistic. In most maxim-makers there is a spice of ill-will, a taint of hostile contempt; and Emerson is ever free from ill-will, from contempt, and from hostility.

In no department of the American branch of English literature is our benevolent optimism more pervadingly manifested than in our humor. American humor is likely to be good-humored; even our satires are not cruelly savage, and our epigrams rarely have a poisoned dart at the tail of them. Our friendliness has prevented most native fun-makers from focusing their gaze on the meaner possibilities of that selfish egotism of which we on the far side of the western ocean have our full share. It is not a little surprising, therefore, that the greatest and most liberally endowed of our later humorists, Mark Twain, should have taken to the making of maxims as disenchanted as those of Marcus Aurelius, although not as acrid as those of La Rochefoucauld. It was toward the end of his career, when he stood pleasantly conspicuous on the pinnacle of his fame, abundantly belauded and sincerely beloved, that his indurated sadness, his total dissatisfaction with life, found relief in chiseled sentences to be set beside the sayings of Epictetus.

Consider this: "Whoever has lived long enough to find out what life is, knows how deep a debt of gratitude we owe to Adam, the first benefactor of our race: he brought death into the world." Note how the same thought is brought forward again in this: "Why is it that we rejoice at birth and grieve at a funeral? It is because we are not the person involved." And yet another twist is given to this thought in a third saying: "All say, 'How hard it is that we have to die'— a strange complaint to come from the mouths of people who have had to live."

Those who knew Mark Twain intimately were well aware of the despairing sadness that darkened his last years. He was wont to don the cap and bells to appear before the public; but in private, or at least when he was alone and lonely, he sat down in sackcloth and ashes. He had always had the melancholy which is likely to underlie and to sustain robust humor, and his melancholy was even more intense and more astringent than that of Cervantes or Molière, although either of these might well have anticipated this saying of their belated brother in fun-making: "The man who is a pessimist before he is forty-eight knows too much; the man who is an optimist after he is forty-eight knows too little." But it may be doubted whether either the Spaniard or the Frenchman would have penned the assertion that "If you pick up a starving dog and make him prosperous, he will not bite you: this is the principal difference between a dog and a man." Here we discover not mere pessimism, but stark misanthropy. There is a sounder philosophy in another of his sayings: "Grief can take care of itself, but to get the full value of a joy you must have some one to share it with."

Quite possibly a majority of casual readers, finding these dark sayings scattered through the bright pages of a professional funny-man, did not feel called upon to take them seriously, and might even have accepted them as merely humorous overstatements intended to provoke laughter by their evident exaggeration. Those casual readers may have discovered no essential difference between the annihilating blankness of the opinions just quoted and utterances avowedly caustic—such as the assertion that "One of the most striking differences between a cat and a lie is that a cat has only nine lives." Yet even in this saying the playful twist serves only to hide from the hasty the solemn warning it disguises.

It is a mark of the superior humorist that he arouses thought as well as laughter; and George Meredith held this to be the test of true comedy of the loftier type. Many a wise man has worn motley that he might win a smiling welcome for his message. When "Josh Billings" was amusing us with his acrobatic orthography, a critic in one of the literary reviews of London was sharp enough to see that the misfit spelling was only an eccentric costume put on to compel attention, like the towering plumes of the quack doctor's hat; and this critic, by stripping off this incongruous cloak borrowed by "Josh Billings" from "Artemus Ward," removed him from the company of the mere newspaper jest-manufacturers and promoted him to the upper class of more penetrating maxim-makers. Professor Bliss Perry recently remarked that the tone of many of the apothegms of "Josh Billings" is really grave, and that often the moralizing might be by La Bruyère.

To the "Josh Billings," who frankly fellowships with "Artemus Ward" we may credit this paragraph: "There iz two things in this life for which we are never fully prepared, and this iz twins"—a bold, whimsical absurdity, which has served its purpose when it provokes the guffaw it aims to excite. But it is to the shrewd observer who is to be companied with La Bruyère that we must ascribe the statement —here deprived of its undignified disguise of queer orthography—that "When a fellow gets going down-hill, it does seem as though everything has been greased for the occasion." That is an echo from Greek philosophy; and here is another saying, in which Professor Perry finds the perfect tone of the great French moralists: "It is a very delicate job to forgive a man without lowering him in his own estimation, and in yours, too." Perhaps it may be well to cite a third equally felicitous in its phrasing and equally acute in its content: "Life is short, but it is long enough to ruin any man who wants to be ruined." These are all assertions of universal veracity, even though they lack any specific American tang.

Local color is lacking also in the motto Washington Allston had painted on the wall of his studio: "Selfishness in art, as in other things, is sensibility kept at home." It is absent also from Thomas Bailey Aldrich's declaration that "A man is known by the company his mind keeps." And it is wanting again in John Hay's distich:

There are three species of creatures who when they seem to be coming are going,
When they seem to be going they come: diplomats, women, and crabs.

By the side of these may be set two of Mr. E. W. Howe's "Country Town Sayings": "When a man tries himself, the verdict is usually in his favor"; and "Every one hates a martyr; it's no wonder martyrs were burned at the stake." Yet even in these remarks from the rural West there is but little flavor of the soil. Perhaps this American savor can be detected a little more plainly in three of the sayings which Mr. Kin Hubbard credits to his creature, "Abe Martin," and which he tries to endow with the unpremeditated ease of the spoken word. One of them is to the effect that "Nobuddy works as hard for his money as the feller that marries it." Another calls attention to the fact that "Nobuddy ever listened t' reason on an empty stomach." And a third asserts that "Folks that blurt out jist what they think wouldn't be so bad if they thought."

There is a homely directness about these rustic apothegms which makes them far more palatable than the strained and sophisticated epigrams of the characters of Oscar Wilde's plays, who are ever striving strenuously to dazzle us with verbal pyrotechnics. The labored contortions of the London Irishman seem to have a thin crackle when we compare them with these examples of rustic shrewdness sprouting spontaneously on the prairies. And in the aphorism, as in every other kind of literature, the fact is more important than the form, the content is more significant than the container.

# ON THE HOSTILITY TO CERTAIN WORDS[1]

*By* Thomas R. Lounsbury

*Professor Lounsbury was one of the brilliant minds employed in the teaching and study of English literature in America of the nineteenth century. His biography of Cooper is still standard, his work on Chaucer was the first effort of modern scholarship in that field, and his* History of the English Language *was widely studied. This essay, first published in* Harper's *in August of 1916, was part of a series upon English usage which later appeared in book form. He was born in 1838 and died in 1915.*

NOTHING IS MORE STRIKING in the history of language than the hostility which manifests itself at particular periods to particular words or phrases. By this is not meant the aversion entertained by individuals to certain locations. This is a state of mind which characterizes us all, and rarely, if ever, does it affect seriously the fortune of the expression disliked. The reference here is to that organized onslaught made by large numbers upon some unfortunate word or construction with the intent of driving it entirely out of use.

This hostility may spring from several causes. Two there are, however, which are conspicuous in bringing about the condition of things denoted. One is that the given locution offends the etymological sense of particular persons or of all persons who care about etymology at all. The word may be or may seem to be unsatisfactorily formed; the phrase may be or may seem to be ungrammatical. Hence those hostile to its use feel that in displaying their dislike they deserve well of their fellow men for standing up for the purity of English undefiled. The prejudice they entertain often owes, indeed, its origin to their ignorance; but that fact renders it none the less potent or effective. But the second agency which produces the hostile state of mind indicated concerns itself not with the form or grammatical nature of a locution, but with its meaning. It is, therefore, directed almost exclusively against the use of certain words or certain senses of words. The aversion usually arises from the fact that such words connote some idea upon which the attention has been made to fix itself. This by being rendered prominent renders the word itself offensive. In both cases the point can be set forth sharply and clearly by giving in detail an illustrative example of each.

Many will remember that a few years ago there went on a violent controversy about the word *tireless*. The discovery had been made that *-less* was a suffix which could properly be appended only to nouns. Hence the form must be discarded, and we must all take pains to say *untiring*. The duty of so doing was preached from scores of professorial and newspaper pulpits. No one seemed to think or care for the various other adjectives similarly formed, and therefore liable to the similar censure which they never received. Hostility was directed against it alone. The actual flaw which vitiated the arguments against *tireless*, its censors never knew or never took into consideration. This was that the fancied rule covering the creation of such words had practically long ceased to be operative whenever a new formation struck the sense of the users of language as being desirable.

Unquestionably in our earliest speech the suffix *-less*, when employed to form adjectives, was joined only with nouns. But the general sloughing off of nominal and verbal endings which went on in later centuries reduced a great proportion of substantives and verbs in the speech to precisely the same form. In consequence the sense of any fundamental distinction between the two broke down in many ways, in one way in particular. There is nothing easier in our speech than to convert a verb into a noun or a noun into a verb. It is a process which has taken place constantly in the past, and is liable to take place at any time in the future, either at the will or the whim of the writer or speaker.

Such lack of distinction in the forms of the two parts of speech, such interchange in their use, naturally affected the derivatives from their stems. So, from the sixteenth century on, we have had a very respectable number of adjectives formed by adding the suffix *-less* to the verb. These have come into general use, and continue in it without protest and apparently without discovery. Others there are which are the coinage of particular writers, and are used only by them or their imitators. Of each of these classes can be given here only a few examples; but they are sufficient to establish the truth of the statement. Who hesitates now, for instance, to say *dauntless*, which has been in continuous use from the time of Shakespeare to the present day? Milton spoke of *resistless*, which was further a favorite word of Dr. Johnson. Gray in his Hymn to Adversity addressed that goddess as "*relentless* power." This same adjective had been employed by great writers before him, as it has been by great writers after him. Coleridge wished to one of his friends a *fadeless* fame—a word which Coleridge's admirer, Lamb, remonstrated with Bernard Barton for using. Lowell was taken to task for saying *weariless*, just as Stevenson employed the corresponding *weariful*. He resolutely refused to give it up. "I don't agree with you about *weariless*," he wrote. "In language one should be nice, but not difficult. . . . I thought of the objection when I was correcting the proof." It is needless to multiply further examples. The so-called rule limiting the suffix *-less* to nouns is no longer deemed binding by the great body of the educated users of speech. With their decisions it is vain for the objector to struggle. His only course is to bear his affliction patiently, and content himself with assuring his misguided fellow men, as in *King Lear* Gloster did the gods, that he will no longer fall

"To quarrel with your great *opposeless* wills."

To the second class here considered belong locutions which, after being held in highest repute, become objects of opprobrium. The fortunes of words, indeed, are subject to as many vicissitudes as the fortunes of individuals. But there is perhaps no one term which just now deserves more commiseration for the hard fate which has befallen it than the substantive *female* used as a synonym for "woman." In reading the denunciations of it constantly met with at this day, the mind instinctively reverts to the line of Goldsmith deploring the lot of the unfortunate being denoted by it. "Turn thine eyes," says the poet, in his "Deserted Village,"

"Where the poor houseless shivering female lies."

The epithets Goldsmith applied to the condition of the character depicted by the word are now, in a certain measure, applicable to the condition of the word itself. It is turned out-of-doors by every corrector of the press. It is contemptuously spoken of as a vulgarism; modern ignorance has sometimes styled it a modern vulgarism. Such by no means has been always its position. Like Goldsmith's "female," the word has seen better days. It was once to be met everywhere in good society. The most pedantic of purists expressed no objection to it; the most scrupulous of writers unhesitatingly employed it. Its story is accordingly worth giving in full; for to it belongs more than the interest of the passing moment. It is the representative of a class, and its varying fortunes show the all-dominating power of usage, and in particular its frequent disposition to frown upon some special locution while receiving into favor some other locution having characteristics essentially similar.

The word female reaches us from the Latin through the French. The remote original in the mother tongue was *femella,* which is itself a diminutive of *femina.* In the daughter tongue it became *femelle,* and so spelled it came over into English. But its original form soon gave way to the present one. This was mainly though not entirely due to the influence of the word *male,* to which it stood in frequent juxtaposition and antithesis.

Both as a substantive and as an adjective *female* goes back to the fourteenth century; but though then occasionally employed as a synonym for "woman," such usage can hardly be called common. Still it is found. The Wycliffite translation of the Bible, for illustration, reads in the twenty-fourth chapter of Matthew that two women shall be grinding at a quern, the one to be taken, the other left. But in the polemic treatise Wycliffe wrote, expounding this same chapter, the two "women" of the gospel appear as two "females." The word turns up occasionally from that time during the three centuries that follow; but so far as any one man's necessarily limited reading justifies the drawing of general inferences it appears but occasionally. In Shakespeare, for instance, in any senses which it has as a noun, it occurs but eleven times, while there are more than four hundred passages where *woman* is employed. In two places, indeed, where the dramatist uses it, the implication is conveyed that the term belonged to what Ben Jonson called "the perfumed phrases of the time."

During the latter part of the seventeenth century and the early part of the eighteenth there was a slowly increasing tendency on the part of good writers to make use of the word. Still, while it is found oftener than before, it is not found often. It was not that there was any stigma attached to it such as now exists; it simply did not occur to men to employ it, save possibly for the sake of giving variety to expression, or because in certain passages it struck them as being somehow more appropriate. All assertions of this sort must indeed be taken with a good many grains of allowance. They represent impressions rather than systematic and thorough investigation; for no wide-embracing study of the practice of our great writers in the matter of disputed usages, either of words or constructions, has ever yet been made. Until that is done something of uncertainty must attach itself to what are on the surface apparently well-founded conclusions.

But by the time we reach the middle of the eighteenth century we have left behind the region of doubt. A complete change has come over the fortunes of the word. *Female* as a synonym for "woman" had become then comparatively common in the very best usage. One may almost venture to say that it sprang into fashion with the appearance of the modern novel. It is far from infrequent in the works of Richardson, Fielding, and Smollett. As we have seen from the line taken from Goldsmith—and to this examples from other authors could be added—it sometimes invaded the region of poetry.

There, however, it was strictly out of place; and so it was perhaps unconsciously felt to be. Certainly its use by the best writers in that form of composition was distinctly limited. In truth, *female* as a noun, in all periods of English, belongs rather to prose than to poetry. It could, of course, have belonged to the latter, had the users of language been inclined so to employ it; as a matter of fact, they have never manifested any such disposition. This limitation to prose conveys no imputation against the propriety or usefulness of the word. It is a characteristic which it shares with many other most respectable terms, with some terms indeed which we could hardly do without; just as there are many valuable and in fact necessary members of society who would not feel themselves, or be looked upon by others, as at home in the most select circles. In a letter to Coleridge, Charles Lamb, in criticising a contribution to the Anthology, declared that "the epithet *enviable* would dash the finest poem." The remark was a just one. *Enviable* is a good word, a proper word. It has been used by statesmen, historians, novelists, and men of science. But it ought to know its place, and its place is not in poetry, save under very peculiar conditions.

*Female* as a substantive is essentially in the same class. Charles Lamb would not have been likely to favor its use in poetry. But in prose, in which, as he said, and very justly said, he considered himself a dab, he employed it not infrequently. In his private correspondence he had no hesitation in applying it to his dearly loved sister. But he probably would have felt that it was a word which did not belong to high-wrought expression, and therefore under ordinary circumstances was out of place in verse, so long as verse retains the associations which are generally connected with it. At all events it rarely puts in an appearance in poetry, and when it does so, it is usually, though not invariably, when the poetry is on a low level.

It is perfectly clear, however, that in the latter part of the eighteenth century and the first half of the nineteenth nothing of its present opprobrium attached to the word. One indeed gets at times the impression that it was beginning to displace the synonymous "woman" in general usage. How little there was of aversion to it during the first of the two periods mentioned, how little there was of any trace of the feelings which now exist, is made very clear by the practice of Madame d'Arblay. In her earlier years, as Fanny Burney, she employed it in her novels. At times the word makes its appearance in her other writings in places where it strikes the sense of the most liberal-minded in matters of usage as somewhat incongruous, not to say queer. In her diary, for instance, under the year 1786, she speaks of the Princess Royal not as the second lady, but as "the second female in the kingdom."

For a hundred years at least the word was not only in common but in the best of use. No one objected to it, no one apparently thought about it. It was not till after the middle of the nineteenth century that the crusade against it seems to have begun; not till the last third of it that it came to be at all effective. At all events it then becomes noticeable; but of course it must have been the object of numerous previous attacks before the hostility could gather sufficient volume to make itself perceptibly felt. The repugnance to it has become so extended that it has led the editor of the New Historical English Dictionary now appearing—a dictionary which no student of the language can afford to be without—to give a somewhat misleading view of the fortunes of the word. While what is said of it may be itself absolute truth, it leaves out so much of the truth that it tends to produce an altogether wrong impression. There is not a single illustration of its employment by any great or even fairly good writer after the early part of the eighteenth century, though such could have been found by the hundred. The citations are taken from authors little known, and in the matter of correct usage carrying no weight whatever. Furthermore, to the section containing the definition of the word as a mere synonym of "woman" is appended the remark "now commonly avoided by good writers, except with contemptuous implication." The only confirmatory authority given for the existence of this asserted contemptuous implication is an extract from a daily newspaper. It comes from no one knows who. Whether the statement made be true or false, it would be difficult to arrive at a nearer approach to no authority at all upon a question of usage.

The inference may be entirely unwarranted, but such a

comment and such a citation lead to the belief that the word has never been at any time in general good use. Moreover, it conveys the impression that it has not received the sanction of the best writers for a long time past; for a feeling such as the one indicated is never the result of any mere momentary or transient hostility. It becomes in consequence a question of some importance to ascertain who were the good writers of the century which has just closed who were careful to avoid it. They may have existed; but they do not appear to have been numerous. Let us, on the other hand, look at some of the favorite authors of this period who have employed the word without scruple. No reader of Scott can be unaware that it turns up with unfailing regularity in his writings. It would probably be safe to affirm that he made as frequent use of it as he did of its synonym, if not more frequent. In the *Legend of Montrose*, for instance, *female* appears twelve times and *woman* has to be contented with six.

In so expressing himself Scott was following the general practice of his age, so far as fictitious narrative was concerned. In so expressing himself he was followed by all his imitators and successors. Cooper, in fact, has been reproached again and again for his frequent use of the word, and the imputation that he was particularly exceptional in this respect has been more than once conveyed by exceptionally ill-informed critics. The accusation can be brought with as much justice against most, and perhaps all, of the tale-writers of the nineteenth century belonging either to the first or second grade. *Female* is contained in Bulwer's novel of *Pelham*, which came out in 1828, and was the one which first brought him reputation; it is also contained in his unfinished novel of *Pausanias*, which was not published till a few years after his death. In a similar way it occurs in the writings of Washington Irving, Disraeli, Dickens, Thackeray, Hawthorne, George Eliot, and Trollope, not to mention others. Some of them use the word only occasionally, some frequently; but whether using it little or much, there is never to be found in any of them an intimation that the employment of it was at all objectionable. Still less, if possible, was there indicated any intention of conveying by it a contemptuous implication.

In fact, were there to be made an exhaustive study of the usage of good writers who flourished during the last century—at least, before the last quarter of it—it would probably be found that there was not a single one of them who did not feel himself fully authorized to employ the word. Take as an illustration the results which are always likely to follow from the examination of some particular instance. Charles Reade's masterpiece, *The Cloister and the Hearth*, was published in 1861. In it *female* as a mere synonym of "woman" occurs more than twenty times. It assuredly never occurred to the novelist that he was making use of either affected or vulgar speech, or that he had exposed himself to the slightest censure on the ground of having resorted to an improper usage.

It is clear that the elder writers, born and brought up amid the linguistic traditions of the earlier half of the nineteenth century, were not in the slightest degree under the influences now prevalent; and that the disrepute into which the word has fallen is mainly the work of the last thirty years. It is hard to tell under what circumstances the feeling of dislike to it arose, or what were the main determining agencies that brought about the state of feeling we recognize as existing to-day. If the remark will not seem invidious, I am inclined to attribute the disfavor in which it is now held to the ill-will entertained and expressed towards it by the members of the sex it denotes. It may be said that they ought to have a determining voice in choosing the appellations by which they are designated. But language is not disposed to accord to either man or woman this liberty of selection.

Furthermore, if it be true now that special hostility exists on their part to the use of the word, it was certainly not true once. Madame d'Arblay's evidence has already been cited. Her course has had plenty of followers among the members of her own sex. Among these, too, must be included our Jane of Janes. She not only applied the word to the female characters in her novels, but used it when she was speaking of herself personally. "I think," wrote Miss Austen in a letter, "I may boast myself with all possible vanity to be the most unlearned and uninformed female who ever dared to be an authoress."

Here are two words employed which are simply dreadful from the point of view of the modern woman. It once fell to the lot of the present writer to have an extended conversation with a noted female author who had very decided opinions as to the character of the sex to which she had the fortune or misfortune to belong. Among other things she expressed the utmost indignation at being styled an authoress. It was not for the likes of me to contend with a goddess who insisted upon being called a god. Being, however, of a dull masculine apprehension, and consequently lacking the delicate feminine perception of the one with whom I was talking, I was unable to detect the great wrong inflicted upon her by having her sex denoted; nor could I understand why she should desire to have her identity as a woman merged in that of a sex physically stronger, to be sure, but in her opinion morally inferior. It flitted through my mind—the thought was left unexpressed—that she would probably have no objection to becoming an heiress, and in such a case might prefer to be designated by that term rather than by heir.

It was in 1815 that Jane Austen termed herself a "female." The indifference manifested by her to the reproach contained in the usage continued with writers of her own sex down even to the close of the century. Recklessly and almost ruthlessly many of the best and ablest among them, unconscious of the rising tide threatening to submerge the word, kept on employing it without scruple and without hesitation. In 1882 Fanny Kemble published her *Records of Later Life*. In it she denounced with vigor the black beetles which overran the rooms in her residence near Philadelphia. They were especially attracted, she tells us, "to unfortunate females by white or light-colored muslin gowns."

But something more painful, not to say more flagrant, belonging to an earlier period, has to be recorded. In January, 1846, Miss Barrett communicated to her future husband certain facts in regard to Tennyson. He was, she told him, writing a new poem. The account she gave of it is now almost harrowing to members of her sex, not for what she says, but for the way in which she says it. From her description it is evident that the work she had in mind was the "Princess." "It is," she wrote, "in blank verse and a fairy tale, and called the University; the University members being all females." It shows how much we have advanced in exquisiteness of taste and in propriety of speech over Jane Austen, Mrs. Browning, George Eliot, and Fanny Kemble, that the thought of being styled females would awaken grief and fiery indignation in the halls of Vassar and Wellesley and Bryn Mawr, and that over the intervening hills Mount Holyoke and Smith would call to each other as deep answers unto deep.

This utter insensibility of the past shows that there is really nothing in the word itself which justifies the sensitiveness of the present; and that the now prevailing prejudice against it is purely an artificial creation. Occasionally reasons for this feeling outside of usage have been paraded as existing in the nature of things. The only one worth mentioning is that the word can be and is used in two senses. It designates the female of the human race and the female of the lower animals. In this it resembles its remote Latin original *femina.* It is doubtless the labored insistence upon one of the meanings denoted by the word that has brought about its present unpopularity. But there is nothing peculiar in its having a double sense. That is a characteristic the possession of which it shares with nearly every common word in the speech. To most of them a variety of significations is attached, and it is the context alone that decides the precise one intended. If the speaker or writer has expressed himself properly, the most profound stupidity cannot miss the meaning, the most perverse ingenuity cannot wrest it from its natural interpretation. When, for illustration, we talk of a bride and groom, no one feels it necessary to explain that the attendant of the former is not a representative of the stables.

Yet, singular as it may seem, the argument has been seriously advanced that the employment of *female* as synonymous with "woman" would result in confusion. It seems impossible for some persons to comprehend the elementary fact that language was not designed primarily for the use of idiots. Both in conversation and writing something must be left to the unaided human understanding. If a man insists in all sincerity that when he meets the word *female* in the sense of "woman," he is unable to distinguish it from the same word designating one of the lower animals, he really has no business to be at large in a civilized community. His proper place of habitation is a home for the intellectually incurable. When it comes to the consideration of questions of usage he will meet in such a resort with many congenial associates.

The purely artificial nature of the present prejudice is further made manifest by the fact that it does not exist in the case of the corresponding noun *male.* Like *female,* this term is applied to the lower animals as well as to human beings. Such was the case also in the language from which it was derived; such it remains in the languages descended from it. The history of *male* with us resembles in most respects that of the word to which it is often so antithetically joined. Like that it came to us from the Latin through the French. Like that it made its appearance in our tongue during the fourteenth century. Like that it belongs to the language of prose rather than of poetry. But for some reason it has never been made the subject of persecution. It has consequently never fallen from its high estate. As an adjective, too, it has intrenched itself in the Constitution of the United States. Having in that instrument secured the right to be connected with the suffrage, it is not likely to suffer from any restriction upon its right to usage.

This last consideration gives additional evidence of the artificial nature of the existing prejudice against the word *female*. The hostility now exhibited towards it is exhibited towards it as a noun and not as an adjective. No reason in the nature of things exists for making any such distinction. Undoubtedly efforts have been or will be made to restrict or discard any such employment of it by those highly intellectual beings who insist that usage must be logical. But unfortunately there is no other word to take its place. *Womanly* conveys ordinarily an entirely different idea, and *feminine* would often be distinctly inappropriate. This is perhaps the reason why no one seems to have risen up publicly to denounce *female* as an adjective; at least if he has, no perceptible heed has been given to his utterances. Nor in regard to the word as thus employed has any pretence ever been put forth that confusion between human beings and the lower animals would be likely to arise in consequence. When a man talks of going into female society, not even the most intellectually obtuse supposes that he is contemplating a visit to the barn-yard in order to see the cows. All of us have or ought to have female friends; we discuss female education; we talk of female beauty; a great poet, indeed, in a celebrated passage, ventured to speak of female errors. We cannot read, in truth, the classic writers of our tongue without constantly coming across some employment of the word in its attributive sense.

But artificial as is the hostility which has been worked up against the use of the word, it has been none the less effective. It has created against it a prejudice so general and potent that every writer who is sensitive to verbal criticism is disposed to avoid it. The same agencies which have brought it into disfavor may, indeed, restore it to favor in the future; just as it has happened to *occupy*, which, as Shakespeare said, "was an excellent good word before it was ill-sorted," but which on that account fell into disrepute in Elizabethan English, and was but little employed for nearly two centuries. However this may be, *female* is now distinctly under the ban. Nor need it be denied that, taking into consideration the practice of the great body of our best writers during all periods, the influence of our highest literature is as a whole unfavorable to the use of the word in nine cases out of ten. But it is the tenth case that counts. The prejudice against it, if carried so far as to cover this, will cripple to some extent the resources of the language. For *female* is not and never has been a mere synonym of "woman." The latter signifies one who has reached a mature age. It would be grossly inappropriate to apply it to a small child, and no one in his senses would think of so doing. But *female* belongs to all ages, from the infant to the great-grandmother. Hence it can be and has been employed where the appearance of any other word would be unjustifiable, and where the non-existence of it would compel the users of language to resort to a clumsy or roundabout mode of expression.

A single example will suffice to put this point beyond dispute. It is taken from a letter of Motley, who, it may be added, like most historians, was in the habit of using the word as a noun. In writing to his mother from Rome, towards the end of November, 1858, he told her that he was in the habit of getting up at daylight, which at that time of the year was about seven o'clock. "Little Mary and I and Susy," he added, "have a cup of coffee at that hour together, the two other females not rising so early." In this instance it is obvious that neither *women* nor *ladies* would have expressed what the writer had it in his mind to say. The only word that would do was the word he employed, unless he forced himself to change the construction of his sentence or went into roundabout detail. Devices of such a sort are distasteful to language. It hates circumlocution much more than in the old physical theories nature used to abhor a vacuum.